KT-134-276

PENGUIN HANDBOOKS

THE COMPLETE GUIDE TO INVESTMENT

Gordon Cummings was born at Carlisle in 1905. In 1928 he qualified as a chartered accountant and a few years later turned to financial journalism, as a result of a keen interest in Stock Exchange affairs. After working for the *Investors' Chronicle* he moved to a national newspaper and soon began to write on investment and economics for a variety of journals. After the war he turned free-lance and began to broadcast regularly: for some years he gave most of the weekly 'Money Matters' talks on the B.B.C. Although now devoting a good part of his time to work as a consultant on financial public relations he still contributes to various publications on finance and investment. His long experience of answering readers' inquiries about savings, investment, house purchase, and other money questions for one of the major publishing houses has given him special insight into people's personal financial problems.

The Complete Guide to

INVESTMENT

GORDON CUMMINGS

SEVENTH EDITION

PENGUIN BOOKS

Penguin Books Ltd, Harmondsworth, Middlesex England
Penguin Books Inc., 7110 Ambassador Road, Baltimore, Maryland 21207, U.S.A.
Penguin Books Australia Ltd, Ringwood, Victoria, Australia
Penguin Books Canada Ltd, 41 Steelcase Road West, Markham, Ontario, Canada
Penguin Books (N.Z.) Ltd, 182–190 Wairau Road, Auckland 10, New Zealand

—

First published 1963
Reprinted 1963
Second edition 1963
Reprinted 1964
Third edition 1966
Fourth edition 1966
Fifth edition 1970
Sixth edition 1973
Seventh edition 1975

—

Copyright © Gordon Cummings, 1963, 1966, 1970, 1973, 1975

—

Made and printed in Great Britain
by Hazell Watson and Viney Ltd
Aylesbury, Bucks
Set in Monotype Times

Contents

Preface

THIS book is the outcome of many years of close association with the various forms of saving and investment and (which has provided a first-hand insight into the problems that puzzle many people) the handling of the financial inquiries of countless thousands of readers of one of the major publishing houses. It is, in other words, based on a combination of inside and outside experience.

One fact is vital, however. It could not have been written without the assistance, guidance, and helpful comments of good friends on the Stock Exchange and in the building society, savings, insurance, and banking worlds. Gratefully, I record my appreciation of their wise counsels and, far from least, of the services they have rendered by their cooperation in ensuring the reaching of a major objective – to present accurate pictures of all forms of investment.

Naturally, some of the figures and examples, particularly those in which income tax is involved, must be those at the time of writing; and I ask my readers to bear this in mind. Subsequent changes, if any, should, however, do little or nothing to alter the basic arguments or general background of information.

GORDON CUMMINGS

Preface to Seventh Edition

TRAUMATIC, that currently overworked cliché, is a mild reaction to the financial, economic and political upheavals which have bedevilled Britain with increasing force since the previous edition went to press late in 1972. Soaring pay packets ... the highest living standards ever known ... personal spending by millions of people outstripping incomes, with other millions struggling to keep above the bread line ... the borrowing of thousands of millions a year to keep afloat internationally ... hopes of salvation pinned on an eventual flow of North Sea oil ... open flouting of the law ... ineffectual governments ... so goes the catalogue of troubles – and anachronisms.

More specifically within the sphere of this book, financial and economic crises and turmoils of a size and type unknown for decades boiled up and overflowed in a few terrifying months. One of the biggest stock market slumps ever known ... Government stocks selling to yield double figures of up to 17 per cent ... local authorities searching around for money at equally costly rates ... inflation leaping ahead from just bearable yearly rates of a few per cent to 10, 12, 15, 18, 20 per cent ... industry, though generally making higher profits, being starved of the new capital needed for expansion and to battle for a much-needed increase in exports ... restrictions on increases in company dividends ... secondary banking, property and conglomerate empires collapsing into receivership or barely staving off bankruptcy, and then only with massive support by the big banks and other powerful financial institutions ... incalculable amounts being wiped off the market values of the stock and share portfolios of life-assurance offices, investment trusts, unit trusts and millions of individuals ... failure to operate a prices and incomes policy as a brake on inflation ... these have been just some of the troubles which began building up at an accelerating pace in 1973.

Over a period of some forty-five years, I, like my contem-

9

poraries, have not previously known such a complexity of difficulties and contradictions; and, of direct importance, the best investment policies to follow in a situation which, if it could not have been avoided, could have been limited in its ferocity. Comparison is naturally made with other crises, particularly that nearest to us in time, the slump of the 1930s. Heartless though it may seem to say so, that crisis was relatively simple in form. The whole economy had crumbled; hardly anyone escaped its financial and social impact. Prices plummeted, unemployment soared, and millions of families struggled, too often unsuccessfully, to keep above a bare subsistence level well below the widely demanded living standards of today. But, despite the harsh severity of the crisis, the recovery issue was clear cut – to boost industrial production, to reduce unemployment (the dole queues), and to improve living standards.

Today we have the awesome paradox of a land of apparent plenty racing head-first into bankruptcy. Like Nero, we fiddle away our resources while our economy burns. We are living beyond our means, trying to get a quart out of a financial pint pot. It is not appreciated, or will not be appreciated, that as section after section of the community demands more and still more of the economic cake, the slices (in *real* terms of buying power, which is what matters) must get less and less. This is no more than self-cannibalism.

Everyone is of course blaming everyone else. Energetic efforts are being made to brush the mistakes under the already-bulging carpets and to avoid nailing the guilty men. It is unarguable that, with the malaise spreading round the world, inflation of some degree could not be averted; that a country dependent on imports for so much of its supplies could not escape the effects of sharply rising prices for raw materials, basic commodities and food; and that a shattering spanner out of the blue like the Arab oil embargo could have been foreseen, or averted. One way or another most of us are, however, guilty of the major mistakes – through greed, lack of thought or terror of the unpredictable future. But, and it has taken time for many sensible people to realize the fact, courageous and firm leadership could have minimized the impact. The guiltiest men have been the politicians – right, left and centre. Wedded, blindly or sincerely, to ideologies or simply clutching at the prestige symbol of 'M.P.' after their names they have failed to do the unpleasant things required in a desperate situation.

The basic mistake was the Heath Government's policy of expansion and economic freedom. It was right to expand the economy; but only under sensible control and with the brakes ready to slow down the rate when our stamina became strained. The yellow light began flashing as long ago as 1972, and turned to bright red early in 1973. Bigger flows of capital into industry and other objectives were being achieved. Unhappily, however, a great deal more credit was pouring into non-essential or fringe activities. Wheeler-dealing in money and property, asset stripping and other 'paper' manipulations stimulated the erection of an inverted pyramid of credit which became ever more unsound and tottery as it multiplied beyond anything known in saner times. Money could be borrowed for almost any venture, often the larger the sum the easier. And who bothered about the interest cost or day of repayment (or atonement)? The financial and property whizz-kids and go-go boys could conjure millions and tens of millions almost out of the air. Secondary banking (really money-lending), insurance, property and industrial empires were born or put together, and paid for with paper in the form of shares or loan stocks or with bank and other loans. Blocks of property changed hands for millions of pounds over one lunch table and passed on over other lunch tables at still more millions, to show paper profits which became huge losses to the final owners when the bailiffs began to move in. Though, as they later learned at some cost, the solidly established banks, insurance companies, pension funds and other respected City institutions could hardly be blamed for jumping on to this politically motivated and lucrative band wagon, they could at least have used more discrimination.

But for its obstinate adherence to a policy which was so plainly leading to financial chaos, the Heath Government could have avoided much of the disaster by admitting its mistake and applying the brakes. When the objective history is written in the full light of after-events it could be found that more harm had been done than in any other economic crisis since the 1920s.

Individual views rightly differ, as they should in a democracy. But the ideologies of the Wilson Government which followed simply threw their own brand of spanner into the financial/ economic machinery. Inflation speeded up; industry had to re-think many of its expansion plans under a threat of nationalization or other forms of State interference; and the Stock Exchange saw share values sheered away to the lowest levels for more than twenty years which, in *real* terms, meant back to below those of the 1930s. One harmful effect of the stock market slump has been an almost complete drying-up in the flow of essential long-term capital into industry and financial institutions such as the big banks which provide shorter-term finance. Investors will not venture savings into shares which are more likely to fall in value than to appreciate and on which dividend increases are restricted. Equally, business hesitates to commit itself to payment of high interest on loan capital for ten, fifteen or more years ahead when, assuming a return to financial and political sanity, rates may drop by half or more to single-figure levels.

More vital in its way has been the effect on the mutual savings of the bulk of families who, through pension-fund contributions and life assurance premiums, are building up financial provision for retirement. It is not sufficiently appreciated that: firstly, between £40 and £50 million a week of new money is so available for investment; secondly, that in normal times around one half of it is invested in industry; and, thirdly, that many millions of men and women are just as closely concerned as individual investors are in the success of such investments, through increases in dividends and capital appreciation. Investment is no longer the prerogative of the so-called rich. Everyone, in some way or another, benefits from the continuing, unfettered prosperity of thousands of companies, large and small. But there must be no more free-for-all in the expansion of money facilities with little or no regard for their economic usefulness or need. And, as the banking system should know, this does not call for nationalization and similar gimmicks.

Individuals, as the ultimate losers or beneficiaries, also have a vital part to play. Far too many save far too little – or nothing at all. Too much is mortgaged to the future by buying on H.P. or other forms of credit. When in money troubles – and this applies equally to mismanaged businesses and all kinds of organizations – there is a scamper for help to some State cash-dispensing department, to Whitehall itself if the sum is large, or to a charity. Something, or someone, will fill the begging bowl. This cadging helps to further debase our money, to boost inflation and to put Britain further in hock to Arab and other foreign money-lenders. Some £4,000 million a year out of taxes and local rates is now spent on education. The average new council house for a working man is subsidized to the tune of over £1,000 a year. True, many families have to be helped, and rightly so. But should we not be asking those who can afford it to pay something – £1 or as little as 50p a week – towards the education of a child and to charge prices nearer to open market rents for heavily-subsidized homes? There would then be greater appreciation of the value of money and of the benefits and pleasures it buys. Through judicious moderation in personal spending we can contribute to the battle against all-corroding inflation – and make what we have left over worth much more. If the politicians have not the courage, or the wit, to chart the way, we ourselves should do the job.

When I wrote the original edition of this book my aims were to encourage saving and to show the ways in which it could be profitably invested to provide for all kinds of needs and, of ultimate importance for most of us, to ensure a better and happier retirement. Those aims are stronger than ever today. Unhappily, the sadly misguided management of the nation's monetary affairs in recent times has caused vast losses; and shaken or destroyed faith in and brought discredit on most classes of saving and investment. However, all is not lost. A return to financial sanity will come; and not too slowly if the majority of us realize that the alternative is economic disintegration and the worst unemployment and poverty for many generations. The fact that the Whitehall pundits have at long last got round to index-linking interest rates and capital values to cost of living changes encourages the cynics to believe that deflation may soon oust inflation. The Treasury has a poor record for anticipating economic changes and devising new ideas to encourage large-scale personal savings! Premium Bonds are about their only success.

While some, or all, may not agree with my strictures and emphasis on the need for much greater saving, again I have to thank many friends in the investment world for their help in providing information, checking facts, giving realistic criticism and, not least, listening to my diatribes against the guiltiest of the Guilty Men. Individual thanks are due to the Department for National Savings; Basil Eckhard of the Leicester Building Society; Norman Griggs of the Building Societies Association; members of the Equitable Life Assurance Society; William Sanders of the Stock Exchange; Barclays Bank and De Zoete & Bevan for their realistic statistics; and Ralph McCarthy, my partner, who so patiently listened to many airings of my views on the sad state of Britain, and who encouraged me to speak my mind.

Because of the awesome uncertainties immediately ahead of the investment world at the time of writing I have divided this edition into two sections. The first, and shorter – 'Investment Strategy '75' – is an attempt to help readers solve the very difficult problems of the safest and most profitable ways to deploy their savings. The second is the original guide to the different forms of saving and investment, brought up to date. It must be stressed in self-defence that both are based on the situation at the time of finalization which is some way ahead of publication. No-one can forecast what further upheavals – or return to normalities – may happen in between, and what changes there may be in taxation and other factors which can affect investment policies.

GORDON CUMMINGS

Investment Strategy '75

WE have, as outlined in the Preface, been dangling on a 'recovery or bust' thread in the economy and, more specifically, in the important investment side of our existence. It is impossible to forecast with anything like complete assurance which way we will end up. Everything depends on how quickly, if ever, there is a return to economic, financial and political sanity. Sticking my neck out, I look for recovery; perhaps not as quickly as we would like but over two or three years.

Progress will depend on how quickly the majority of us realize that without an adequate flow of new permanent capital into industry it will be an even more rapid run down to overall bankruptcy; and that everyone now has an interest in successful investment of savings which will look after not only present needs but a happier future. In the meantime, the question in the minds of millions of direct savers and investors is: What do we do? The following commentary may help you to make the right decisions, whether only a few pounds or many tens of thousands are at stake.

SHORT-TERM INVESTMENT

Individual circumstances such as the sum involved, when the entire amount or part of it will be needed, the purpose of saving or keeping money handy, speed of withdrawal, handiness and personal inclinations or biases will largely decide the choice, or choices, of the various media available. Generally, however, some part of most people's capital should be kept liquid, at least until stock markets show signs of moving more certainly from the bear tack to a bull, or recovery, tack. There are two sectors of choice – really short term, and longer term.

First, if quick withdrawal is wanted at any time under, say, a year, there is the choice of Savings Bank ordinary accounts; deposit or savings accounts with Commercial Banks; Building

15

Society share accounts; Local Authority deposits or short-term loans; and Finance Company deposits. The amount is a factor. But if it is a small sum or up to £10,000, it will be difficult to beat a Building Society, particularly if there is one handy enough to be able to do business over the counter. It is essential, of course, to compare like with like, to take account of income tax liabilities or exemptions and whether interest is paid gross or net of tax. Rates offered should therefore be put on a common basis. Taking base rate tax at 33 per cent, the following table of net and gross interest rates should help:

Net %	Gross %	Net %	Gross %	Net %	Gross %
4	5·97	7	10·45	9	13·43
5	7·46	7½	11·20	9½	14·18
6	8·96	8	11·94	10	14·93
6½	9·70	8½	12·68	10½	15·68

Only investors paying tax at well above base rate can benefit to the maximum from ordinary accounts in the National or a Trustee Savings Bank with the first £40 of interest completely tax free. The main advantage is therefore the handiness with which small amounts of cash can be withdrawn, particularly through the 21,000 Post Offices offering National Savings Bank facilities. Commercial banks are limited at the time of writing to paying no more than 9½ per cent on deposit accounts under £10,000; and the whole of the interest is liable to tax. If ready to take amounts under, say, £10,000 to £20,000, Local Councils may be offering 10 to 13 per cent or so on deposits subject to ten days' notice, or similar notice after one to six months. Only the large, well-backed finance companies should be considered in these uncertain times; and they might have minimum limits of, say, £1,000 or more for short-term deposits. So, unless a relatively substantial sum is involved, Building Societies have a very good edge on other media. The current general rate of 7½ per cent tax paid (equal to 11·2 per cent grossed up for a base rate taxpayer) could come down to 6½ per cent net (9·7 per cent gross) before most of the others could begin to compete.

Secondly, if withdrawal is unlikely under one year, a consideration will again be the amount to be invested. If more than £100, some of the Building Societies offer term share accounts on which interest is, say, $\frac{1}{2}$ per cent above the share rate for an investment fixed for one year, 1 per cent over for two years, and $1\frac{1}{4}$ per cent more for three years fixed period. Local councils offer two choices – mortgages for one, two, or three years or more at current rates of up to 14 per cent or over (the amount invested is taken into account) or 'yearling bonds' which, as described on page 68, can be bought through the Stock Exchange to give somewhat similar interest. High-rate taxpayers also have the choice of short-dated Government stocks standing at a discount on their repayment price *at least* one year ahead and on which the capital profit is free of gains tax after twelve months of purchase.

GILT-EDGED STOCKS

Assuming a return nearer to financial sanity, interest rates should begin to fall, perhaps not within months but over the next year or two. This will bring fixed-interest stocks back into favour, both through rises in market prices and because of the good yields offered on them. The choice in government and similar gilt-edged stocks is wide. Inflation is rightly a consideration; but if its velocity is abated, current yields and capital profits on redeemable stocks will go some, if not all, of the way to counteract its ill-effects. Once more, choice is dictated by each investor's tax position. High-rate taxpayers should give priority to low-yielding issues showing capital profits (free of gains tax) redeemable in more than one year and up to, say, ten years.

For income, and on the longer term view, undated stocks are likely to do well. A popular choice, largely because of the big amount in issue, is $3\frac{1}{2}$ per cent War Loan. Far better however, and a really worthwhile stock to pick, is $3\frac{1}{2}$ per cent Conversion Loan. As detailed on page 161, it is not generally realized that a sinking fund is rapidly reducing the amount outstanding – over the past ten years alone the total has fallen by not far short of £200 million to under £300 million. True, as the one per cent half-yearly sinking fund is based on the stock outstanding, the sums available will fall. But when, as has been happening, the

17

market price has been as low as £21 per £100, the annual average of over £6,000,000 cash which will be applied in the next few years will buy a large amount of stock. 3½ per cent Conversion will become a steadily scarcer 'commodity'. So, unless there are valid reasons against it, concentrate on this redeemable maverick.

A safer way into gilt-edged is what I call the EACH WAY INVESTMENT method in a definitely redeemable stock and an undated issue. One way is to take a unit of cash, for illustration £1,000. First, buy £1,000 *nominal* of a stock repayable in up to, say, 10 to 15 years and standing at a discount. Second, put the *cash* left over into an undated stock. As usual, the choices depend on income and other needs. As various factors may have changed by the time for action, the two examples must be 'notional'. However, with all reservations, taking 3½ per cent Treasury, redeemable February 1979/81, at an all-in price of 70 as the low-yielder, 6½ per cent Funding Loan, redeemable May 1985/7, at 60 as the high-yielder, and 3½ per cent Conversion at 24 as the undated stock, this is what could happen:

LOW YIELD

Stock – amount	All-in price	Cost £	Income £p
£1,000 3½% Treasury	70	700	35·00
£1,250 3½% Conversion	24	300	43·75
		£1,000	£78·75

With 3½ per cent Treasury repayable at par by 1981 at the latest, the £1,000 invested would be recovered, the investor would be left with £1,250 3½ per cent Conversion for nothing, and he would in the meantime get a gross yield on his money of £7·875 per cent.

HIGH YIELD

Stock – amount	All-in price	Cost £	Income £p
£1,000 6½% Funding	60	600	65·00
£1,666 3½% Conversion	24	400	58·31
		£1,000	£123·31

Here the 6½ per cent Funding will recover the £1,000 invested by 1987 at the latest; there will then be left £1,666 3½ per cent Conversion at no cost, and the interim gross yield will be £12·331 per cent.

An alternative to the cash basis is to buy equal nominal amounts of the respective stocks; which would mean cash investment of £940 for the low-yielder and £840 for the high-yielder, in each case being left finally with £1,000 Conversion for nothing. A variety of permutations is open, but whichever is used 3½ per cent Conversion Loan is the best undated stock.

A pertinent comment here is that it is more than time that some government got round to giving dates to the eight undated stocks now in issue, of which the notorious 3½ per cent War Loan accounts for £1,909 million out of the total of just over £3,400 million. Alternatively, with 3½ per cent Conversion as an example, sinking funds could be started of, say, one per cent per half-year or two per cent a year. This would provide around £68 million a year and would have an increasingly noticeable effect in reducing the amount – and, in time, raising the price – of stocks standing in the market at a value of barely £750 million at my latest count. A practical guideline is that the longest *dated* issue at present – 7¾ per cent Treasury Loan – is repayable by January 2015 at the latest, or some forty years ahead.

FIXED INTEREST STOCKS AND SHARES

For reasons similar to those applying to gilt-edged there could be bargains amongst company debentures, straight loan stocks and preference shares. One difficulty is that the market in the smaller issues is limited and at times it is impossible to buy, or patience is required in waiting for offers of stock. Substantial amounts of the many issues are held by life offices and pension funds, which are also steady buyers. The attractions are double-figure yields and, in the case of many debenture and loan stocks, capital profits on redemption in anything up to 10, 12, 15 years or more ahead. With the exception of some water-company stocks, very few preference shares have the benefit of repayment dates; they are fixed capital. Big issues apart, the market is thin and, again, patience may be needed to pick up fair lines. Current yields are, however, high and run up to almost 20 per cent on some of the not too well-covered shares.

CONVERTIBLE STOCKS

Convertible loan stocks, of which there is a varied choice, are, as explained on page 133, a good way of combining some security with equity risk. If equity prices recover there will be the chance to get on to the ordinary share wagon; if they do not, there is still a good-yielding fixed-interest stock repayable at a definite date or dates. With few exceptions convertibles currently offer double-figure fixed-interest yields and eventually, even if conversion rights are not exercised, capital gains for those standing below redemption prices; which means most issues. Many stand, however, at a premium on the conversion price. For example, an 8 per cent issue with a conversion option of 100 shares for each £100 stock may be bought at, say, £56 when the price of the ordinary is only 28p a share. Anyone unwise enough to convert would thus be paying 56p a share, or twice the price at which it could be bought in the market. Another key point which calls for much greater consideration is the latest conversion date. It should be at least three or four years ahead, especially if the conversion 'premium' is high. Otherwise, unless equity shares recover very sharply very soon, an investor stands to be left with a fixed-interest stock only.

ORDINARY SHARES

The equity share market has suffered the rudest and most costly shocks. The nerve-wracking drop in share prices has dealt a shattering blow to the cult of the equity – the one investment which should be able to ride inflation through the rising profits of soundly-managed companies which could pay increasing dividends paralleling or beating the rise in the cost of living. But, no. First dividend limitation, designed by the Heath Government,

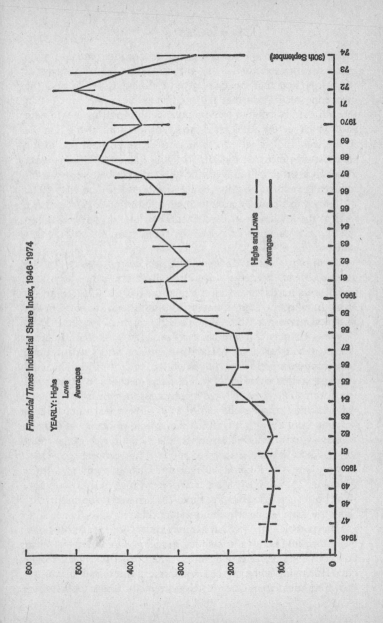

Financial Times Industrial Share Index, 1946 - 1974

YEARLY: Highs
Lows
Averages

Highs and Lows ——
Averages ——

to show that the *rentier* class was making sacrifices equal to those asked of the wage and salary earners. Then failure to agree a prices and incomes policy. Lastly zooming inflation and the increasing realization that the politicians had lost control, that the communist-inspired trade unions could flout the law to gain ends which merely accelerated the inflationary spiral and that the future was riddled with uncertainties. These brought one of the sharpest and most costly falls in living memory. The *Financial Times* Industrial Share Index, the U.K. market bell-wether, summarizes the sad story. After rising to a peak 543·6 in May 1972, it slumped in a bare 2½ years to 164·6 in November 1974, or back near to the low levels of the 1950s. The chart on page 21 shows the highs, lows and averages of the Index from 1946 to the first nine months of 1974.

Unhappily, the F.T. Index is based on current values. Taking account of inflation, the *real* fall in share prices has been very much greater. Based on an average of 100 for 1963, Barclays Bank Intelligence Unit estimates that, although the U.K. index in actual terms was up to 173·9 in 1973, after 201·2 for 1972, it was only 100·4 at constant prices against 126·9 for 1972. In other words, it had barely moved and, to make matters worse, there was a much more severe fall after the end of 1973. The only comfort, if it is comfort, is that the real declines in other main European stock markets were mostly more severe.

So, writing towards the end of 1974, investment in equities is very much an act of faith. At the very worst, prices could drop to give-away, or unsaleable, levels. On the medium view, they could move sideways with chances of modest, but erratic, recoveries. At the best, there could be real and strong recovery with a doubling, or more, of prices from recent lows. Given courage, this could be a good buying time. If risks are to be minimized there are two buying ways into the market.

First is the Each Way Investment system as outlined for gilt-edged stocks. Though the formulae are basically similar, the scope is not so wide because of a more limited selection and the difficulty of buying some of the fixed-interest stocks going into the mix. The constituents are: (a) Debentures or loan stocks repayable in not more than, say, ten to fifteen years standing at a good discount and (b) Ordinary shares at prices below around 30 to 40 pence; both in the same companies. As many changes could take place in the coming months, the name of the company selected as an example is not given. Taking a £1,000 *cash* unit the purchases at all-in prices would be:

Nominal amount	All-in price	Cost £	Income £p
£1,000 6½% Debentures 1981/86	£57	570	65·00
1,344 Ordinary shares	32p	430	28·90
		£1,000	£93·90

When the debentures are repaid by 1986 at the latest the original investment of £1,000 will be recovered and, assuming no change in the gross ordinary dividend of 2·15p a share, the annual gross yield in the interim will be £9·39 per cent. The main difference compared with gilt-edged is that the profit of £430 on redemption of the debentures will be liable to capital gains tax, so that, if this is still 30 per cent, the cost of the ordinary shares will be £129 or only 9·6p.

If equal amounts of debentures and shares were bought the outlay would be £890 – £570 for debentures and £320 for 1,000 shares – and the income would be £86·50 a year. The ultimate net cost of the 1,000 ordinary shares would be only £19 – £320 *less* £301 net profit on the debentures. These shares were as high as 89p in 1972!

The second method is to spread the risks as widely as possible. For most investors this is achieved most easily by leaving the job to investment experts such as investment trusts, unit trusts and, in a slightly different form, insurance companies. Some of these experts were not, it is true, quite so prescient as they might have been in anticipating the bear market of 1973/4. Still, on past records, selected investment trusts are one of the cheapest ways of taking a wide interest in equity shares. In view, however, of the possibly still uncertain political outlook in the U.K., companies selected should have at least 30 to 40 per cent of their

23

portfolios in North American and other overseas shares. But why not unit trusts as a first choice? The answer is that, because of the management loading and some other costs, you buy unit trusts at above their net asset value whereas shares of investment trusts usually stand in the market at a discount which has ranged up to 30 per cent or more in recent times. In other words, if say the net asset value of an investment trust share is 100p and it is bought at an all-in price of 75p, you get £100 worth of a diversified portfolio for £75.

On the other hand, for the small investor, unit trusts are easier to buy and if done by regular monthly savings there is the possible advantage of 'pound-averaging'; which means that if prices fall more units are acquired for the same money and if the prices rise fewer are bought. A brief, and exaggerated, example shows what might happen with four monthly subscriptions of £20 each:

Month	Price	Units bought
	p	p
1	40	50
2	50	40
3	35	57
4	25	80

For £80 a total of 227 units are bought, to give an average price of about 35¼p each. If the whole £80 had been invested in Month 2 only 160 units would have been acquired, but if Month 4 had been picked there would have been 320 units for the same money.

Direct investment in ordinary shares of individual companies may, however, be wanted. Naturally, it is not practicable in a book of this nature to give specific recommendations. Some ground-rules should help, however, in making the choice:

Spread the risks as widely as possible.

Unless big risks can be taken, stick to industries which have the best chances of weathering the worst economic (and political) storms. Obvious choices are industries whose goods will always be wanted – food, household goods, chemicals and retailers. Prices and profit margins may be controlled, but these are industries which can recover quickly.

Pick only companies with good, proven management.

Profit records should be progressive, with an upward trend in pre-tax profits as a percentage of sales.

The net asset value should at least equal, or be not too much below, the share price.

The liquid position should be strong, with current assets at least twice current liabilities including any bank and/or short-term loans repayable within five years.

The total of debenture, loan stock, bank and other loan debt should have a low ratio to assets. Watch carefully if an unduly large proportion of debt is repayable within five years.

Cash flow – retained profits plus depreciation and other provisions not entailing cash outlays – should be substantial in relation to assets.

Available profits should cover ordinary dividends at least twice. The price–earnings ratio – the number of years needed for current earnings to equal the share price – should, in existing circumstances, be not more than 10 to 12. While it was not very long ago that a price–earnings ratio of around 15 was not excessive, it was nearer to 4 in late 1974!

The market in the shares should be relatively free, even in the worst of times, which means that the company should be fairly substantial.

Adherence to the traditional emphasis on U.K. industrial, commercial and financial companies could be profitable. But if government and trade-union interference, plus nationalization threats, are to be intensified, a more promising field will be companies with complete, or large, overseas activities. The two broad types are, first, those registered in the U.K., and therefore prone to domestic interference and taxation but doing all or most of their business abroad; and, second, completely foreign companies which may or may not have some U.K. interests. A good choice of both is dealt in on the Stock Exchange.

In the first type there are two broad divisions – single-industry companies operating in only one overseas country; and multi-industry or trading groups operating in a number of countries including perhaps the U.K. Single-industry companies are mostly tin miners in Malaya and West Africa; rubber and tea planters in South East Asia, Ceylon, India and Kenya; and other base-metal producers in Australia, Southern Africa, Portugal and other countries. The multi-industry groups are diversified over wide areas, and include well-known concerns such as Inchcape and Dalgety with trading, pastoral and/or other activities; and mining finance houses like Charter Consolidated, Consolidated Gold Fields, and Rio Tinto-Zinc whose interests take in gold, copper, uranium and other mining together with industrial and oil activities.

The second type, the overseas registered companies, which in themselves are outside the vagaries of British politics, offer a wide choice from single-industry concerns to groups widely diversified by activity and geographical position. A possible deterrent to some investors is that, as foreign companies, the investment (or dollar) premium has to be paid when buying their shares and on a sale 25 per cent of it has to be surrendered. There are thus two factors to watch – the local share price and fluctuations in the dollar premium; the latter has been very wide recently. Both can go the same way, up or down; or contrariwise, which can mean some cancelling out. Still, for investors ready to take a fair risk and a longish view, this is a good market to look to. Despite threats of much greater taxation of mining and oil ventures, Canada is worth consideration. Racial biases excepted, South Africa also offers some exciting prospects, particularly if gold continues to rise in price and uranium comes back into strong demand.

NATURAL RESOURCES INVESTMENT

Providing the so-called advanced nations can work through their inflationary problems without creating slumps, improvement in living standards and growth of population in both advanced and backward countries are bound to increase demand for natural resources such as basic raw materials. Unlike manufactures, you can take out of a mine or oil well only what is in it; there is no question of replacement. The search for new sources of supply must therefore intensify, while existing producers should benefit from rising prices should demand keep on outstripping supply, as it has done at various times in the past.

North Sea oil ventures apart, natural resources investment has to be in companies operating entirely, or almost entirely, abroad. A cautionary consideration is the recent tendency of local governments, of which Australia, Canada, Zambia and Papua New Guinea are examples, to take a larger slice of the cake through increased taxation, production royalties, direct share participation, or partial or complete nationalization. Some governments are, however, beginning to appreciate the vital fact that by going too far they may stifle or kill the initiative to explore for and develop new resources. Mining and oil explorations are highly risky operations of which only a relatively small proportion are successful, and demand the outlay of vast sums of money by private enterprise. There is thus a good argument for spreading investment risks. One way is through mining finance houses as already mentioned, together with powerful overseas groups such as Anglo-American Corporation of South Africa, De Beers Consolidated Mines (diamonds are only part of its interests), and North American companies like Amax, American Smelting, and Cominco. An even broader spread of interests is provided by Canadian Pacific and some of the U.S.A. railroads like Burlington Northern, Union Pacific and Southern Pacific which own, in addition to extensive and successful transportation organizations, large acreages of land beneath which are coal, oil and mineral deposits and on which are huge timber forests and areas ripe for urban and agricultural development.

Footnote: Because of the time-gap between finalizing this strategy and publication it should be appreciated that much may happen, financially and politically, and that detailed action may need adjustment. Broadly, however, the general policies advised may not be far off beam and whatever the state of stock markets could still be profitable ones.

CHAPTER 1

Savings and Other Bank Accounts

A BANK account is the simplest, best known, and most widely used means of keeping money in safety. Cash can be paid in and drawn out over the counter. It provides an easy and secure way of transferring money to someone else. Two types of bank – Savings and Commercial – have been known to and used by generations of savers. A third and much newer type which has sprung up in recent years is the 'Industrial Bank' or – an apter description – the hire-purchase or credit-finance company. Each type has its particular features and uses.

Most people at one time or another have had an account with the National Savings Bank or one of the Trustee Savings Banks. Though the younger by some fifty years, the Post Office Savings Bank (since October 1969 re-named the National Savings Bank) is the largest organization of its kind in the world. There are now two types of account – *Ordinary* and *Investment*. Balances to the credit of over 21 million accounts amount to the very sizeable figure of some £2,000 millions, or an average of about £97 per account. Its popularity and usefulness to a vast range of customers are shown by the fact that it has an annual turnover of around £1,400 million in approximately 66 million separate transactions. Although the name has been officially changed to 'National' there must be millions of savers who will continue to think of it as the 'Post Office' Bank.

The idea of such a bank was first mooted while Napoleon was struggling to master the world. As far back as 1807, Mr Samuel Whitbread, an M.P. member of the famous brewing family, presented to Parliament a Bill designed to set up a bank for the 'labouring classes'. This far-sighted proposal did not, however, get any further. More than fifty years had to pass before it took practical shape. In 1859 a measure put forward by a Mr William

Sikes achieved success, partly because it had the blessing of Sir Rowland Hill, the then Secretary of the Post Office and initiator of the penny post, and the formidable Mr Gladstone, who was Chancellor of the Exchequer at the time. Mr Gladstone, who is said to have looked on the results as one of the finest achievements of his illustrious career, piloted through the legislation which in May 1861 founded the Post Office Savings Bank.

When the doors were opened to business on 16 September 1861, 435 deposits totalling £911 were paid in through 301 Post Offices. Deposits per account were limited to £30 a year and an overall total of £150, or £200 including accumulated interest. They were, however, guaranteed by the State and the interest fixed at $2\frac{1}{2}$ per cent per annum. By 1880 the Bank was so successful that facilities for investing in Government stock were added.

Today, although deposit limits have been greatly extended and services widened, the founding basis remains unchanged. The State guarantees every penny invested in the National Savings Bank. An important change is however that interest on *ordinary* accounts, after remaining at $2\frac{1}{2}$ per cent for nearly 110 years, was increased to $3\frac{1}{2}$ per cent as from 1 January 1971 and by a further $\frac{1}{2}$ per cent to 4 per cent from 1 January 1973.

An account can be opened with as little as 25p at any of about 21,000 Post Offices, which means all but the very smallest in Great Britain, Northern Ireland, the Channel Islands, and the Isle of Man. The procedure is about as simple as any form-filling can be and one of the attractions for those who like to have written evidence of their financial transactions is that all deposits and withdrawals are entered in a pass book as they take place. Everything is there, clear to see. Other basic facts about National Savings Bank *ordinary* accounts are as follows:

Accounts: Anyone over seven years of age can open one *or more* accounts. Individuals and Trustees can also have joint accounts. Friendly Societies, Thrift Clubs, Church Funds, and similar bodies can apply to have accounts. Arrangements can be made for firms to credit direct to their account savings deducted from the earnings of employees.

Children under seven years of age can have accounts in their own name, but withdrawals are not allowed until they reach that age.

Deposits: After opening an account (minimum 25p), any sum from 25p upwards can be paid in in cash, cheque, money or postal order, dividend or interest warrant, National Savings stamps, or National Savings Gift Tokens. Although an individual is normally limited to a total of £10,000 in one or more accounts, this may be exceeded by the crediting of interest; by interest from stocks or bonds on the National Savings Stock Register (referred to later); or by transfers from a deceased depositor's account. A previous limit to the amount which could be deposited annually no longer applies; up to the maximum of £10,000 can be paid in at any time.

Direct Credits: Simple arrangements can be made for interest and dividends on Government securities, and on other stocks and shares payable in sterling, to be credited direct to accounts, a service which saves investors the trouble of handling such income themselves.

Withdrawals: One advantage of an N.S.B. ordinary account is that up to £20 cash can be drawn on demand during long hours of the day from any of around 21,000 branches on mere production of the pass book. Larger amounts, up to the limit in the account, can be withdrawn within a few days.

Larger sums up to £25 a day can also be drawn at any specified office by two-way telegram and authority to draw up to £50 will be given by telegraph on the day a postal application is received at the National Savings Bank Headquarters.

Crossed warrants, similar to a cheque, may be obtained on application to Savings Bank Headquarters for payment to the depositor, or any Bank, person, etc. to whom he has to send money. This simplifies the transmission of money by post. The minimum amount for a crossed warrant is £1.

Periodic payments of regular fixed outgoings such as rent, mortgage repayments, insurance premiums, subscriptions and other items due not more frequently than once a calendar month can be arranged to be paid direct. Acceptance by the National

Savings Bank of such orders is naturally subject to keeping a reasonable balance on the account. The charge is 10p per payment, payable yearly in advance.

Interest at the rate of 4 per cent per annum is credited annually on 31 December. It starts to accumulate from the first of the month following the deposit of money and ceases from the beginning of the month in which it is withdrawn.

Income tax: Compared with £21 previously, individuals get the first £40 of annual interest free of income tax starting from the 1974/5 year of assessment but are liable on anything over this amount. Husband and wife are each entitled to this relief, so that on a joint account, or their separate accounts, the combined tax-free limit is £80. Interest on any ordinary department account with a Trustee Savings Bank must however be included in all cases. For example, if an individual has £25 interest on both National Savings Bank and Trustees Savings accounts the taxable amount will be £10, i.e. £50 less £40. Exemption now applies to all rates of income tax.

Bank books should be made up once a year if interest or dividends are being credited direct to accounts, or if periodic payments are being made from them.

Death: Providing action is taken during lifetime, depositors can dispose of Savings Bank moneys on death by completing a nomination form obtainable from National Savings Bank headquarters.

In June 1966 a new service was launched – the *Investment Account*, paying a much higher interest, the rate of which is flexible and depends on the income earned from invested deposits less expenses of operation. Although the initial interest was 5½ per cent, it has since risen steadily and the rate current at the time of writing has been 9 per cent since 1 January 1974. *All* the interest, which is credited yearly on 31 December, is liable to income tax and must be included in tax returns. Anyone (including trustees, societies, and the like) can open an investment account and add to it – a requirement to keep a minimum of £50 in an ordinary account was abolished as from 1 May 1974. The minimum deposit is £1, and one month's notice has to be given for repayments. A limit of £10,000 total investment was removed in the March 1974 Budget and there is therefore now no maximum to the balance which can be held. Accounts can be opened in the names of children but withdrawals cannot be made until the child reaches the age of seven years.

The overall position for individuals is thus that they can have up to £10,000 in an ordinary account and any amount they like in an investment account. It should be noted that while a husband and a wife can *each* have up to £10,000, in *separate ordinary* accounts, their maximum in a *joint* account is limited to £10,000.

In addition to its bank services the Department for National Savings provides other saving and investment facilities. British Savings Bonds and most Government stocks such as Treasury Bonds, Funding Stocks, and War Loan can be bought through Post Offices. These services are dealt with in the appropriate chapters which follow.

Save-As-You-Earn, or contractual savings, is easily the most revolutionary newcomer to the range of facilities offered by the National Savings Movement. Announced in the April 1969 Budget, the scheme was a useful case of necessity stimulating invention, the necessity being the desperate need to encourage personal savings to play a much greater part in getting the country out of its balance-of-payments troubles – the less spent on consumer goods the greater the volume of goods available for export and the easier the chance of slowing the inflationary curse. A second issue, offering better terms than the original issue, was launched on 1 July 1974. The essence of the contracts for both issues is the same – *the schemes must be completed* to get the full benefits of S.A.Y.E., details of which are:

Savings must be fixed monthly sums in round pounds with a minimum of £1 and a maximum which was raised from £10 to £20 as from 1 September 1971.

Any individual aged sixteen and over (but not joint holders, trusts, societies, or any other bodies) can enter into a non-transferable contract to save up to the limit of £20 a month.

Savers who do not initially go for the £20 a month limit can take out additional contracts providing there is a gap of at least one month between starting each one.

Savers with contracts for the first issue can also invest up to the limit of £20 monthly in the second issue; which, for anyone already paying the maximum into the first issue, means up to £40 for the two.

The contract period is five years, at the end of which the bonus – free of income tax and capital gains tax – will be the equivalent of 12 monthly payments for the first issue and of 14 monthly payments for the new, second issue. This means compound *net* yields of 7 per cent and 8·3 per cent, respectively; and gross yields, at 33 per cent basic income tax, equal to about 10·4 per cent and 12·4 per cent, respectively.

Completed savings left in for an extra two years, making seven in all, qualify for doubled bonuses of 24 months on the first issue and 28 months on the second issue. This will raise the interest to yearly *net* rates of almost 7·5 per cent and 8·6 per cent, respectively; or to *gross* averages with tax at 33 per cent of some 11·2 per cent on the first and of 12·9 per cent on the second issue. Investors paying tax at the higher rates will benefit even more.

Monthly subscriptions can be paid by standing order on a bank or the National Giro; in cash over a Post Office counter (or at a Trustee Savings Bank or Building Society office, if saving through these media); or by voluntary deductions from pay if employers are participating in the scheme.

Savers will be sent yearly statements of their accounts.

Up to six payments can be missed during the contract period without loss of the bonus, *provided* that all missed payments are made up in the months immediately following the fifth anniversary of the starting date. The bonus date will be deferred by an equivalent number of months.

Savers wanting to discontinue their contracts can withdraw *all*, but not part, of their savings. In place of a bonus, compound tax-free interest will be added on first-issue contracts *over one year old* at (a) 2½ per cent on withdrawals after the first but before the fifth year; (b) 4½ per cent on savings 'frozen' for the rest of the five years; and (c) at 4½ per cent when a saver dies before completing the five-year contract. On the second issue interest is added at the rate of 6 per cent per annum on uncompleted contracts repaid *after* the first year but before the end of five years. This equals a gross yield of 8·9 per cent at basic tax rate of 33 per cent.

The financial attractions of S.A.Y.E. are shown by the way in which savings of various monthly amounts grow, as follows:

		FIRST ISSUE		SECOND ISSUE	
Monthly saving	Total saved	5-year bonus	7-year bonus	5-year bonus	7-year bonus
£	£	£	£	£	£
1	60	12	24	14	28
5	300	60	120	70	140
10	600	120	240	140	280
15	900	180	360	210	420
20	1,200	240	480	280	560

A monthly saving of £10 in the first issue thus grows to £720 in five years and to £840 if left in for the extra two years; the corresponding totals for the second issue are £740 and £880.

Two general points of value to savers interested in this new method of accumulating capital are:

1. *Each member* of a family who is 16 years old or over can invest up to the monthly limit of £20.

2. In addition to running a plan with a savings bank an individual can also, as shown on page 81, invest up to £20 a month in a similar plan with a building society. Which means that *as much as* £40 *per month in all* can be saved by having accounts with both a savings bank *and* a building society.

A new 'index-linked' S.A.Y.E. scheme is scheduled to be launched this year, so it may pay to await the detailed terms before starting this type of regular saving.

Trustee Savings Banks began their useful life in the earliest years of the last century, well before the launching of the Post

Office Savings Bank. Like the latter, their aims are to encourage thrift and provide a safe home for savings. Aptly, in view of the thrifty habits attributed to the Scot, the initiation of the first trustee bank has been credited to a small community in Dumfriesshire, where the local minister, Dr Henry Duncan, was active in encouraging his flock to put by some of their income for future needs and rainy days. As imitators, or as original ideas, other banks were soon formed in other parts of Britain, and by the time (in 1817) when Parliament passed its first Act to control their activities, there were no less than eighty-four of them.

Since those pioneering days further Parliamentary legislation has enabled the Trustee Banks to expand their facilities. While each bank is a separate non-profit-making unit, directed by unpaid local trustees and managers, the general methods of operation are common to all. Interest on what are known as ordinary department accounts is fixed, as with the National Savings Bank, and after remaining static for many generations at $2\frac{1}{2}$ per cent it was increased to $3\frac{1}{2}$ per cent as from 21 November 1970 and still further to 4 per cent as from 21 November 1972. Deposits are guaranteed by the State; and each bank is under Government supervision.

Today, after some fluctuations of fortune over the decades, and after amalgamations and branch development, they range in size from single-office concerns with assets of under £1,000,000 to some with funds approaching or exceeding £300 million and some dozens of branches serving the larger cities and surrounding areas. Between them, the seventy-two banks now in operation have some 1,550 offices. (The first of what should be a series of moves to regionalize banks into bigger units will be the merger of six of them in and around London into the South East Trustee Savings Bank with 228 branches and funds of £525 million.) Through mutual facilities they give depositors a country-wide service which is geographically almost as extensive as that of the 'National' Bank. A measure of their popularity is that total funds multiplied almost $3\frac{1}{2}$ times from £1,100 million in 1953 to more than £3,800 million in 1973. Active accounts of all kinds total more than 13,800,000.

While they do not have as many branches as the National Savings Bank, the Trustee Banks offer more services to their customers. Most of them divide their business into three departments: Ordinary; Special Investment; and Stock. Almost all banks in England, Scotland, and Wales provide one of the newest services, Cheque Accounts. All banks participate in the National Giro system described on page 46 and in the new Save-As-You-Earn scheme.

Ordinary Department accounts are akin to National Savings Bank accounts. Interest is a fixed 4 per cent, and up to the first £40 (£80 in all for husband and wife) is free of income tax at all rates. Anyone seven years of age or over can open one or more accounts in his or her own name. Accounts can also be opened on behalf of children under seven years old, as well as by certain types of friendly society or club, trusts, and schools. The limit of deposits is £10,000, and money can be paid in over the counter in cash, cheque, or other acceptable form; by post; or, as with interest or dividends, by direct credit to individual accounts. Many Trustee Banks also have schemes whereby firms can directly pay in savings deducted from employees' wages or salaries. Money can be drawn on demand up to any amount, the only stipulation being that if it is more than say £50 or £100, short notice may be needed. Arrangements can be made to draw money at other branches of the bank or through another Trustee Bank. Banks have in fact arrangements to enable depositors to get cash almost anywhere, including emergency withdrawals of up to £20 on demand at any T.S.B. Most of them will likewise make regular payments such as rent, mortgage repayments, insurance premiums, hire purchase instalments, rates, and gas and electricity bills; and provide travel drafts in denominations of £10, £20 and £50 up to a total of £200. Travellers' cheques for use in the U.K. or abroad are also available in convenient amounts.

Special Investment Departments are run by most Trustee Savings Banks. Though still subject to Government control, such departments have much wider latitude in investment. The Bank management can select fairly freely from local authority, Government and other gilt-edged stocks, which means that with interest rates higher than the Government allows on the ordinary department business, depositors can be paid a better rate on their investments. In fact, while it varies from Bank to Bank, interest in recent times has been up to as much as 9 per cent and, due to the general upsurge, to even higher rates. A long-standing rule that at least £50 should be in an ordinary account before a special investment account was maintained was abolished in the March 1974 Budget, as was the limit of £10,000 – now any amount can be invested. *All* the interest is however liable to income tax as well as surtax; *there is no £40 exemption limit.* Withdrawals, it is important to note, are subject to notice which may be anything from one to three months, depending on the current regulations of each Bank. A higher rate of interest is sometimes offered in return for longer notice, such as an extra ½ per cent for three months and 1 per cent or more for six months or longer.

Government Stock Departments provide services similar to those of the National Savings Bank for buying and selling most of the Government securities quoted on the Stock Exchange. Dividends are credited direct to the accounts of depositors, without deduction of income tax. Details are given in a later chapter.

Save-As-You-Earn facilities are now a feature and can be used in the same way as the scheme provided by the Department for National Savings and as outlined on pages 32–4.

Cheque Accounts are a newer service offered by the Trustee Savings Banks. Some banks began operating the system almost immediately from the official starting date in May 1965; others followed more slowly. Today all banks except the very smallest operate the system. The following general requirements have to be met by depositors wishing to open such an account:

1. He or she must already have an *ordinary department account.*

2. At the time of opening (a) there must be a credit balance on the ordinary account of at least £50 (some banks may slightly vary this figure) or (b) an account must have been held for at least six months.

3. References will usually have to be given, but the name of an employer may suffice.

4. A specimen signature must be supplied and an undertaking

given that the account will not be used for business or trade purposes.

5. Overdrafts will not be allowed.

6. No interest will be allowed on cheque accounts.

When the balance over the six-monthly 'charging' period does not fall below £50 no charges are made; but if below this amount cheques cost 2½p, including any drawn for cash. Arrangements can be made for employers to pay money directly into cheque accounts. And, on the other side, regular payments such as mortgage repayments, T.V. rentals, insurance premiums, H.P. instalments, etc., can be made on standing order. Approved account-holders can have *cheque cards* entitling them to cash cheques for up to £30 at any Trustee Bank or the Birmingham Municipal Bank. The cards are also useful for identification if paying by T.S.B. cheque for up to £30 worth of goods bought in shops and elsewhere. Cards are valid for twelve months, and holders have to apply for new ones towards the end of each period. Statements, giving details of payments in and out, charges, and the balance, are sent every six months but, for a small charge, these can be supplied more frequently.

A radical change was announced at the end of July 1973, when the Government stated that legislation was on the way to giving the Trustee Savings Banks powers to develop a comprehensive banking service which would compete with the commercial banks and which would enable them to make personal loans to their customers. They would also be freed in due course from specific Government controls.

In addition to this useful range of saving and investment facilities, Trustee Savings Banks offer other services of considerable value to millions of their customers. Most of them will keep in safe custody customers' valuable documents such as Savings Certificates, stock and share certificates, insurance policies and deeds of property. Their managers and staff are also available for advice on normal financial problems and explaining how to buy and sell shares. In other words, the Trustee Banks provide a much more personal service than the National Savings Bank.

Trustee Banks now run their own Unit Trusts which provide

simple facilities for block purchases and regular monthly or other periodical investment. Investors can draw their dividends half-yearly or leave them to be re-invested. A measure of the popularity of the first T.S.B. Unit Trusts is that in late 1974 the fund was valued at over £18 million. As with most other unit trusts, investment values have been hard hit by the 1974 stock market collapse; but there should be recovery prospects. Life assurance can be linked to a regular savings plan of £5 *or more* per month. There is also a trust plan to save money for children to draw on their eighteenth or twenty-first birthday.

Harvest Bonds provide a useful and simple way of investing lump sums in round £'s from £10 upwards. Subject to a small deduction of a once-for-all expense the money goes into T.S.B. units at the ruling price of the day an application is received. All net dividends are re-invested, to give automatic accumulation of savings. Bonds can be cashed at any time at the ruling bid price of the T.S.B. Units. By treating them as a gift, put into a parent's name, Bonds can be bought for children. Built-in insurance provides against loss if a holder dies before cashing them.

An *Income from Growth Plan*, in which any amount from £500 upwards can be invested, provides for a regular income (part interest and part capital) at any selected rate between 5 per cent and 10 per cent a year net of tax.

No so many years ago few weekly wage earners even thought of having an account with one of the Commercial Banks. If they did open one it was probably a deposit account with no facilities for drawing cheques. The general increase in incomes and living standards in recent years has however brought about a considerable change. More and more people are realizing the advantages of, and ease of payment by, cheque.

The more obvious advantages of having a current account are:

The simplicity of drawing a cheque for all kinds of payment.
Reducing cash carried about or kept in the house.
Cash, cheques or other money can be paid in at any branch of the bank, or any other bank.

Subscriptions, rent, hire-purchase instalments, mortgage repayments, insurance premiums and other regular payments can be made direct by the bank on standing orders.

One or more bills can be paid with *one* cheque by using the banks' Giro credit system, which also saves postage on sending individual cheques and keeps down the number of debits.

Interest, dividends, salaries, and other regular income can be paid direct into the account.

Documents, jewellery, and other valuables can be left with the bank, permanently or for short periods while on holiday.

Arrangements can be made for cashing cheques at other branches or other banks, travellers' cheques can be bought and facilities provided for other means of transmitting funds. The last two facilities are also available to non-customers. Credit cards enabling holders to draw money away from home or for buying at shops and for other uses are the latest service.

Investment advice can be obtained through the bank's stockbrokers, and stocks and shares bought or sold through its agency.

Banks also have specialized departments, staffed by experts, usually called *Trustee*, to look after, advise on and administer trusts and deceased estates; and to manage investment portfolios, to give advice on estate planning with a view to minimizing taxation and death duties, and to provide for particular needs such as children's education.

A newer type of financial facility is what Barclays call their 'Money Doctor Service' which is designed to help individuals of all kinds with their financial management problems. Specialists advise on investment, taxation, estate administration, assurance, pension arrangements, fire and other insurance, loans and credit facilities, and the other problems which today need attention if one is to make the best use of capital and income and to provide for the future. Fees rightly depend on the work involved, but are kept as moderate as possible.

Some banks also now operate their own Unit Trusts and provide simple facilities for buying shares in them over their counters or by regular monthly or other periodic purchase. Some of the bank-operated trusts are linked with life assurance.

Loans can be arranged for house purchase, home improvements and 'bridging' the financial gap between paying for a new house and getting the money from selling an existing property. The bank will however want the longer term types of loan repaid over no more than, say, ten years or by normal retirement age.

Then there is that valuable financial reserve the overdraft, which, used prudently, can be helpful in case of emergency or for some special short-term purpose. Overdrafts, it must be appreciated, are not given as of right. There must be a justifiable need. Satisfactory security must generally be provided. And the manager, however willing he may otherwise be to help, may have his hands tied by Government-imposed credit squeezes.

Overdrafts, as I have said, usually have to be backed by acceptable and readily realizable security such as stocks or shares with a market value, life assurance policies with surrender values, or deeds of properties. Life or endowment assurances, it is well for the hopeful borrower to note, do not usually have surrender values until two or three years' premiums have been paid; and even then the amount in the early life of the policies is no more than one-third to one-half of the total payments. A bank may also be ready to give an overdraft if repayment can be guaranteed by someone of adequate financial substance. Such loans, whatever the security, must not be treated as permanent arrangements. An overdraft or loan is a relatively short-term affair which is subject first to reconsideration by the Bank every six months or less, and secondly to fairly steady reduction during its currency. Despite the high interest rates of recent times an overdraft can be a cheaper, and usually simpler, means of short-term finance compared with say hire purchase and other forms of instalment buying on which the *real*, effective, rate of interest can be up to 20 per cent or more. Depending on individual circumstances, interest on an overdraft can be 2 to 3 or 4 per cent over the bank's base rate. This means that if the latter is, say, 11 per cent the interest is 13 to 15 per cent.

Some of the banks, when credit restrictions permit, are ready to make *Personal Loans* for the purchase of durable consumer goods such as a car, refrigerator, kitchen equipment, central heating, and furniture, or heavy repairs to a house. Unlike an overdraft, no security is required – the loan is made on the credit standing of the customer. The maximum is normally £500 or £1,000, interest is charged on the original loan, repayment is spread over say two to three years in equal monthly instalments, and free life insurance provides for extinction of the outstanding balance if the borrower dies at any time.

Tax relief on bank interest has become a political yo-yo. Up to the Labour budget of 1969 all of it was eligible for relief, but from then until the Conservative budget of 1972 it was allowed only on loans for housing and business purposes. From 6 April 1972 to the Labour budget of March 1974, relief was given on all interest above £35 a year. Now, at the time of writing, relief will not be given on interest paid on overdrafts arranged *after* 26 March 1974, with the exception of loans not exceeding £25,000 for owner/occupier property purchases or improvements. An exception to this rule covers overdrafts existing *before* 26 March 1974; subject to disallowance on the first £35, relief will be given on interest paid during the tax year ending 5 April 1975, but on nothing thereafter.

Bank charges were until fairly recently a cause for criticism and misunderstanding. 'Why', it was often asked, 'should I pay for using my cheque book when I am not getting any interest on the credit balance in my current account?' The bank's answer was that, unless the balance was large enough in relation to the transactions on the account, it had to charge something towards the cost of 'processing' the debits and credits passing through it. That was when interest rates were much lower than the levels to which they soared in the earlier 1970s. Starting in mid-1972, base rate rose (with some breaks) from 7 per cent to a previously undreamt of 13 per cent by November 1973. This, combined with an official freeze to $9\frac{1}{2}$ per cent interest on deposit accounts below £10,000 and a sharp increase in business, meant bigger profits for the commercial banks and intensified the pressure for cuts in charges. Today, all the leading banks have abolished, or largely done away with, charges on personal accounts kept in credit of as little as £50, or less. There is thus no merit, or profit, for the average individual to keep little more than the minimum on current account. Surpluses should be put to profitable use.

Banks do not usually pay interest on current accounts. Deposit accounts are, however, a different matter. Until imposition of the 'freeze' mentioned above, interest was usually $1\frac{1}{2}$–2 per cent below the base rate of each bank. At the time of writing $9\frac{1}{2}$ per cent is paid on amounts below £10,000; but for larger sums there is no restriction and, depending on the amount available and time it will be left on deposit, interest can be 10 to 11 per cent, or more. Deposit accounts are a handy and useful means of investing funds which may be needed at a specified date ahead or at short notice. Subject to giving the agreed notice, normally seven days, interest is paid from the day of lodgement to withdrawal. All such interest is liable to income tax and has to be included in annual returns. Most banks also offer Savings Accounts at fixed interest rates.

An interesting break with generations-long tradition has been the entry of merchant banks into the 'small-man' deposit business. Interest is calculated daily up to date of withdrawals and these can be made on demand instead of being subject to seven days or other notice.

Hire purchase and similar ways of buying goods on credit are now an accepted way of life. Something like one-third of household goods are bought in these ways. It is not surprising therefore that, despite the various Government-imposed curbs of recent years, the total H.P. and other instalment credit debt of individuals and businesses averages some £2,000/£2,500 million, a sum which calls for considerable financial resources. While substantial amounts of such credit sales are financed by retailers, distributors, and manufacturers from their own resources, much the greater bulk is handled by specialist finance houses which are loosely termed industrial banks or (more correctly, in the opinion of some experts) hire-purchase or credit-finance companies with resources running up to tens or hundreds of millions of pounds.

Hire-purchase finance companies, as we shall call them, get the bulk of the capital for their operations from three sources. First is their issued share capital, which may be privately or publicly held, together with trading profits ploughed back as reserves.

Second are loans from banks, which are secured by charges on hire-purchase contracts and perhaps other assets. Third are deposits which generally do not have any specific security and may rank as ordinary creditors in the event of a company having to be wound up. It is this latter source with which private investors are mostly concerned.

Some H.P. finance companies restrict the acceptance of deposits to relatively large amounts such as a minimum of £5,000 or £50,000, and look for them to other financial institutions or companies with temporarily surplus funds. Others, particularly the small to medium-size undertakings, openly invite deposits from the general public in amounts of as little as £100 and upwards. Such money can be deposited for a fixed period of say six months or more; or be subject to withdrawal at one, two, three, or six months' notice. One attraction in comparison with the Savings and commercial banks is that the interest is higher, for the simple reasons that the risk is greater and the H.P. companies earn enough to offer more. Rates naturally depend on the financial standing of individual companies, the terms of withdrawal, perhaps the amount deposited, and the trend of interest rates generally.

While the interest offered varies, the Finance Houses Association, of which the leading companies are members, has, like the commercial banks, its own base rate. This is fixed objectively on the last business day of each month on an eight-weekly average of what is known in the City as the three-month inter-bank rate as calculated at 11 a.m. each day by a leading firm of money brokers. The base rate applies from the first day of the following month. An indication of the interest rates offered to investors, and of the violent fluctuations which can take place, is that the year 1972 started at 5 per cent and ended at 8 per cent, while the corresponding range in 1973 was a rise from 8½ per cent in January to a peak of 14 per cent for December with quite wide fluctuations in between – double-figure rates continued into 1974. Looking at the other side of the picture, these high levels of interest paid for the money needed to lend on to borrowers underlines the costliness of this type of finance and explains why charges of 18–20 per cent and upwards have to be made. So, as mentioned earlier, it pays borrowers to shop around and, if possible, to get a bank overdraft.

Legislation lays down some stringent requirements from those inviting deposits. Though many of the finance companies therefore now offer fair to top-rate deposit facilities, some may be weakly financed, having expanded too rapidly to build up adequate reserves, or having taken on too much speculative business. Care in selection is therefore vital. In addition to a clear statement of the nature of its business, the examination of any concern should have in mind such considerations as those set out below:

The first factor is the interest rate. A well-tried test of any investment is that the higher the yield the greater the risk. If more than 1 or 2 per cent over the Finance House base rate is offered, look elsewhere, or get expert advice from your Bank Manager or the City Editor of one of the national newspapers or weekly financial journals. The next test is whether the company is a member of the Finance Houses Association.

Whatever the answers, there should be no hesitation in supplying to all who apply for it an up-to-date and *audited* balance sheet which should give certain basic information and pass some simple checks. On the left-hand or liabilities side, the total of bank and other loans, deposits, and other liabilities should not exceed much more than some five times the issued capital and reserves shown higher up. H.P. debts owing to the company, as shown on the assets side, will include interest which has not been earned at the date of the balance sheet. Prudent finance dictates that no credit should be taken for such unearned profits, and that (as a specific item on the liabilities side, or as a deduction from the outstanding debts) there should be a reserve to allow for this. If no such reserve can be found – or it is less than 8 to 10 per cent of the outstanding debts – choose another company for your deposit account. The profit and loss account is equally important in showing whether the business is operating profitably. Work out the number of times available profits cover deposit interest paid; and whether after meeting all expenses, providing for losses or bad debts and paying dividends on the share capital, a good margin is left over for strengthening reserves.

The sudden outburst of crashes in what is now called the 'secondary banking' sphere towards the end of 1973 and first half of 1974 brought out the weakness of many of these companies, large and small. Far too many had relied on excessive amounts of deposits and loans repayable on demand or short notice for the bulk of their finances for all kinds of credit lending, including second mortgages repayable over relatively long periods. They had also taken on a lot of dubious business at exorbitant interest rates and, in some notorious cases, advanced money to property speculators and developers who were caught up in the sudden bursting of a property boom, as well as investing at high prices in the shares of industrial, financial and property companies which suddenly developed liquidity or other troubles.

A tax point which can cause misunderstanding is that the whole of the annual interest on a hire-purchase finance-company deposit account is liable to income tax, and must be included in annual returns. There is no £40 a year or other special exemption. The misunderstanding may arise because of two methods of accounting for income tax. If the deposit runs for more than twelve months, the interest is technically of the 'annual' variety, and tax at the standard rate should be deducted from it by the company. If however the deposit is repaid in not more than eleven months, the company does not have to deduct tax; the depositor must account for anything due. Any statement which implies that deposit interest is tax free is wrong and misleading.

Lastly there is the Post Office Giro, which provides all and sundry with a sophisticated, computerized means of settling money transactions speedily, safely and with the minimum effort. It is, as the dictionary defines the word, a 'circuit' which switches payments to and from its users' accounts with the minimum of paper work. To open an account money can be paid in by cheque or in cash at any time at all but the smallest of post offices or by cheque direct to the National Giro Centre at Bootle, Lancashire. Each account-holder is given a number which must be used on all transactions. Subject to making the necessary, but simple, arrangements direct payment can be made into an account of (a) part or all of weekly, fortnightly, or monthly wages or salaries; (b) interest and dividends from investments; and (c) other regular income. Irregular payments can also be made into a Giro-holder's account free of charge from another holder's account or by using a simple 'in-payment' system through almost any post office.

Electricity, gas, rates, rent, telephone and other bills can be paid by completing a transfer form (provided by whoever is owed the money or by the Giro) and sending it to the Giro Centre in a pre-addressed, post-paid envelope. Regular fixed payments such as life assurance premiums, mortgage repayments, and hire-purchase commitments can be looked after automatically by standing order. Money can be paid to anyone by an authenticated payment order exchangeable into cash at a post office. Payment orders can also be sent to individuals or organizations who do not have Giro accounts but only ordinary bank accounts. Account-holders can easily arrange to draw cash themselves at a nominated post office up to a limit of £20, or larger sums by getting an authenticated payment order from the Centre.

SUMMING UP

Every saver, whatever his or her circumstances, should have a Savings Bank or Commercial Bank account. It is the simplest and safest way of accumulating money where it can be readily available for a multiplicity of needs.

Post Office or Trustee Savings Bank accounts are well-tried, safe, and simple means of starting to save. One account will serve all purposes, or separate accounts can be opened for specific saving such as holidays, Christmas, a car, motor-cycle, new furniture or household equipment, payment of rates and other regular outgoings, and school fees or insurance premiums. But, as there are more profitable and equally sound investments, the balance on ordinary accounts should be kept to minimum workable limits of say £100 to £200 at the outside.

Sooner or later most people handling a fair amount of money, or with bills to pay, need a Cheque Account with a Commercial or Trustee Savings Bank. But again credit balances should be kept to a workable figure, which may be a minimum of £100 or more, or enough to cover payments out for two or more months ahead. Unless cash may be wanted quickly for some particular purpose, the surplus should be put to profitable use by transfer to a deposit account with the bank, transferred into a building society share account or lent to a *sound* finance company, or invested in stocks and shares. When saving for some particular purpose, arrangements can be made with a bank to transfer to a deposit account fixed monthly sums or the surplus over a stipulated balance on the current account.

CHAPTER 2

National Savings: Savings Certificates

SAVINGS Certificates, British Savings and similar Government Bonds, and Premium Savings Bonds are basically extensions of the Savings Bank idea of encouraging thrift. They are a major part of what are collectively and correctly called National Savings and – though not so aptly nowadays – Small Savings. Over the years they have provided, first, many thousands of millions of pounds for Government finance, and, secondly, handy investments for tens of millions of men, women, and children. Their main attractions are simplicity of buying and selling; competitive rates of interest; and, for what it is worth in inflationary times, £1 invested is always equal to 100p plus accumulated interest.

The first of this well-tried trio, Savings Certificates, was introduced in February 1916 as a novel and attractive way of encouraging the 'small savers' to help finance the First World War. Called War Savings Certificates, they were sold in units of 15s. 6d. which instead of having interest paid in the normal way increased in value month by month, to become worth 26s. at the end of ten years. (The life of this historic first issue has since been continued indefinitely, with interest being added at the rate of one old penny ($\frac{5}{12}$p) per month.) Particular attractions were that the interest was free of all taxes, and units could be cashed at any time at their face value plus accumulated interest. Tax exemption naturally meant that individual holdings had to be limited to a maximum which would not benefit wealthy investors to the detriment of the small savers.

To date, there have been sixteen different issues of Savings Certificates, including a conversion issue in 1932 and a special 'extra' issue of £1 units during the last war. The value of all issues outstanding nowadays is about £2,500 million, including some £600 million accrued interest, held by some 6·5 million investors. The terms on which the different issues have been made have naturally depended on monetary conditions at the time of launching. But the fundamental principles of continuing accretion in value and tax exemption have not changed.

The issue on sale at the time of writing (late 1974) is the fourteenth. Terms, as with its immediate predecessor (the Decimal), depart in some ways from those of most earlier issues. First, the issue price is £1. Second, the initial life is only four years compared with five or more for issues up to the twelfth – superstition got the better of numerical sequence by calling what was No. 13 the 'Decimal' issue. Third, a particular departure, the growth rate is steadier, thus reducing the penalty for holders who withdraw before the maturity date. Individuals can buy up to £1,000 worth of certificates in £1 units or in various multiples up to £500. Over the four-year life a £1 unit will grow in value to £1·34, to give an average yearly interest of £7·59 per cent, tax free, or the equivalent of £11·33 per cent gross to a holder paying 33 per cent income tax, the highest rate ever offered on this form of saving. The first interest – of 6p – is not added until the end of the first year. But thereafter additions are made every four months; at the rate of 2½p in the second year, 3p in the third year and 3½p in the fourth year, with a final payment of 1p at the end of year four, making 34p in all. Growth, tax-free yield, and equivalent gross yield allowing for basic rate income tax at 33 per cent for each year are as shown below:

FOURTEENTH-ISSUE YIELDS

| Years held | Year-end value £p | Yearly yield % | |
		Tax free £p	Gross £p
1	1·06	6·00	8·96
2	1·13½	7·08	10·56
3	1·22½	7·93	11·83
4	1·34	9·39	14·01
Average yield		7·59	11·33

Holders paying more than basic rate income tax do even better. Gross yields over four years for some higher tax rates as laid down in the March 1974 budget would average:

Tax rate %	Gross yield %
43	13·32
53	16·15
63	20·51
73	28·11
83	44·65

The investment morals are twofold. Providing inflation can be kept within more reasonable limits, Savings Certificates are profitable holdings for income-tax payers, particularly those liable at above the basic rate. But, as I have explained, because of these tax advantages, there must be limits to the number which can be bought. For the current fourteenth issue this is £1,000 worth. Husband and wife can, however, each hold up to the limit, and further investments can be made for children. A family of five could, for example, have 5,000 units between them. Holders can also have the maximum of previous issues, the normal limits being:

Issue	Maximum units
7th and earlier	500 in all
£1	250
8th	1,000
9th	1,400
10th	1,200
11th	600
12th	1,500
Decimal	1,500
14th	1,000

Hence, including 1,000 of the fourteenth, it is possible to hold up to 8,950 units of all issues. When two or more people hold certificates in their joint names for their joint personal benefit the full number is however counted against each holder in reckoning the individual maximum. For example, if two people have 500 fourteenth issue units in a joint holding they could each buy up to only 500 units in individual sole holdings, which would give them 1,500 units in all. If, therefore, husband and wife are investing fairly substantially in Certificates, it pays them to have separate holdings.

An exception to the maximum rule is that the limit for any issue can be exceeded when additional Certificates are inherited. For instance, if a holder has already bought 1,200 twelfth-issue units and 500 eleventh, and inherits 600 of each issue, he does not have to cash the extra 300 twelfth and 500 eleventh units.

A question often overlooked is whether it is profitable to continue holding older issues of Savings Certificates. The answer is mainly a matter of tax and individual circumstances. Generally, however, it pays to look carefully at holdings of the earlier issues. It is all very well to point out that $\frac{5}{12}$p (1d.) a month is still being added to first-issue Certificates. Though this looks very attractive on the cost price of 15s. 6d., it is relatively meagre when calculated, *as all such interest should be*, on the present value. A first-issue Certificate bought, say, fifty-five years ago is now worth £3·55 (71s.) so that the 5p (1s.) a year interest gives a *real* yield of only £1·43 per cent; and the rate of yield will continue to fall as the units continue to grow in value. At the time of writing, there are no time limits to all issues up to the sixth – they can be held indefinitely. The range of yearly interest for different times of holding such issues, which were on sale up to November 1939, is now no more than about 1·30 to 2·50 per cent. As it happens, there are only about £6 million worth at issue price still outstanding; and of these it is possible that a good many will never be claimed because of death or lack of knowledge of ownership. Anyone who still has any of these issues should cash them and, if still wanting this type of investment, should put the proceeds into the current issue.

Issues launched between November 1939 (seventh) and March 1966 (twelfth) had original lives varying from ten years down to five years; but in every case there have been extensions of one or more periods, mostly on better terms. As with the pre-1939 issues, there have however been persistent encashments by holders, particularly of seventh to tenth units and the £1 issue, of which barely 1·5 million are still outstanding. Reasons have included switching to the newer, more profitable issues; transfer to other types of investment offering better terms; and the normal one of the need for cash. It is fairly certain, however, that the eroding effects of inflation, which have wiped out or largely offset the tax-free increments, have speeded up the move. The Committee to Review National Savings (popularly called the Page Committee after its chairman Sir Harry Page) in its report of June 1973 calculated that in terms of purchasing power values had not kept pace with inflation; which, for more recent times, was putting it mildly.

Leaving inflationary factors aside for the present, it is important that holders of older-issue certificates should know what they are worth and are earning in interest. In almost every case, extension or no extension of life so far, interest now being credited is less than the four-year *average* of £7·59 per cent on the current (four-teenth) issue. Details which follow should help holders to decide whether to switch immediately; to wait for any bonus due at the end of a 'holding' period; or to do nothing.

Sales periods, present lives and range of maturity dates for issues between 1939 and 1966 can be summarized as under:

Issue	On sale		Life	Maturity dates	
	From	To	years	Earliest	Latest
7th	Nov. '39	Mar. '47	36	Nov. '75	Mar. '83
£1	Jan. '43	Mar. '47	33	Jan. '76	Mar. '80
8th	Apr. '47	Jan. '51	29	Apr. '76	Jan. '80
9th	Feb. '51	Jly. '56	25	Feb. '76	Jly. '81
10th	Aug. '56	Mar. '63	19	Aug. '75	Mar. '82
11th	May '63	Mar. '66	12	May '75	Mar. '78
12th	Mar. '66	Oct. '70	9	Mar. '75	Oct. '79

Prime considerations in the decision of what to do are the current and future annual interest rates. The next tables show these for the years still left, together with the accumulated values.

SEVENTH ISSUE			£1 ISSUE			EIGHTH ISSUE		
Years held	Value	Yield %	Years held	Value	Yield %	Years held	Value	Yield %
	£p	£p		£p	£p		£p	£p
28	1·67½	3·07½	28	1·57½	2·44	24	1·02½	3·80
29	1·75	4·48	29	1·66	5·55½	25	1·07½	4·88
30	1·81	3·57	30	1·73	4·06	26	1·12	4·18½
31	1·89	4·14	31	1·80½	4·33½	27	1·16½	4·02
32	1·96	3·97½	32	1·88	4·15½	28	1·21	3·86½
33	2·04	3·82	33	2·00	6·38½	29	1·30	7·44
34	2·11	3·68						
35	2·20	4·14½						
36	2·32	5·45½						
Issue prices: 75p			£1			50p		

The Complete Guide to Investment

NINTH ISSUE			TENTH ISSUE			ELEVENTH ISSUE		
Years held	Value % £p	Yield % £p	Years held	Value % £p	Yield % £p	Years held	Value % £p	Yield % £p
19	1·40	3·70½	12	1·19	3·26	9	1·40	3·70½
20	1·45	3·57	13	1·22½	3·16	10	1·45	3·57
21	1·50	3·45	14	1·26	3·06	11	1·50	3·45
22	1·57½	5·00	15	1·32½	4·95	12	1·60	6·66½
23	1·63½	3·81	16	1·37½	3·77½			
24	1·69½	3·67	17	1·43½	4·36½			
25	1·80	6·19½	18	1·49½	4·18			
			19	1·60	7·02½			

Issue prices: 75p   75p   £1

N.B. Because of decimalization after issue some values and yields are not absolutely exact; differences compared with the actual amounts are, however, very small.

Initial life of the *twelfth issue* was five years, with the £1 units increasing from £1 to £1·25 to give an average annual yield of £4·56½ per cent. A four-year extension gives interest additions of 1½p for each completed period of four months and a bonus of 7p at the end of the ninth year. Year-end values and yields are: year 6, £1·29½ and 3·60 per cent; year 7, £1·34 and 3·47½ per cent; year 8, £1·38½ and 3·36 per cent; and year 9, £1·50 and 8·30½ per cent. Average interest for the extra four years is thus 4·66½ per cent.

Terms for the *Decimal issue* of October 1970 were the addition of 3p interest to the price of £1 at the end of year 1, followed by 1½p for each completed four months in year 2; 2½p for each completed four months in year 3; and 3p for each four months in year 4 with an extra 1p at the end, to make 25p in all. Growth details are:

DECIMAL ISSUE

Years held	Value £p	Yield % £p
1	1·03	3·00
2	1·07½	4·37
3	1·15	6·97½
4	1·25	8·69½

– to give an average yield over the four years of 5·73½ per cent, tax free.

An interesting move to look after 1939/1970 issues maturing during the period August 1974 to May 1975 is a two-year extension only. This indicates that a major reorganization and consolidation along the lines suggested in the Page Report could be on the way – and may have taken place by the time this edition is out. Key details for the extra two years, where applicable, are:

Issue	Maturity value Basic	After 2-year extension	Overall annual interest rate
	£p	£p	%
7th	2·32	2·65	6·88
£1	2·00	2·28	6·77
8th	1·30	1·48	6·70
9th	1·80	2·05	6·72
10th	1·60	1·83	6·95
11th	1·60	1·83	6·95
12th	1·50	1·71	6·77
Decimal	1·25	1·43	6·96

Again, yields are tax-free.

Some general rules may help to summarize what has been written about Savings Certificates. Subject to the rate of increase – or reversal – in inflation, action would be:

They are a priority investment for the 'old oak chest' reserve fund. Unless money is being accumulated for some short-term need, the general run of saver should make them his first investment choice, after a Savings Bank account, and not look elsewhere until £100 worth or more has been salted away.

They can be attractive to savers paying income tax, particularly those liable at above the basic rate.

It pays however to look regularly at holdings of the earlier issues. It may be profitable to transfer to the current issue, or to some other investment. The guiding rules are:

Providing the limit of £1,000 will not be exceeded it can pay to switch into fourteenth issue Certificates from earlier issues up to the twelfth.

It is almost generally beneficial for holders paying only base rate tax who would otherwise exceed the £1,000 limit for the fourteenth issue to cash all issues up to the twelfth and to re-invest in a building society at 7½ per cent, or even 7 per cent, tax paid.

If no income tax is paid, it is profitable to cash all issues up to the Decimal and to re-invest in equally safe securities like British Savings Bonds, Local Authority loans, and Government stocks offering substantially higher interest.

High income-tax payers with the maximum of the current issue should look carefully into the profitability of keeping all issues from the seventh onwards. Medium tax payers should however cash all issues up to the sixth.

The simplest way of transferring from older issues to the current issue is to complete a repayment form, which can be obtained at the Post Office, and asking for re-investment at a chosen Post Office which will issue current issue certificates in exchange for the repayment warrant; and pay in cash any balance left over.

CHAPTER 3

Government Bonds, Premium Bonds, and Local Authority Loans

NOVEMBER 1939 brought a new form of National Savings to encourage investors to help in financing the cost of another world war – *Defence Bonds*. Sold in units of £5 at Post Offices and through the Savings and other Banks, the fundamental differences compared with Savings Certificates were that (a) interest was payable half-yearly; (b) they had a maximum life of seven years; (c) at the end of this period they were repayable with a tax-free bonus of one per cent, or £1 per £100 of Bonds; and (d) holders could cash them previously at their full face value on giving six months' notice, or immediately subject to the loss of the equivalent of six months' interest. Another major difference was that, in the appropriate cases, interest was liable to income tax and surtax, though no actual deductions were made from the half-yearly payments; which saved tax-exempt investors the trouble of making repayment claims. Interest on the historic pioneer issue was 3 per cent, and the initial limit which an individual could buy was £1,000 worth.

Various issues followed at interest rates attuned to financial conditions at their launching and which varied from as little as $2\frac{1}{2}$ per cent for those on sale between May 1946 and January 1951, to 5 per cent on the issues sold between 1 May 1958 and 12 March 1963. Lives were either seven or ten years, and, with one exception, the bonuses for holding the various issues to maturity ranged between the original one per cent to as much as five per cent. Limits were also altered upwards to a maximum of £5,000 for later issues, in addition to which there could be held extra amounts arising from the different conversion offers made when older issues reached their maturity dates, and by inheritance. During their time Defence Bonds brought in some thousands of millions. All issues have now been repaid, or converted into National Development Bonds and/or later into British Savings Bonds.

The name 'Defence' was a misnomer after the end of the Second World War. It persisted, however, issue by issue, until 1964 when, on 15 May, *National Development Bonds* took over the financial running. Up to 10 July 1966 there were five issues (including three conversion offers to holders of maturing Defence Bonds) at 5 per cent interest. These were followed by three issues (including two conversions) at 5½ per cent on sale up to 30 March 1968. Basic differences were that (a) all issues had only five-year lives; (b) the tax-free bonuses on repayment at maturity were 2 per cent; (c) the limit of purchase by an individual investor was £2,500 per issue; and (d) the repayment terms prior to normal maturity were eased. All National Development Bonds have been repaid or converted into British Savings Bonds.

Another change came on 1 April 1968, when the first issue of *British Savings Bonds* went on sale through the usual sources. While there were no changes in the basic ideas attaching to this type of National Savings, the interest was 6 per cent and the purchase limit as much as £10,000. Taking account of the 2 per cent tax-free bonus payable on normal maturity at the end of five years the effective average yield was about £6·35 per cent for non-taxpayers and some £6·50 per cent for investors liable at 30 per cent. Although encashment of Bonds within six months of purchase meant the loss of interest for up to such a period, those held for more than six months could be cashed at their full face value on giving only one month's written notice.

Little more than a year later a fresh issue came on sale as from 28 April 1969. Designed to encourage the much-needed increase in personal savings the interest was put up to 7 per cent. Otherwise, the terms were similar to the 6 per cents: 5-year life; 2 per cent tax-free bonus on maturity; purchase limit per individual £10,000 in multiples of £5; and, after the initial six months of holding, encashment at full face value on only one month's written notice. Taking into the reckoning the 2 per cent bonus, the average yield over the five years to normal maturity was £7·34 per cent for investors paying no income tax, and around £7·50 per cent for those liable at 30 per cent.

A second 7 per cent issue was launched on 3 May 1971 with one important change: the tax-free bonus was raised one point to 3 per cent. Held for five years, the average yield is in the region of £7·8 per cent if tax is paid at 33 per cent.

A further issue came on sale in May 1973 at the still higher interest rate of 8½ per cent, with a tax-free bonus of 3 per cent at the end of five years and a £10,000 limit. Allowing for the bonus the average yield over the full five years is £8·99 per cent for investors exempt from income tax and £9·28 per cent for those paying a basic rate of 33 per cent.

With inflation blazing away, still another increase in interest followed in June 1974, when a 9½ per cent issue of British Savings Bonds was inaugurated. With interest payable in January and July, and the established limit of £10,000 purchases per individual, the tax-free bonus is also 3 per cent at the end of five years. The average yield is thus £9·98 per cent for non-taxpayers and £10·26 per cent gross for those liable at 33 per cent. Bonds can be bought in the usual multiples of £5.

With these issue details in mind it is time to summarize the key points about British Savings Bonds in general, as follows:

Limits are put on the total of each issue which can be bought. It is £10,000 for each issue. Holders can, however, have up to the limits of previous issues and can go over the £10,000 limit by means of conversion offers such as from maturing Bonds; or through inheritance.

Each member of a family can invest up to the limit.

Cashing Bonds is simple. An application form, obtainable at post offices, should be sent with Bond Book or Certificate to: The Bonds & Stock Office, Lytham St Annes, Lancs FY0 1YN.

Transfers of Bonds are possible if they are not in the nature of sales. Permission has however to be obtained from the Director of Savings or, in the appropriate cases, from the National Debt Commissioners.

Proceeds from cashing older issues cannot automatically be reinvested in the current issue, for the simple reason that an application form for investment in new Bonds must be completed. A repayment order for old Bonds can, however, easily be handed over the post office counter in payment for new Bonds, with any small difference either way being settled in cash.

Income tax, as already explained, is not deducted from the half-yearly interest. But such income is *liable to tax* in the appropriate cases, and the total received for each year ending 5 April must be entered in annual tax returns. Tax payable, if any, will of course depend on the income from all sources and the tax allowances of each investor.

Collection of any tax due on Bond interest usually takes one of two forms. First, and simplest, is when tax is paid under P.A.Y.E. The annual interest is deducted from the tax allowances when the code number is being fixed and the appropriate tax is then deducted weekly or monthly from wages, salary or pension. Accumulation of arrears and bother are saved by notifying the tax office immediately of all purchases of Bonds, while overpayments of tax can be avoided by notifying sales. The second form applies where Bond-holders such as self-employed or retired people pay their income tax direct; they are assessed on the interest applicable to each particular tax year.

Bonuses payable on maturity of all issues are exempt from income tax and capital gains tax. Only the annual interest is taxable.

An important problem facing holders of older issues of Bonds is that of switching to the current, 9½ per cent, issue of British Savings Bonds. The tax-free bonus is usually the decisive consideration, particularly for investors liable to tax on the interest. Broad guide lines are:

The first consideration is an investor's tax position. As already shown, the tax-free bonuses on redemption are worth more to the tax payer than to one who is tax exempt. The second factor is the time still to run until redemption. The third point is the total of the older holdings and whether a switch would mean going over the £10,000 limit for the current issue. Lastly, there must be some speculation on the length of time Bonds will be on sale at 9½ per cent – the next issue, when it comes, may be at a higher, or lower, interest rate. However, 7 per cent Bonds, particularly the second issue with their 3 per cent bonus, should be held if there are only some 12 to 18 months to go; otherwise a switch is profitable. In view of their launch date, there can be little argument, subject only to the £10,000 limit rule, against *not* cashing 8½ per cent Bonds and re-investing to get the extra 1 per cent interest from the current issue.

The advisability of switching from old issues of Bonds to the current issue must also rightly take account of the interest which could be earned on other types of investment. If older issues are worth cashing before maturity it might be more profitable to re-invest outside this field. For example, local councils may be offering substantially more on money lent for periods of up to five years or longer; building societies, after allowing for income tax, may be giving the gross equivalent of ½ to 1 per cent extra; and Savings Certificates, again after allowing for tax, may have a useful edge on Bonds.

A very general guide based on interest rates ruling at the time of writing is that (a) investors paying no income tax can certainly do better by investing in local council loans, always providing they are ready to lock up their money for a *fixed* time, or in long-dated or undated Government stocks; and (b) those paying tax should normally do a little better with share accounts in sound building societies and Savings Certificates.

Retired people should also consider the merits of the 'Index-Linked' Bonds which are likely to be issued later this year, the details of which were not available at the time this edition went to press.

Premium Savings Bonds, or *Premium Bonds* as they are more popularly called, are the third leg of the National Savings group. They are the twentieth-century version of the State lotteries which flourished during the Napoleonic Wars – but with one vital difference: Premium Bonds are a safety-first speculation, not a win-or-lose-all gamble. They are a means of saving, offering some of the attractions of the football pools and catering for the pretty general human inclination to 'have a go' on something. *Their particular merit is that an investor cannot lose his investment*. Premium Bonds can be cashed any time after purchase at their full face value. Every Bond held for the basic qualification period has however a chance of winning tax-free prizes up to £75,000 in the monthly draws, and from July 1974 of a single prize of £50,000 and 25 prizes of £1,000 each every week – and of going on winning them. Their popularity is shown by the fact that from the date when this unorthodox and controversial means of raising money for Government purposes was introduced, in November 1956, gross sales have exceeded £1,800 million and the number of bond-holders is well over 21 million, with average holdings approaching £50.

The basic difference between Premium Bonds and the other forms of National Savings is that they do not offer the usual type of interest to holders. Instead, the equivalent of interest is put into a fund each month and distributed as prizes from the draws, which are made by the now familiar robot character 'ERNIE'. Bonds first qualify for the draws three clear months after purchase. A bond bought any day in March will, for instance, go into the July draw and every one thereafter, until the holder cashes it. Draws start on the first day of each month, but if this is a Saturday, Sunday, or public holiday the draw is deferred until the first weekday after. The special weekly draw is announced each Saturday.

As with other National Savings, there is a limit to the Premium Bonds which can be held. For the first issue, which was on sale from 1 November 1956 to 31 July 1960, it was 500 £1 Bonds. The limit has since been increased four times – to £800 on 1 August 1960, to £1,000 on 21 April 1964, to £1,250 on 14 April 1967 and to £2,000 on 1 April 1971. Though there are now in issue two series – A and B – all Bonds are treated equally and in accordance with the issue terms of series B. The distinguishing letters A and B are simply administrative codes.

Anyone of sixteen or over can buy Premium Bonds at a post office, through a bank, or by debit to a National Savings Bank account, in quantities ranging from two £1 units to £500 worth. Prior to 5 February 1972 the minimum purchase was one £1 Bond; but the change to a £2 minimum makes no difference to the basic unit of £1. They can also be bought by parents or guardians on behalf of children under sixteen years of age. Each £1 unit has its own six-figure number and (a matter of some controversy and mis-understanding, discussed later) two letters. The first letter indicates the value of the Bond, A being for £1, B for £2 and so on up to z for £500 worth. The second letter is the million figure, with z representing zero, B one million, F two million, and K, L, N, P, S, T, and W the million figures up to nine million. A number in front of the letters means tens of millions, while two figures indicate hundreds of millions. An example shows how this works.

A buyer of £10 worth of Bonds might be allotted, say, 2KN423981/423990, which means that he or she holds Bonds 25,423,981 to 25,423,990 in the £10 series. Details of every sale are filed in alphabetical and numerical registers at the Premium Savings Bond Office. Bonds are then brought into the monthly draws as soon as they complete the qualification period of three clear months.

Until Premium Bonds were created, the popular conception of the right way to make prize draws was to put every single 'ticket' into the drum. The option of buying Bonds in single units or blocks not unnaturally raised the question as to which method gave the better chances of winning prizes. The answer is unequivocal. Whatever the size of a holding – 1 or 2,000 Bonds – each £1 unit has an equal chance. With many tens of millions going into each draw, it would obviously be far too cumbersome, slow, and costly to follow the traditional custom of putting single £1 'tickets' into a drum. It was for this reason that 'ERNIE' was created. He has now done his job for many years, and the official mind is confident that he is absolutely fair to all comers.

Electric Random Number Indicator Equipment, to give 'ERNIE' his full name, was made by the Post Office Research Department specifically to generate numbers at random, without fear or favouritism. The method of operation has been officially described as follows:

ERNIE is electronic, although it may be helpful to think of it as a box containing ten wheels spinning behind small windows – rather like a fruit machine, but showing numbers and letters around the rim of each wheel. Reading from left to right, the first and second wheels will represent the hundreds and tens of millions, the third will have letters representing Bond values, the fourth will have ten letters indicating the millions figures 0 to 9, and the remaining six each have ten figures 0 to 9. If the wheels were driven round independently and erratically for a time, then stopped simultaneously for the letters and figures to be read as a Bond unit number, this would correspond broadly with the method used in ERNIE. The next number would be selected in a similar way, and so on.

All substances contain millions of minute particles called atoms, each comprising a nucleus with electrons revolving around it like planets around the sun. The numbers generated by ERNIE depend on the haphazard movement of electrons in a device called a 'Noise Producing Diode', made from a substance called a semi-conductor. When a specific electric current flows through this device, some of the electrons leave their 'parent' nuclei and move in a haphazard fashion until they find another orbit. Sometimes a collision takes place, forcing another electron into free motion.

Each unpredictable movement of an electron contributes minutely towards a fluctuating amount of energy within the diode, thus producing, at completely random intervals, pulses of energy of differing magnitude. These pulses are fed into an electronic counter and, so as to doubly ensure randomness, two counts are effectively added together to generate one of the ten characters of the Bond number. The whole Bond unit number is produced by recording the characters generated by ten pairs of counters, and this process is carried out at the rate of 1,000 complete unit numbers every minute.

ERNIE thus generates separately, but simultaneously, each of the ten characters which make a complete Bond number and puts them together. During the draw, a special part of ERNIE is told which ranges of Bonds have not yet been issued for sale. Since there would be no point in recording these, any numbers generated within these ranges are rejected automatically. All the rest are stored on magnetic computer tapes. ERNIE produces two of these tapes and, immediately after the draw is completed, special equipment compares the two tapes to ensure that they are absolutely identical.

The order of prize-winning is foolproof: ERNIE prints a draw serial number showing the order of 'drawing' as each winning Bond comes up. The method of selection means that Bonds which have not yet been sold, or which have been cashed, cannot qualify for prizes. All drawn numbers are checked and counter-checked against the numerical register already mentioned, and any not on it are rejected. Thus 'live' Bonds only can qualify for prizes; and the lucky numbers are not published until the essential facts have been verified. Constant checking of the equipment and registers ensures that *all* units eligible for each draw are included and that ERNIE maintains his strict impartiality. Two new ERNIES, which began work recently, have speeded up the draws.

The method of calculating the prize funds is simple. They are determined by calculating one month's interest at an annual rate on the Bonds going into each month's draws. From 4 per cent originally, the annual interest rate has been increased five times, and from 1 July 1974 has been $5\frac{1}{2}$ per cent compared with $4\frac{7}{8}$ per cent for the previous twelve months. Division of the monthly fund as from July 1974 has been:

Weekly Prizes	*Monthly Prizes*
1 of £50,000	1 of £75,000
25 of £1,000	1 of £25,000

Monthly Prizes
Each remaining £100,000:

1 of £5,000	25 of £100
10 of £1,000	850 of £50
10 of £500	1,400 of £25

Each remaining £10,000:

1 of £1,000	80 of £50
1 of £500	140 of £25
10 of £100	

Any balance under £10,000 is divided into £25 prizes.

A previous £250 prize category was abolished and the number of £50 prizes almost doubled.

A typical draw for a month with four Saturdays in it produced 97,121 prizes valued at £4,622,975 and distributed as shown overleaf.

Every Bond going into the draw contributes one month's interest to it. The odds are in this way kept at the relatively stable level of around 10,560 to 1.

Denomination £	Number
75,000	1
50,000	4
25,000	1
5,000	42
1,000	522
500	422
100	1,070
50	35,860
25	59,199

While a Bond unit can win no more than one prize in a draw, it can go on to win further prizes in future draws. A holder of more than one eligible unit has the chance, of course, of winning more than one prize in each draw. *Prizes have the particular advantage of being free of income tax, surtax and capital gains tax.*

Prizewinners are notified by post, which is one good reason for immediately notifying a change of address to the Premium Savings Bond Office, Lytham St Annes, Lancs FY0 1YN. Most newspapers publish lists of the numbers winning, at least the larger prizes. The full list of numbers only – names and addresses of holders are strictly confidential – is however printed monthly in the *London Gazette*, copies of which are at main Post Offices.

All £25 and £50 prizes are paid direct. Winners of £100 or more must however complete a claim form which is sent to them with the good news.

Luck, as in any sweep or draw, is a major part of prize-winning success. A holder of one unit may win the first time the Bond goes into a draw, while other holders with the maximum of £2,000 worth may go prizeless month after month. A natural question after months of waiting may therefore be whether it is worth while holding on, in the hope that luck will turn, or whether to transfer the money to an interest-paying investment. To give a comprehensive answer is not easy; so much depends on individual circumstances. Some general rules may help.

Give 'ERNIE' a fair run of at least two or three years.

If the Bonds represent 'spare money' which is not needed to earn a steady income, hold them all.

But if income is needed to help with living expenses, do not keep an unduly high proportion of savings in Bonds. A practical compromise in such circumstances is to cash say half.

Premium Bonds can be cashed easily within a few days by completing a withdrawal form, which can be obtained at the Post Office or a bank, and sending it to the Premium Savings Bond Office. The actual Bonds should be enclosed if payment is wanted by crossed warrant; otherwise they have to be given up at the Post Office if payment is made in cash. When part of a block is cashed, a certificate is issued for the balance.

Bonds cannot be transferred to a new holder.

When a unit-holder dies, all eligible Bonds can be *repaid* on application by the next-of-kin or the legal personal representative, or *left in* for all draws held in the month of death and in the following twelve calendar months. After this they cannot win prizes and should be cashed.

Another form of investment similar to National Savings, which has grown widely in popularity during recent years, is the mortgage loan to Local Authorities. Though this is a far from new means of raising money for housing, schools, street and road development, and other public services, councils have had to revert to this method of 'tap' financing, largely as a consequence of Government financial policy. For a few years after the last war attempts were made to control their capital spending by insisting that borrowings were made from what is known as the Public Works Loan Board, which receives its funds through the Exchequer. The bulk of such funds came in fact from Budget surpluses of tax and other revenue over ordinary Government spending. This control was dropped some years ago when, though funds could still be obtained through the Public Works Loan Board, local councils were encouraged to go direct to the public for their capital requirements.

Local Authorities now have four main methods of raising money. First they can make a public offer of a fixed amount of stock, say five million pounds' worth, which – as it is usually dealt in on the Stock Exchange – is susceptible to fluctuations in price. Secondly, they can raise what are generally known as 'Euro-loans' through the international money market and which largely consist of dollar and Continental funds subscribed by banks and overseas institutional investors.

Thirdly, they can issue *Yearling Bonds* which get their name from the fact that they have a one-year life. Each Tuesday a batch of bonds is issued on behalf of a number of local authorities, each of which has its due proportion, in its own name, at a common rate of interest. Controlled by the Treasury and the Bank of England, the interest rate is based on current conditions in the money market, as is the total offering, which may be, say, £12 million. Interest rates have varied widely since the beginning of 1973 (when they were under the 10 per cent mark) to over 15 per cent. Anyone can buy Yearlings through the Stock Exchange in minimum amounts of £1,000 and, equally, can sell them before maturity at the end of their twelve-month life. A tax pointer is that if bonds are sold before they are quoted ex-dividend any profit is liable only to capital gains tax; which can help investors who pay high rates of income tax.

Fourthly, councils can let it be known, generally by advertisements in local and other newspapers, that loans will be accepted at a stated rate of interest for periods of one year, or from two to five years or more. There is no limit to the amount which a council can raise in this way, and it has become the most popular method, particularly amongst the smaller Authorities which have had little chance of getting into the queue formed by their bigger brethren for the opportunity of making the older type of block offer. The 'tap' can be turned on and off as funds are needed.

The main attractions of Local Authority mortgage loans are that investors know they will get a fixed rate of interest for an agreed period; there are no expenses such as brokerage or Government stamp duty to add to the cost of the investment; and there is no risk of fluctuation in value as with Stock Exchange securities – £100 invested always equals £100. On the other hand, although most councils will consider prior repayment or transfer in cases of need or special circumstances, or offer a 'break' clause, the money is otherwise tied up for the agreed period.

The general rules are that the minimum investment is say £100 to £500; interest, which begins immediately, is payable half-yearly on specified dates; and income tax is deducted at the standard rate from all interest payments. Investors who are exempt from tax can of course make repayment claims by getting in touch with the appropriate Income Tax office in April, or (if the amount is fairly large) half-yearly in October and April. Some councils offer slightly higher interest on minimum investments, of say, £1,000, £5,000, £10,000, or more. Here again, there was a steep rise in interest rates in the second half of 1973, which carried through into 1974. From single-figure rates, interest soared at one time to over 16 per cent, with the actual rate partly depending on the period of loans.

A variation of this 'tap' type of investment, which can be useful when money may be wanted at short notice, is a deposit account with one of the councils ready to accept such funds. The usual terms are two or seven days' notice of withdrawal and interest of 1 to 2 points below the longer term mortgage rate; which, in recent dear money times, has meant rates comfortably into double figures and ranging up to 14/15 per cent. Large sums running into tens and hundreds of thousands of pounds get even better terms, especially when short-term money is hard to come by – interest of 20 per cent has been known to be paid in periods of acute stringency in money markets.

Local Authority mortgage loans are specially useful for retired people who want income and absolute security and who do not pay income tax. They can also be profitable for investors wishing to put away money for a definite period, knowing that it will be repayable in full on a specified date.

It is sometimes objected that deduction of tax from interest payments involves the trouble of making repayment claims, and that British Savings Bonds are so much easier in this respect. The answer is that if the interest is a good deal higher, as it has been in 1973/74, it is well worth the work of making repayment claims in return for the greater income. In the vast majority of cases, once the formalities of the first application are over, they are quite simple to carry through.

Short-period deposits and Yearling Bonds are the better choice for money which will be needed fairly quickly or within a few weeks or months.

Another useful rule is to invest (a) for the longest period when interest is high, and (b) for the shortest period when it is low.

CHAPTER 4

Building Societies

BUILDING societies have an even longer record than the Savings
Banks as means of encouraging thrift. The first societies were
formed some 200 years ago. The earliest to be traced was one
called Ketley's Building Society, which started business some-
where about 1775 at Golden Cross, Birmingham. The basis of
operation of the pioneers was mostly similar. A number of people,
mainly artisans and higher paid manual workers, combined together to build their own houses. Each member of the society
undertook to pay in a fixed 'share' per week or month, the funds
so provided being used, first, to buy land and, secondly, to start
building houses, usually one at a time. As each house was completed, the shareholders drew lots for it. If the lucky drawer
changed his mind about home ownership he could sell his rights,
or shares, to another member. Whatever the fortunes of the draw
each member, house-owner or not, continued to pay in his share
subscriptions until all members had their own dwellings. The
society was usually then terminated, which gave rise to the word
'terminating' in the names of many of them.

Land societies provided an early variation, and received a
powerful stimulus when the bitterly contested Reform Act of 1832
was passed. Under an old Act of 1430, the owner of a freehold
with an annual value of not less than 40s. was entitled to a Parliamentary vote. Cobden, the determined advocate of free trade, was
amongst the first to appreciate the value of the land society 'as an
engine that might be successfully and legitimately used for ex-
tending the franchise'. Whigs and Tories alike hastened to promote freehold land societies. These bought land, generally large
estates, for division into lots which were sold to individuals with
the right political allegiance. Any doubt as to the value of the
plots was taken care of by granting ninety-nine-year leases of a

71

few, at a ground rent of not less than 50s. a year. Payment for plots was made by instalments.

Although the combined assets of building societies are marching towards the £21,000 million mark and overall membership exceeds 19 million, there has been no change in their basic idea. Savings of investing members are used to assist borrowing members to buy or build their own homes. A few facts show their usefulness. Despite the cash shortage problems of the last half of 1973 and the earlier months of 1974 – caused, incidentally, through no fault of the societies – expansion has been largely unbroken for many years. Total assets at the end of 1973 of more than £17,500 million were over four times the 1963 figure of £4,300 million and compared with £15,250 million in late 1972.

During the ten years to 1973 the number of investment accounts grew from 5,486,000 to more than 15,000,000 and the savings in them from £4,000 million to £16,600 million. In the same period the total of 'live' borrowers expanded from 2,625,000 to over 4,200,000 and their mortgage debt outstanding from £3,556 million to £14,532 million. New loans for house-ownership, which were only £850 million in 1963, rose to a record level of £3,630 million in 1972 before slipping back slightly to £3,513 million in 1973. Investment in building societies is today getting on even terms with life assurance and is approaching double the total invested in the once dominant National Savings sector.

Every community of any size has at least one building society. It may be a relatively small, purely local concern with assets of no more than a few thousand pounds, or a branch of one of the big regional or national societies which count their funds in tens or hundreds of millions of pounds and which may have a dozen or more offices scattered over Britain. Mainly owing to amalgamations and the absorption of smaller concerns by larger ones, the number of societies has been steadily falling, the 1973 aggregate of 447 being only about one-fifth of the 1900 total and comparing with 807 in 1951. While in some ways this contraction is to be regretted, its continuance is inevitable, for the simple reason that this is the age of the big unit. And, as experience generally shows, the bigger concern with its large resources often can give better service to both investor and borrower. Some mergers, like that of the Leicester Permanent and Leicester Temperance, the biggest 'marriage' up to May 1974 and creating the seventh largest society, are geographically and managerially logical. Others, equally, will be of ultimate benefit to the whole movement.

A long-established and guiding principle of British financial institutions is to keep to a minimum the policy of 'borrowing short' and 'lending long'. In other words, if a large part of their funds is subject to withdrawal on demand or at short notice, as is the case with the commercial banks, the bulk of their assets should be invested so that realization is speedy. Building societies provide the classic case of the reverse policy proving financially sound and profitable for both classes of member. The major portion of their investment funds is repayable on little notice from investors. On the other hand, up to 80 or 90 per cent of their assets are mortgages, which, though mostly repayable by monthly instalments, represent money lent for periods of up to twenty years or more.

Long experience has shown that, boom or slump, financial ease or crisis, the average building society investor does not panic or withdraw more cash than he may require for pressing needs. On the other hand, the zoom in interest rates, which began in mid-1973, did have two unpleasant effects. 'Hot' money was withdrawn, and invested in the money market and with local councils on much more profitable terms than the societies could match. And, for similar reasons and because of the steep rise in living costs, there was an acute drop in net new investments. Retention of 15 to 20 per cent of a society's assets in cash and readily realizable investments has been proved, however, to be more than enough to meet any 'run' of withdrawals and to fulfil commitments on mortgage advances.

Building societies, though individual policy varies, generally offer four general types of investment facility. These are deposits, shares, subscription shares, and 'term' deposits or shares.

Deposits, which can be accepted up to a maximum of two-thirds of a society's mortgage assets, have a first call on profits and assets. They must be accepted on terms providing not less than one month's notice of withdrawal. In practice, most societies will generally repay reasonable sums in a few days or on demand. Interest, in view of the additional security, is usually $\frac{1}{4}$ or $\frac{1}{2}$ per cent less than on shares. Deposits in societies which, as mentioned later, qualify for the necessary status are now authorized investments for trust funds.

Shares, sometimes described as 'fully paid-up', 'A', 'B', 'Ordinary', or by some other tag, may or may not have a fixed value such as £1 or £20; and for all practical purposes it does not usually matter. As a rule, the normal share account is like a Savings Bank account: and many investors, particularly in the North and Midlands, use it as such. Interest on most share accounts starts from the day money is paid in, or within a few days, and is credited up to the day of withdrawal. The great bulk of building society 'capital' is in this type of account, which for the majority of investors is the best and most profitable. Share accounts in a 'designated' society also qualify for trustee status.

Subscription shares, as they are often called, are designed to encourage regular saving. Names vary, such as 'Regular Savings', 'Savings Plan', 'Planned Savings', 'Extra Yield Savings' and 'Build-up Share' accounts. An agreed amount is invested monthly – sometimes weekly – for a stipulated or selected number of years, which may be two, three, five, or more, depending on the particular society's scheme. Extra amounts may also be paid in providing the total for a month does not exceed a stipulated limit such as, say, £50. In return for this regularity of saving, which is particularly useful for investors saving ahead to buy a house or for some other long-term project, societies pay extra interest of between $\frac{1}{2}$ per cent and $1\frac{1}{4}$ per cent above the rate paid on 'Ordinary' share accounts. For instance, if the latter is 7·50 per cent, the subscription rate could be as much as $8\frac{3}{4}$ per cent, tax paid. At least one society has a guarantee plan for 'first home' buyers using regular savings accounts which ensures that they will be able to borrow up to ten times their savings with a maximum of £13,000. If subscriptions are not kept up, or those paid in are withdrawn, the investor must naturally suffer some penalty. With most societies this is normally limited to loss of the 'bonus' interest. Not all societies offer this useful means of accumulating funds; but those which do so invariably fix a minimum of £1 and maximum of up to, say, £50 a month and an overall investment limit such as £2,000 or £3,000.

Term investments, mostly called term shares or term deposits, though not universally popular amongst managements, are accepted by some societies. The main attraction is that in return for leaving money for a minimum period of one, two, or three years, or as little as six months, an investor gets between $\frac{1}{4}$ per cent and $1\frac{1}{4}$ per cent more than the current rate on share accounts. For instance, if the share rate is 7·50 per cent, 7·75 will be paid for a six-monthly minimum term; 8 per cent for a one-year term; 8·5 per cent for two years; and 8·75 per cent for three years. The minimum initial investment may be £100; but, except perhaps for a six-month account, the maximum is the limit of £10,000 which an individual may have in any single society. A possible disadvantage is that such investments may not be withdrawable until the end of the agreed period. Some societies will, however, repay earlier in cases of urgent financial need, though naturally at a lower rate of interest. Subject to this contingency, term investments can be a profitable way of investing money for use some time ahead.

Monthly income shares are a new facility offered by a few societies. Subject to a minimum investment of say £1,000, the society posts a cheque direct to the investor or to his bank each month for the appropriate income. Assuming that the current rate of interest paid by the society is 7·50 per cent (income tax paid) the *net* monthly income per £1,000 invested is £6·25. Investments in excess of the minimum can be made in multiples of say £100 up to the maximum of £10,000 which an individual can invest in any one society; which means that a husband and wife could have £10,000 each in such accounts and, on the above basis, draw a combined net income of £125 a month. Retired people and others exempt from income tax should note that under arrangements in force at the time of writing no tax can be reclaimed and the interest received may affect special tax reliefs open to investors aged 65 or over. Withdrawals of capital are usually subject to 1–6 months' notice.

The choice offered to investors by individual societies clearly depends on management policy. Some favour all the facilities described above. Others restrict themselves to deposits and ordinary shares, or even shares only. Although each society decides its own interest terms, most stick to the rates recommended by the Building Societies Association, which speaks for a large proportion of the movement. Noteworthy exceptions to this general policy are the smaller societies in the London and bigger provincial areas, which generally offer say an extra ¼ per cent, in order to compete for investment funds against their larger competitors. Strong efforts are made by all to keep investment interest in line with the rates of the main competitors such as National Savings and hire-purchase finance companies.

A particular feature of all interest is that individual investors receive it income-tax paid at the equivalent of the base rate, which at the time of writing is 33 per cent. Societies pay the income tax under special arrangements with the Inland Revenue at what is called the 'composite rate'.

While the tax-paid arrangement benefits investors liable to income tax, it is not so beneficial to those who are exempt. The latter cannot reclaim any of the tax paid by the society; the interest they get is both net *and* gross. Equally, investors liable to tax at rates above the base level have to pay the extra on the 'grossed up' interest – if the interest received is, say, £7·50 the amount to take into account is £11·19.

Because of the tax arrangement it is important when comparing building societies with other types of investment to *gross up* the interest at base rate income tax. The effect, taking the latter at 33 per cent, gives these results:

Net %	Gross %	Net %	Gross %	Net %	Gross %
6·25	9·33	7·25	10·82	8·25	12·31
6·50	9·70	7·50	11·19	8·50	12·69
6·75	10·07	7·75	11·57	8·75	13·06
7·00	10·45	8·00	11·94	9·00	13·43

Tax, as will have been seen, is an important factor when considering the investment potentialities of building societies. Two general rules should be helpful:

1. Whatever the tax rate, they provide more profitable SHORT-TERM investments than ordinary department accounts in the National Savings Bank or a Trustee Savings Bank, and Savings Certificates held for, say, less than two years. Though not fully on a par with such Government-backed investments, the security is first class, *provided that the choice is made from societies which pass certain tests mentioned later*.

2. The LONG-TERM value, however, largely depends on each investor's tax position. While, as has been shown in the above table, gross equivalent rates of interest are attractive, it is a different matter if there is tax exemption. Accordingly, although useful for the safekeeping of money which may be needed quickly or has to be invested for a relatively short time, they are not the most profitable for permanent investment if no tax is paid. Local authority mortgage loans, British Savings Bonds, medium and long-dated and undated Government stocks, and similar securities should then be the choice.

Building society accounts can generally be opened with as little as £1, perhaps less, and added to at any time. The only restriction is that individuals cannot have more than £10,000 in any society, although husband and wife can *each* invest up to the £10,000 maximum in a single society. There is nothing, however, to stop anyone having up to the limit in more than one society – two, a dozen, or even fifty or more.

Investment facilities are simple and varied. Money can be paid in over the counter, if an office is handy; by cheque or, for regular saving, by banker's order; or by credit transfer facilities through the local branch of a bank designated by the society or by using the National Giro. Arrangements may also be made for the direct credit of interest and dividends on other investments to the account of the holder.

Withdrawals are made with the minimum formality. Most societies will pay out on demand up to £100, £250 or more, and though the rules may stipulate that notice of one month or some other period should be given, larger sums are usually repayable within a few days in cases of emergency.

Interest on most building society share and deposit accounts starts from the day money is paid in, or shortly after, and is credited up to the date of withdrawal, or nearly that date. Investments are therefore earning their keep pretty well all the time they are held. As some societies do not start interest from the day of payment, or do not pay it right up to the day of withdrawal, it is sound policy to get a clear-cut answer on this point when choosing a society.

The choice of building societies, though amalgamations are steadily reducing the overall number, is wide. Selection should not however be completely indiscriminate. Though the vast majority, large and small, are sound, well-run, and safe concerns, not all of them can be recommended to the investor. Despite the greater powers given to the Chief Registrar of Friendly Societies under the Building Societies Acts 1960 and 1962, the description 'Building Society' is not a universal guarantee of soundness. During the years immediately preceding the strengthening of the Registrar's powers, a crop of mushroom societies attracted some tens of millions of pounds of investors' money. A few of these were moribund societies whose attraction for those who got control was that they had been in existence for many years. Others were new concerns which often were given impressive names. Both types attracted investments by offering higher rates of interest than the orthodox societies. The inevitable result was that in order to pay share interest and running costs they had to invest their funds at well above normal rates in somewhat doubtful mortgages or for speculative building and property dealing operations far beyond the general run of building society business. The second result was that this rapid expansion made the building-up of the necessary reserves lag well behind the growth in assets. Action by the Registrar to stop new investment and to transfer the management to new and experienced boards of directors has fortunately given investors in most of these mushroom concerns a reasonable chance of getting back their money over a period of years.

The Building Societies Act 1962, which (as already indicated) gives the Government department concerned – the Registry of Friendly Societies, 17 North Audley Street, London W1 – much greater control over all such ventures, has made a repetition of this outcrop extremely unlikely. Before the new Act, any four people could form a building society with only £20. Now at least ten people must each put up £500 initial capital and leave it invested for five years. Similar rules can be applied to a small society which the Registrar considers is being expanded to evade the provisions. Moreover, new societies cannot advertise for funds until the Registrar gives permission to do so. Other safeguards applying to new and old concerns are that the Registrar can prohibit the acceptance of investments from the public; prohibit advertising and make general regulations governing the contents of advertisements; refuse to register a name which is considered to be undesirable or misleading; and exercise wide powers of investigation. Stricter rules apply to annual audits by professional accountants, and every new investor must be given a copy of the latest audited accounts when opening an account.

Despite this strengthening of control, not every building society (as already indicated) can be treated as 100 per cent sound and suitable for investment. Before putting money into one, the investor should measure its strength by applying some simple tests.

The first check is to find out if it is a member of The Building Societies Association, whose headquarters are at 14 Park Street, London W1. The Association, which does much useful work in coordinating policy amongst its members, has its own rules for financial soundness. It has long insisted that member societies should adhere to minimum financial requirements which are dealt with below. Unfortunately we cannot make this the only rule, for, although membership now covers some 280 societies holding about 99 per cent of the assets of the whole movement, not all are in the B.S.A. There are some very sound societies outside it.

The second check is whether the society has qualified for trustee status under the House Purchase and Housing Act 1959. The main qualifications are that total assets are not less than £1,000,000; net reserves, after allowing for any depreciation on gilt-edged and other investments, must equal specific percentages of the assets, with a minimum of 2½ per cent on the first £100 million and decreasing ratios on amounts over this figure; liquid funds in the form of cash and investments must not be less than 7½ per cent of total assets; and investment and mortgage lending policies must conform to the best practices. A society with trustee status can thus be looked on with confidence.

If, however, it is not in the B.S.A. and is under £1,000,000 trustee limit, other checks must be applied. The last audited balance sheet should show that net reserves are equal to at least 2½ per cent of the total assets; a minimum of 7½ per cent of the latter should be in cash and realizable investments; not more than 10 per cent of the total mortgages should be in amounts of £13,000 and upwards owing by individuals plus sums due by bodies corporate – such details should be shown in the balance sheet – and the rates of interest paid on investments or charged on mortgages should be the same as or not much more than those of the larger well-known societies. Many 'small' concerns amply measure up to these tests.

The particular advantages of investing in properly-chosen building societies can be summed up as security, a competitive rate of interest, freedom from income tax, easy withdrawals, freedom from fluctuations, simplicity, no cost or expense, and service. To these must be added their specially valuable use in saving to buy a house or other needs. Being an investor known to a society is not a specific guarantee of obtaining a mortgage, but it can be helpful in realizing home-ownership plans. A building society account is therefore virtually a must for engaged people, newly-weds, and others looking forward to buying their own house; as shown in a later chapter, a substantial part of the cost generally has to be put down in cash, and only a proportion can be raised on mortgage.

Two questions that should be asked if a society's reserve position is not much above the minimum trustee level are: Has it recently revalued its own office and other property and added the surplus to its reserves? If substantial proportions of its 'reserve' investments are in loans to local authorities at relatively low rates of interest, are these worth their book value in comparison with similar investments quoted on the Stock Exchange and which would have to be taken into the reckoning at market value? It is possible that, quite legally, some societies may have retained trustee status because of property revaluations and/or not having to value unquoted investments at current market worth.

A recent, and revolutionary, development is life assurance linked with regular monthly saving which some societies are offering to investors aged 18 to, say, 55. Allowing for tax reliefs on the life assurance part of the premiums it is claimed that such 'Bonds' can show annual returns of 10 per cent or more to income tax payers. Unit-linked savings plans have also been devised, their basis being regular investment, backed by life assurance, divided between a building society and a unit trust in a ratio of say 50-50, 75-25 or 25-75, respectively, as selected by the investor – the investments so made are usable as backing for a mortgage.

A further innovation is the 'Property Bond' which is designed to add to the normal type of investment a growth element in the form of direct property ownership. For example, after deduction of say 5 per cent to cover initial expenses and life assurance cover, money subscribed is divided equally between an investment with the building society and in property. While the former gives a steady income the latter is expected to provide capital growth and thus provide protection against inflation. Minimum investment is say £100 and the life cover per £100 can range from £150 for ages up to 35 down to £100 for investors of 56 and over.

Another new and profitable addition to building society invest-ment services is the extension of the *Contractual Saving*, or S.A.Y.E., scheme to them. Individuals of 16 years or older can open accounts of up to £20 a month on the same terms and con-ditions applying to the savings bank scheme outlined on pages 32–4. *It is thus possible to save a maximum of £40 a month – £20 each in a savings bank and in a society.*

Putting part or all of S.A.Y.E. savings in a building society can be attractive to those young people who can look ahead *not less* than five years to buying a house. While no society can guarantee that a saver will qualify for a mortgage, it is a widespread practice that special consideration is given to anyone who has been investing for a reasonable time. S.A.Y.E. is a profitable way of qualifying for this consideration by potential home-owners who will not expect to become borrowers less than five years ahead. The tax-free bonus at the end of five (or seven) years will be a useful addition to the cash needed to bridge the gap between what the building society will lend and the cost of the house. With the bonus free of all taxation, the scheme is also attractive to surtax-payers.

CHAPTER 5

Life Assurance and Annuities

MAKING financial provision for a family can be a serious problem for a married man with little capital. A single man or woman may also have the problem of accumulating a sufficient sum to provide a worthwhile income on retirement. The best method of achieving such objectives is regular saving in sound investments. Voluntary saving is, however, something which can too easily be put off on the pretext that 'as I can't manage it this month I'll double my saving next month'. Judicious compulsion can help to keep to a savings plan. One good well-tried way is life assurance. It combines the necessary compulsion to save with the desired family protection – the sum payable on death or normal maturity is an assured minimum. A large proportion of personal saving is done through life assurance.

Life assurance is no modern invention. The first record shows that Richard Martin, an alderman of the City of London, insured the life of William Gybbons, a salter, for one hundred pounds for twelve months at a premium of eight pounds – and paid up when the insured died before the end of the year. The first collective effort was started in 1706, with the formation of the 'Amicable Society for a Perpetual Assurance Office'. Although the earliest ventures have gone the way of those whose lives they insured, it is significant of the success of this type of protection that one Society formed in 1762 has happily celebrated its second centenary and that other concerns which are now well to the forefront began life a hundred years or more ago. There has, it is also significant to record, been no great change in the basis of life assurance, which can be simply summarized as pooling the risk of mortality. All that has happened in fact is that the concept and its advantages have grown tremendously, refinements have been added, estimation of the average expectation of life has become more scientific, and

83

changes in the methods of investing insurance funds have enabled the 'offices' to quote more attractive terms.

Two broad groups of 'office' transact life assurance business. Some are *companies* with capitals owned by substantial numbers of shareholders, the shares of which are quoted on the Stock Exchange. The others are *mutual offices*, which (as they have no shareholders) belong in effect to the policy-holders. This means that unlike the proprietary companies, which allocate their surpluses between shareholders and 'with-profits' policy-holders, all the profits go to the latter – in practice all offices follow the prudent financial course of putting part of their surpluses to reserves. Some offices, company and mutual, transact two kinds of life assurance – industrial and ordinary.

Industrial is the type of endowment and whole-life assurance where premiums of relatively small sums are collected weekly or monthly by agents. For this reason it is generally described as 'home service' insurance. In view of the cost of maintaining a large number of agents calling at millions of homes, the expense of such business is relatively high. Against this must be set the fact that this type encourages regular thrift, and although not quite so important in these days of National Insurance death benefits and generally higher incomes, it continues to serve one of its original aims of providing cash for funeral expenses and towards retirement. It is not unusual to find mothers or fathers insuring all members of the family, and paying the weekly premiums.

Ordinary branch business covers endowment and whole-life assurance on which premiums are on an annual basis – payable yearly or in half-yearly, quarterly, or monthly instalments – and which are usually for policies of at least £200 to £500. With expenses on a lower ratio, premiums are relatively cheaper than on industrial policies.

A variety of assurances are available through the two kinds of office. They include whole-life, endowment, temporary, convertible life, mortgage protection, educational, children's deferred assurance, income benefits, house purchase, and pensions, to-gether with annuities. There is a tendency today to call these types of assurance *long-term* to distinguish them from fire, accident and other *short-term* insurance. Before we summarize the salient features of the various types it should be noted that in most groups the assured has the option of taking out a non-profits or a with-profits policy.

Non-profits policies do not share in the surpluses earned by the office. They are for a fixed amount. For instance, a £1,000 non-profits whole-life or endowment assurance is for the fixed sum of £1,000, neither more nor less. The holder therefore knows that a definite sum will be paid on death or maturity. Premiums are less than on the other type, for reasons explained below. This is the kind of policy to take out when the maximum cover at the lowest cost is wanted.

With-profits policies share in the surpluses earned by the office. The amount insured thus rises in proportion to the profits so allocated after each valuation of the liabilities and income earned. While an increasing number of offices value annually some still adhere to the older method of valuing at longer intervals. On their completion, the company declares the rate of bonus, which may be a *simple* addition to the sum assured or a *compound* rate calculated on the sum assured plus accumulated bonuses. If a triennial bonus is at the rate of £4 a year, the simple addition to a £1,000 policy for the three-year period is £120. If, however, it is a compound rate, and the accumulated value of the policy is £1,250, the new addition is £150 – 12 per cent on £1,250. All offices have increased their bonus rates in recent years, largely as a result of successful investment. With-profits policies thus provide some protection against inflation.

Although it is impossible to make any firm forecast, it is likely that present bonus rates will not be reduced and that given a return to more normal investment conditions than those of 1973/4, many offices may be able to increase their rates over the coming years. This prospect is enhanced by the ten-dency to take into account some of the capital appreciation on equity share investments when calculating the profits to be allocated to policy-holders under bonus schemes. Policy-holders usually have the option of leaving bonuses to accumulate (the better alternative wherever possible) or of turning them into cash at a lower rate. With-profits assurances should be the choice, once the minimum family protection has been provided.

A few examples show how actual bonuses can make policies worth more than their estimated value at the time of taking them out. One mutual office has increased its normal compound bonuses over a twenty-year period from £2 a year to £2·50, to £3·25, to £4 and, currently, to £4·25 per cent. Another office records that in addition to the normal bonuses the extra 'capital' bonuses coming from appreciation on its investments have added £45 per £100 of each sum assured over a twenty-year period and as much as £76 for a forty years' old policy of £100. A third office shows the benefits accruing from a £1,000 with-profits policy taken out by a 30-year-old man at different times over a period of 25 years:

No. of years ago	25	20	15	10
Value	£2,648	£2,221	£1,784	£1,433
Net outlay	£864	£877	£892	£950
Effective gross annual yield	13·5%	14·0%	13·8%	12·3%

Net outlay and yield assume payment of income tax at standard rates.

The attractions of with-profits assurances are enhanced, as already indicated, by the payment by a growing number of offices of *terminal bonuses*. A good answer to the unit-trust-linked assurance plans discussed in a later chapter, these add to the value of a with-profits policy part of the capital gains accruing up to the year in which the policy matures. The insured thus gets some of the benefits of the investment success of the life office during the term of his policy. Such extra bonuses can add quite a high percentage to the ordinary reversionary bonuses, and so to the 'profit' on the net cost of the assurance. It should be noted, however, that terminal bonuses are liable to fluctuate; and one adverse effect of the 1974 slump in stock markets was a reduction in the new declarations by some offices. However, like traditional bonuses, once added to the sum assured they are a permanent increment.

Whole life, as the term indicates, provides the assurance benefit only on the death of the policy-holder. It is therefore the most suitable where the maximum provision has to be made for some specific requirement or liability which would arise on death. Premiums, which are relatively cheaper than the other types, may be payable up to the date of death, be limited to a specified number, or cease at say age sixty-five. This is one of the two best types of policy for the family man who wishes to provide the maximum protection for dependants at the lowest cost; in other words, to get the greatest capital benefit for his money.

Endowment assurances do a double job. They provide full death benefit from payment of the first premium. But if the assured lives an agreed period of say twenty-five or some other number of years, or to a specified age, he or she will draw the money. Such policies are the better choice when saving for retirement; to provide a lump sum for repayment of a fixed mortgage; paying for a child's university or professional training; for some other purpose some years ahead; or for the single man or woman who does not have to provide for dependants.

(These two types are dealt with in more detail later.)

Temporary, or short term, assurance against death only can be arranged for as little as one day or for much longer periods such as, for example, death occurring before age sixty-five. Premiums are cheap, but of course on survival of the agreed period the policy expires and there is nothing to come. It is, however, the second of the two best and cheapest ways for a young married man to get the maximum protection for his family. For as little as around £9 a year a 25- to 30-year-old man can take out a £5,000 assurance for a ten-year period and have the option, when he can afford the extra premium, to convert it to a whole life or endowment assurance. Such insurance can also be useful to cover the risk of death over a special period or for some specific event such as entering into a commitment to meet a future liability, death duties on gifts given during lifetime, extensive travelling, or to cover a particularly expensive period of a child's education when the death of the breadwinner might mean the drying-up of funds.

Convertible life policies, which go under various names, are particularly useful for the young married man or the youngster who expects to get married. They start as whole-life policies and so give greater cover than endowment assurances for the same premium. At the end of five years or some other specified time the holder has the right to convert the policy into an endowment on payment of the appropriate higher premium. This means that if he has made progress he can begin to think in terms of providing for retirement as well as for family protection. Amongst the other attractions of these 'young people's' assurances may be the right to take out extra assurance without medical examination or to step up the whole-life or endowment cover after stated periods.

Mortgage protection, or reducing-term assurance, is a simple and cheap way of providing for repayment of the 'reducing' type of loan provided by building societies and local authorities if the borrower should die at any time before the normal redemption date. The amount insured falls roughly in line with the reduction in the debt. As the greater part of the mortgage repayments are for interest in the earliest years, the benefit is especially high until well after half-way through the loan period. The cheapest form of policy merely provides for repayment of any balance normally owing at death – the insured gets no benefit on survival to the end of the mortgage-redemption date. Premiums, as with all life assurance, depend on age, the mortgage repayment period, and the rate of interest. Such protection can cost only a matter of a few pence a week. A typical premium on a 25-year mortgage for £5,000 at 11 per cent taken out by a man aged thirty next birthday would be about £12, payable however for only 20 years. Premiums qualify for the usual tax reliefs mentioned later. Building societies can arrange such insurance on the basis of a single premium, which may be added to the mortgage loan. If, however, the borrower wants to make sure of a maximum cash sum over and above whatever is owing on the mortgage during its currency (or on normal repayment) he can do so for a substantially bigger premium. The cash sum can be a proportion of one-fifth or one-quarter of the original amount covered, such as £200 for each £1,000. An even larger cash sum would be provided by taking out a with-profits policy. Allowing for tax relief on the premiums, the net cost of this type of mortgage protection can be little, or nothing. Other advantages are that a cash sum may be useful to help with heavy repairs, additions, or modernization when the mortgage is repaid, or as a form of saving for retirement. *Income benefits* for the balance of the mortgage repayment period can also be provided at an extra premium; which can be valuable to a widow and for educating children after their father's death. In fact, it is a good idea to look into the comparative costs and advantages of such a policy – an income benefits assurance providing the equivalent of the mortgage repayments can be less costly than a mortgage protection policy for the capital sum.

Educational assurance is a good way of providing for the most expensive part of a child's schooling, university fees, or professional training. The parent takes out an assurance on his own life, and this provides annual payments over a period of fifteen terms, or five years, commencing when the child reaches say thirteen or a later age. Premiums depend on the age of the parent and the term of policy – the lower the age of the child at the time of taking it out, the longer the term and the lower the premium rate. Most policies provide for the cessation of premiums if the parent should die before benefits are scheduled to begin; and some add an income benefit during the intervening period, or extend the 'school' benefits for a further period. One useful method is to take out a series of policies maturing over, say, five years. For example, a thirty-year-old father wishing to provide £1,500 a year for a son's or daughter's public school education to start at the age of thirteen, and who begins the insurance payments at the time of the birth of the child, would pay (after tax relief) £222 annually for thirteen years, followed by £168 in the fourteenth year; £118 in the fifteenth year; £75 in the sixteenth year; and only £36 in the seventeenth year.

Other arrangements can be made to provide preparatory school fees and, at the longer educational end, university fees. It is also possible, under a scheme which may be useful when grand-parents are meeting school bills, to pay fifteen terms' fees in a lump sum – around £5,500 down payment would, for instance, produce £500 a term, or a total of £7,500.

Children's deferred assurance is a useful way of (a) providing a cash sum on a child's twenty-first birthday, or (b) insuring his or her life on ground-floor terms. Up to the age of twenty-one the assurance is in effect an endowment without death benefit on the child's life but with life cover for the parent, who can claim the appropriate tax reliefs on the premiums. On reaching twenty-one the child has, however, the option of continuing the policy – at the same premium and without medical examination – as a whole-life assurance or as an endowment payable at a selected age. Taking a representative selection, an annual premium of £30 paid from birth will provide at the age of twenty-one a sum of £538 plus a share in the profits which, at current rates, would add more than £700. Instead of taking everything in cash the child could continue the assurance at the same yearly premium and, at current rates of bonus, have a policy worth some £6,000 at age 46 and of over £11,500 at age 60.

Income benefits, which are usually tax free under the present law, can be provided up to an agreed age or over a specified number of years, either as an addition to whole-life or endowment assurances or as a separate insurance. Their main advantage is the provision of an income for dependants should the insured die during the earlier years of married life when expenses of bringing up children can be the heaviest and when there has not been so much opportunity to accumulate savings. Taken out as a separate insurance – it is easy to link income benefits with life or endowment policies at all-in premiums – a man of 30 could ensure for his dependants a tax-free income of £1,000 a year for up to twenty years for an annual premium of only some £16, which would be increased to around £22 for 25 years' cover. A useful refinement for these inflationary times provides an annual increase in the income benefit of say 3 per cent. Thus, while death in the first year would provide for each £100 cover £100, the rate for the fifth year would be £115·90 and by the twentieth £180·60. Naturally, premiums are higher.

Deferred house purchase policies are basically endowment assurances, with the addition that they can be specifically used for the repayment of a mortgage advanced by the insurance office, which undertakes to consider lending increasing proportions of the value of a house the longer the policy has been in force. For instance, whereas 80 per cent of the valuation may be lent in the first year, the proportion may be 90 per cent after three years and even 100 per cent after six years. The rising proportion is made possible because of the value of the premiums paid. Some companies will add to the basic proportion of loan the whole of the premiums paid. Although these assurances are very good ways of saving to buy a house, it should be clearly understood that they do not give an unqualified guarantee of a mortgage. This, as explained in another chapter, depends on the valuation of the house; the current lending policy of the office; and the sum assured being at least equal to the mortgage advance. The persistent rise in house prices over recent years has in fact caused disappointment to some such policy-holders. It can therefore be preferable to save funds for house buying through a building society.

Pension benefits can be provided under a specific policy or by transferring part or all of the proceeds of a matured endowment assurance into an annuity. Although there is a tendency in these days of rapid expansion in pensionable employment to assume that such income and the State pension will be sufficient to provide for retirement, it is well not to overlook the fact that even though living expenses may fall at retirement, there may also be an even sharper drop in income. It is therefore a good idea to make some personal provision for retirement, and as already indicated, endowment assurance is a good and profitable means of regular saving. It is surprising and encouraging how relatively small proportions of current income can grow into sizeable capital sums. Provision against retirement is particularly important for the individual in business on his or her own account. It can be equally important when a married man in a pension scheme decides to sacrifice part of his retirement income in order to provide a continuing pension for his wife. His own separate provision can close or narrow the resultant gap.

Self-employed people have to provide their own pensions, a fact which the Inland Revenue recognizes by allowing full tax relief up to certain limits on the annual premiums on policies taken out for such purposes. The general basis for those born in 1916 or later – higher limits apply to older people – is that the maximum premiums qualifying for full tax relief are £1,500 or 15 per cent of the net earnings for the year of assessment, whichever is the less. The problem of keeping premiums within the tax limits, or of annual resources, can be looked after by taking out a variable premium assurance or by single-premium policies bought year by year. Whatever the method, the insured can start to draw his or her pension at any agreed age between sixty and seventy, whether then retired or still working. Subject to limits imposed by the Inland Revenue, provision can be made for a pension to a widow or for a lump sum payment of part of the assurance. All pensions are taxable as earned income. These policies are also available to people in non-pensionable jobs. Two examples show the attractions of this way of saving for retirement:

1. A self-employed man aged just under thirty invests £600 a year steadily for a pension starting at age sixty-five. Assuming tax relief at the current base rate of 33 per cent, the net annual cost is reduced to £402 and the total net payment over thirty-six years is £14,472. In return, his 'pension' at current bonus rates paid by the life office would be £22,128 a year; or he could take a cash sum of about £46,000 and an annuity of £15,362 per annum.

2. Assuming the same man progresses in his business, he can pay bigger premiums in later years, and attract higher rates of tax relief. Say he pays annual premiums of £600 for 5 years, costing a net £402 with tax at 33 per cent; then £900 for each

of the next 5 years, when his tax rate is 43 per cent and net cost £513; then another increase to £1,200 for the following 5 years, when his top tax rate is 53 per cent and net yearly outlay £564; and finally, £1,500 for the last 21 years, when his top tax is 63 per cent and net cost £555. Total net premiums will thus be £19,050, or a yearly average of about £530. His 'benefits' at current bonus rates would be (a) an annuity of £35,888 a year; or (b) a cash sum of almost £75,000 and a reduced annuity of £24,916.

Some points are common to all or most of these various methods of assurance.

Premiums depend on age, type, and amount of the policy, and state of health. The greater one's age on taking out assurance, the greater the premium. Again, where applicable, the rate for a with-profits policy is naturally greater than for a non-profit one. Examples based on the average of rates quoted by some leading offices indicate the variations:

WHOLE-LIFE ASSURANCE

Age next birthday	Premiums per £1,000	
	Non-profit	With-profits
	£p	£p
18	9·13	18·37
25	11·11	22·50
30	13·10	24·34
40	19·07	32·30
50	29·37	45·05

These rates are for premiums payable throughout life. Premiums can however be limited to a specified number or age on payment of higher rates. For example, if a man aged twenty-five next birthday decides on a limit of twenty-five annual payments the non-profit premium is £12·75 and with-profits £27·25.

Examples of endowment assurance premiums are given on page 94.

A variation which could be worth consideration is the 'Reduction of Premium' policy offered by one of the life offices which does not pay commission. It is unique in the way premiums can cease after ten years. The method is the simple one of applying bonuses towards payment of premiums. Assuming full tax relief at the 1974/5 rate of 16·5 per cent, a policy with an annual

ENDOWMENT ASSURANCES

£1,000 – Payable at death or end of

Age next birthday	15 years		20 years		30 years	
	Non-profit £p	With-profits £p	Non-profit £p	With-profits £p	Non-profit £p	With-profits £p
25	54·29	73·00	38·03	54·40	22·35	35·33
30	54·40	73·24	38·14	54·64	22·82	35·92
35	54·64	73·59	38·50	55·34	23·63	37·09
40	55·22	74·41	39·43	56·40	25·15	38·96
50	58·38	77·80	43·52	61·07	—	—

premium of £100 would mean a net yearly cost of £83·50 in years 1 to 8, followed by £16 in year 9, £8 in year 10 and *nothing thereafter* – a total net cost of £692. Yet, at current bonus rates, the sum payable on death at age 75 would be not far short of £20,000. In the meantime, the minimum payable would have been around £3,225 on death at any time and there would have been options to convert to endowment assurance after year 10.

It is important to note that many life offices now make a basic annual charge on each policy whatever the amount of the assurance it provides. Although allowed for in the above examples, the basic addition to each policy could range from £2 to £4 whatever the sum assured.

Premium rates may be reduced for larger policies, but most offices insist on a minimum assurance of £200 or £500. They recognize the fact that women live longer on average than men, and quote lower rates accordingly – in terms of years the difference can be say five; a 30-year-old woman would pay at the premium rate for a 25-year-old man. On the other hand, male or female, higher premiums may be asked if the health record is not good or the insured is engaged in hazardous employment. It is generally possible to pay premiums monthly, quarterly, or half-yearly by banker's order, the nominal addition for the facility being mostly around 1½–3 per cent.

Medical examinations may be dispensed with if the health record is satisfactory and the proposer is in the younger age-groups. However, examination is necessary if there is any doubt on health, for older proposers, or if the policy is for a substantial sum.

Income-tax relief, which can bring a useful reduction in the cost of assurance, is given on the annual premiums payable on whole-life, endowment, and other policies providing a benefit on death. The allowances for policies taken out after June 1916 are:

If the total premiums do not exceed £20: 33 per cent on the full amount or on £10, whichever is the less.

If the total allowable premiums exceed £20: 16·5 per cent.

The premiums taken into account are limited (a) to 7 per cent of the sum assured, excluding bonuses, under each policy, and (b) to a total of one-sixth of the net total income. If the premium on a policy for £1,000 is £85, the amount on which the allowance is calculated is restricted to £70. Again, if the net income assessed to tax is £1,200 and the total of the premiums is £250, the allowance is calculated on one-sixth of £1,200, i.e. £200. Where a capital sum is *not* provided on death the allowance is limited to tax at the appropriate rate on a sum of not more than £100. Moreover, for policies taken out after 19 March 1968 there are other restrictions, the chief of which is that premiums must be paid for a period exceeding 10 years. The Autumn 1974 Budget, it should be noted, does away with the 7 per cent restriction on certain policies. As already noted, *premiums on 'self-employed' assurances rank within certain limits as a full deduction.*

Planning life assurance is important. On the one hand, as already stated, it should be adequate to provide family protection, to meet some particular commitment such as repayment of a fixed mortgage, or to provide capital for retirement. On the other hand, commitments by way of premiums should be kept to a reasonable proportion of income and the risk of finding them a financial strain avoided. Putting first things first, most young people setting out in life should have an assurance policy of some kind, even if it is for only a few hundred pounds. At worst, they have provided for funeral expenses and settlement of any debts owing at death. At best, they have started to build up family protection in the event of marriage or a retirement fund. The first objective of the young married man should generally be to obtain the maximum cover for the minimum cost, which can be done by taking out first, a short-term assurance and, secondly, a non-profit whole-life assurance. Later, however, as income expands, he can turn from provision for dependants to his own needs; which will mean taking out endowment assurance. The best of these two worlds, as already shown, can be achieved by means of a convertible assurance. It can be based on a short-term policy or a whole-life assurance carrying the necessary option.

Another useful idea is to review one's life assurance every few years, as income rises or as personal circumstances (such as family or job) change. By setting aside a reasonable proportion of income, substantial capital sums can be built up against retirement. Fixing the maturity date of endowment assurances is important, particularly for self-employed people. It may be a good idea to have all policies maturing at the likely retirement age, or to have the dates spread over say the ages of fifty-five, sixty, sixty-five, or later. On the whole, however, the average man will probably find sixty-five or seventy to be the best maturity age.

Uses to which assurance policies can be put are varied. They can, as already shown, provide family protection, cover children's education or training, and form a retirement fund. Endowment policies can be applied to repayment of mortgages, and – up to their surrender value – perhaps be used as additional security for a building-society advance. Assurance is also a useful means of providing for estate duty – in addition to the fact that the money due can be arranged to be payable immediately on satisfactory proof of death, and so be available for early clearance of part or all of the duty, such provision may avoid the necessity to sell investments, a house, a business, or other assets. Finally, although a credit squeeze can be restrictive, policies are available as security for a short-term loan or overdraft from one's bank, up to their surrender value; or a loan can be raised on them direct from the insurance office.

Surrender values sometimes cause misunderstanding. Until a policy matures it is never worth its full value. In most cases, there is in fact no value until say two years' premiums have been paid. And then the value for loan purposes, or surrender if the holder wishes to give up the assurance, is perhaps only one-third in the early years, though rising much higher as the maturity date nears.

'Why,' it is asked, 'should I not get back all I have paid in, if I do not want to carry on with the policy?' The perfectly reasonable answer is that from the minute of paying the first premium, the life office is liable to pay out the full amount of the assurance if the individual covered dies, and it must allow for this; also that certain expenses are involved in 'writing' the policy, and these must be spread over its life. *Once a policy is taken out, every effort should thus be made to continue it.* If future premiums cannot be afforded, the best way of dealing with the problem is to make the policy a fully-paid-up assurance for a smaller sum, the amount of which will be determined by the number of premiums paid and the normal maturity date. A temporary financial embarrassment may be met by borrowing the premium from the office, or, if bonuses have accumulated on a with-profits policy, by taking part or all of their cash equivalent. *Surrender is the very last resort.*

Other personal insurances include cover for hospital and medical expenses; sickness; accident; travel; winter sports; and liability to third parties for accident or death. There has in fact been a sharp increase in recent times in *sickness and disablement* insurance. It is true that Social Insurance provides basic benefits and that many employers keep employees on full, or partial, pay for a time; but in most cases incapacity to work by the breadwinner can cause hardship. It is therefore worthwhile taking out insurance which provides income for a maximum period or indefinitely. Subject to the nature of one's work and age this can be done at really low cost. For example, if benefits are deferred until 13 weeks after suffering the incapacity a thirty-year-old man can provide for £20 a week up to age 65 for an annual premium of only £22.

EQUITY-LINKED ASSURANCE

Unit trusts were the first to launch into a type of regular monthly saving which linked share investment with life assurance. The early schemes put the buying of unit trust shares first and added some form of life assurance cover as a secondary feature. While the assurance side varied in the cover offered – a guaranteed minimum sum on maturity or earlier death, a reducing life cover, or the undertaking that a plan entered into for a fixed number of years would be completed free of cost if the investor died in the interval – a universal attraction was tax saving on the monthly investment. Subject to the normal rules for tax relief, all or most of the monthly payments into the plan are treated as life-assurance premiums. Which means that for taxpayers the unit trust shares being bought each month are acquired at a discount even after allowing for the cost of the life assurance. Put another way, this is a cut-price way of investing in unit trusts.

Soon the idea became an active competitor with normal life and endowment assurance. The life offices just had to take notice of its growth; which they did by starting their own unit-linked plans. Today all the leading offices are in the market. Some, including the biggest, have started their own unit trusts. Others have created a separate fund which, in effect, operates apart from the traditional funds in their organizations. And some have tied up with established unit trusts. Whatever the method of operation, the basic ideas are however that the policy-holder's interest is directly linked to the performance of the fund and that, in turn, his ultimate benefits partly depend on such performance. Investment tactics for such funds may of course change; but at present the main force is concentrated on equity shares or property.

The right and natural question is which type of assurance – traditional or unit-linked – will be the more profitable. Without any attempt at begging the question the answer must be that time alone will tell. We must wait until some of the plans begin to mature, which may be ten, fifteen or more years. If equity shares once again rise in value unit schemes should comfortably beat the traditional ones. Equally, if equity share markets run out of steam, fall back or run into a bumpy, up-and-down long-term trend, the traditional type with-profits assurance should do better.

Three factors give a useful measure of stability to the traditional type. First, the investments of the average life office are spread over a very wide field which takes in fixed interest securities giving a steady income in good or bad times; in property; in mortgages; and in equity shares. Secondly, once a reversionary bonus has been allotted to a policy it is part of it and unchangeable; it cannot become less. Thirdly, if past history is any guide, bonus rates have better chances of going up than staying put or falling; and the newest development, special terminal bonuses, may add to the maturity value of with-profits policies.

Taking a count at this stage it is probably a fair assessment to say that there is little to choose between the traditional and the new. But it is of course the coming years which will be the most vital to policy-holders, particularly those about to take out life assurance. Risking the criticism that it is nothing more than trying to play safe my advice is:

(1) Use, say, the first £5 a month which can be invested in life assurance to 'buy' a traditional policy.

(2) Use the next £5 a month for a unit-linked plan.

(3) Divide anything over £10 a month between extra traditional and extra unit-linked plans.

And lastly, keep in mind the key financial fact that comparison of the merits of *all* life assurance plans is the measure of the difference between what goes in by way of net premiums after tax reliefs and what comes out by way of basic assurance and reversionary bonuses. The ratio of the ultimate profit to the net premiums paid over the life of the policy is the test of success.

BONDS

A newer kind of savings scheme now offered by most insurance offices is *bonds*. Though varying in detail, they generally provide for regular monthly savings or a lump sum investment. The savings method is very much like the unit-linked assurances. A typical capital scheme would provide however for a ten-year investment with the right to withdraw at any time on the basis of a surrender value of 95 per cent of the single premium plus 5 per cent per annum compound interest, and on death before the end of ten years of a return of the capital plus 5 per cent per annum compound interest. At the end of the ten years an investor with a £1,000 bond could take a cash sum of £2,015, equal to a gross annual yield of 10·35 per cent; or an annuity for life (with guaranteed payments for at least five years) which, for a man or woman aged 65 at the start of payments, would be £108 and £96 a year, respectively. There are a number of variations such as lump sum investment which gives a tax-free annual income of say 9 per cent or more plus return of the original investment after ten years or on earlier death.

PROPERTY BONDS

This type of investment grew very rapidly until the severe setback in property prices in 1974 played havoc with many of the optimistic forecasts of capital growth and, unhappily, brought to a costly end some of the more speculative ventures. It is relatively easy to buy property; but it is a very different matter to value it, say, month by month in order to fix up-to-date prices for the bonds or monthly subscriptions. Valuations downwards, by as much as 10 to 25 per cent in some cases, have been much more the feature in recent months, while liquidity problems have not made it easy – in some instances, impossible – to repay investors wishing to cash their bonds. While a revival of confidence in property values could bring improvement in such investments, only investors ready to take a big risk should put money into property bonds.

ANNUITIES

Annuities are a useful but sometimes not too well understood means of providing an assured income on retirement. In return for a capital sum, the insurance office undertakes to provide an annual income until the death of the annuitant. In effect, the purchaser of the annuity thus gets interest and a part return of capital; but except where annuity payments are guaranteed for a minimum period of say ten years or some other period, 'the capital dies with the annuitant'. It is this point which causes misunderstanding and which is a vital factor when considering such an investment.

The general rule in making the decision is: buy an annuity only if you are prepared to use up the capital. If you wish to leave your capital to dependants, choose some other form of investment giving reasonable assurance of keeping its value over the years. If, however, a married man is concerned about provision for his wife should he die first, the problem can be solved by taking out a *joint annuity* on the two lives, or by a *survivorship annuity* which continues at a reduced rate on the death of one party. A practical compromise where it is not desired to part with all one's capital is to apply say one-half to the purchase of an annuity and to invest the other half in the ordinary way.

Annuities are based on expectation of life, so it is inevitable that the older the age at the time of purchase the greater the annual income. This is one reason for not buying them until the age of at least sixty or sixty-five. At the latter age, £1,000 will, for example, buy a man an annuity of say £155 a year and (because the expectation of life is greater) a woman £142.

A money-saving feature of an annuity is that as part of the income represents return of the capital invested, tax is payable on only part of the annual income. In the above examples, the capital or tax-free portions are £71 and £58 respectively. Largely because of the rise in interest rates and dividends earned on their investments, life offices have substantially improved their terms in recent years. Changes in annuity rates have in fact been quite frequent, which makes it essential to get up-to-the-minute quotations from several offices or ideally through an insurance broker. The following table must therefore be taken as only as approximate guide to the annual income to be expected at different ages.

ANNUITIES FOR £1,000 PURCHASE PRICE

Age at purchase	MALE		FEMALE	
	Gross annuity £	Tax-free portion £	Gross annuity £	Tax-free portion £
50	124	39	120	34
60	140	57	131	47
65	155	71	142	58
70	175	91	157	73
75	204	120	178	95

Some offices sell *increasing annuities* which provide for increases of say 10 per cent in the annual payments after agreed periods which may be every three or five years. Although the initial 'income' is less than with the ordinary type of annuity the upward variation gives some cushion against inflation or allows for rises in spending commitments.

The proceeds of endowment assurances, as already seen, can be invested entirely or in part in annuities. Where maturity comes before there is need of such income, the annuity can be *deferred* to an agreed age; in which event, as the insurance company has the use of the capital for a time, the annual payments will be greater than the normal rates. A particular point to watch in any such deferment is to ensure that if death occurs before the date the annuity is scheduled to start the capital will be repaid in full, together with reasonable interest.

A consideration of use to those in poor health is that they can look for higher rates of annuity, the extra annual amount depending on the likely impairment of life. Medical examinations are naturally essential before the life insurance office can assess the exact position; but it can be worth while to look into the possibilities.

Before launching into any form of life assurance or buying an annuity it is advisable to follow a few simple, but very important, rules:

Be very careful in choosing the life office for *your* money. Some of the newer offices have gone bankrupt or have failed to live up to their promises.

Stick to the soundly established and solidly financed offices even though their terms may be not quite so promising as those of the newer concerns.

Shop around. Do not be talked into specious propositions by a doorstep salesman. Consult an expert – a reliable, established insurance broker.

But remember that, as most brokers live on commission, they, as human beings, may naturally not include in their recommendations the old-established mutual offices which do not pay commission.

So, it may pay to compare brokers' recommendations with the terms offered by the 'no-commission' offices such as The

Equitable Life Assurance Society; The London Life Association; or The Ecclesiastical Insurance Office. Which is a strong argument in favour of brokers charging their clients fees for advice instead of relying on commissions for their income.

CHAPTER 6

Buying a House

BUYING or building a house is the biggest and most important financial transaction undertaken by many people. They make an *investment* which calls for a large sum of money, the carrying-out of certain commitments, and the possibility that they may spend the rest of their lives in the property. Despite the importance of the operation it is surprising how many buyers rush into it with insufficient thought of what is involved and the long-term merits of the venture. It is a fact of course that the post-war shortage of houses has created a scarcity demand which leaves the seller with all or most of the advantages – unless a prompt decision is made, the house may be snapped up by another buyer. But this should be no excuse for ignoring or brushing aside the necessary precautions to ensure that the property fills the essential requirements and is fair value for the money, and that the project can be financed. As the chairman of a leading building society once warned: 'A little more care by purchasers could contribute to price stability as there is no doubt . . . that some buyers approach house purchase more casually than buying a motor car or even a television set.' Would-be home-owners should know how to set about this important business and – if the property cannot be paid for outright – the best means of raising a mortgage or loan.

The tenure of the land is the first consideration, whether building or buying a house. In England and Wales it may be of one of two legal types. If *freehold*, the purchaser becomes the outright owner. If *leasehold*, ownership is enjoyed for only a limited period, which may be any number of years but usually not more than nine hundred and ninety-nine; and a rent is payable to the ground landlord. But whatever the type, there will almost certainly be covenants and restrictions on the use to which the land can be put, the kind or style of house which can be built, the alterations which can be made to existing buildings, and the standards of maintenance.

Full knowledge of any restrictions is specially important when buying a plot of land for building – it may not be possible to put up the style, size, or height of house in mind.

It is equally important in every case to know whether the area is zoned for industrial development; whether there are airfields, sewage disposal dumps, or other works near by which could cause inconvenience, spoil the outlook, or reduce the value; whether there are *any rights of way* running through the land; and whether the local council or other authority has in mind taking over the property or part of the plot. Details of the type of land and covenants should be obtainable from the vendor or his agent. Other matters should be checked by local examination and inquiries of the local council and local planning authority.

Further points to consider are the nature of the soil, its suitability for gardening and liability to flooding; and the siting of the land in relation to light, sunshine, vistas, and contours, rivers, streams, or other water, and trees which may overshadow windows, create obstructions, or attract undue moisture. Availability of shops, schools, churches, places of entertainment, recreational facilities, and road and rail transport are of equal concern. The cost of travelling may also be a factor. If building, the handiness of mains for drainage, gas, water, electricity, and telephone must be taken into account. If the roads have not been made up, it should be found out what plans are in hand, the likely cost of the work, and who is responsible for it. Local building bye-laws should not be overlooked – they may limit the height, width, or depth of a new building, ban the use of certain materials, prohibit certain styles of structure, or otherwise run contrary to the plans in mind for a new house or to alterations or additions to an existing one.

Such factors emphasize the importance of making the fullest inquiries and of consulting the necessary experts before entering into any binding undertaking to buy a plot of land for building or an existing house. The golden rule is to make any arrangement to buy '*subject to survey and contract*'. You are then legally protected should it be necessary to withdraw. Otherwise you may well have entered into a binding contract which could mean having to complete the transaction or, at the very least, losing part or all of the

10 per cent deposit which generally has to be put down by way of compensation to the vendor.

The first expert who may have to be consulted is a *surveyor*. He will advise on the suitability, value, and condition of the house or land. It is best to engage an independent surveyor who is a member of one of the recognized professional bodies such as the Royal Institution of Chartered Surveyors or the Incorporated Society of Valuers and Auctioneers. The extent of the survey and its cost will depend on the nature of the property. A general report on condition and value may be sufficient, if it is a reasonably new house put up by a reputable and known builder. If, however, it is old, or obviously needs extensive repairs, the survey should be complete and cover drainage, dry rot, roofs, ceilings, electric wiring and other essentials, and the estimated cost of putting everything into good condition. As the cost of a survey depends on the work done, it is essential to instruct the surveyor clearly on what is required and to arrange the fee with him. The normal scale of fees for valuation only are £1 per cent on the first £1,500, then £0·50 per cent on the next £11,000 and £0·25 per cent on any balance, with a minimum of £10. Fees for additional work are a matter of arrangement and should be agreed beforehand.

The need for a survey when buying a new house put up by a builder on his own account or by estate developers depends partly on their reputation and standing, and – often a key factor – on whether they are on the approved list of the National House Building Council. The Council, amongst its valuable services, lays down minimum standards of construction and materials, inspects the work at all stages, and on completion issues a certificate of soundness if the work has been properly carried out. A builder in the scheme is bound to put right any defects resulting from non-compliance with Council standards which occur within two years of completion. In 1966 the Building Societies Association took the excellent step to eliminate jerry-building of recommending to its members that newly built houses considered for mortgaging should be constructed by N.H.B.C. members, the one exception being properties built under the supervision of an architect or qualified surveyor employed solely by the purchaser. One effect is that the buyer is protected for ten years from completion against major defects such as collapse, distortion, dry rot, subsidence or chemical failure of materials up to a total of £5,000. The address of the N.H.B.C., which should be contacted if there is any doubt whether a builder is a member, is 58 Portland Place, London W1.

The next expert to be consulted in the early stages of any negotiations is a *solicitor*. He will advise on vital matters such as the draft contract for purchase, covenants restricting the use to which the property could be put, undertakings which the buyer must take over, rights of way, and the possibility of compulsory purchase; and if it is advisable to go ahead, the solicitor will investigate and verify the vendor's title to the property, as well as drawing up the document needed to vest it in the buyer. Until quite recently a solicitor charged fees at scale rates with minimum levels. Now, however, for this and all other essential work he may charge fair and reasonable fees having regard to all the circumstances, including the purchase price, the complexity of the business and whether or not the title is registered at the Land Registry. Where the title is already registered – registration is compulsory in some areas – fees should normally be lower because of the smaller amount of work involved. On the other hand, if a property has to be registered for the first time following a sale, the usual fee will be that for an unregistered house plus a fee for making the registration. A client who is dissatisfied with the fee charged can require the solicitor to obtain a certificate from the Law Society as to what is 'fair and reasonable' without prejudicing his right to have the final bill taxed (in effect, investigated) by the Court. For guidance, some typical old scale fees in England and Wales – in Scotland, different laws tend to make costs somewhat higher – for values under £30,000 were:

Value £	Registered £	Unregistered £
5,000	43·75	67·50
7,000	51·25	82·50
10,000	62·50	105·00
13,000	73·75	120·00
15,000	78·75	130·00
20,000	89·75	155·00

Land Registry fees depend on whether a property is already registered or is being registered for the first time. Following a reduction in July 1973, the cost is, however, relatively small. For example, the fee on a price of say £5,000 is £8·10 on a first registration and £11·70 if the title is already registered. There is no longer any further fee for registering a mortgage arranged simultaneously with a purchase.

Stamp duty is payable if the purchase exceeds certain figures. From mid-1974, *nothing* is payable if the price is not over £15,000. Thereafter it is at the rate of 25p per £50 above £15,000 and up to £20,000; 50p per £50 above £20,000 and up to £25,000; 75p per £50 above £25,000 and up to £30,000; and £1 per £50 above £30,000. In percentage terms the rates are thus $\frac{1}{2}$ per cent, 1 per cent, $1\frac{1}{2}$ per cent and 2 per cent, respectively.

The services of an *architect* will be required when building to one's own design. His job is to plan what is wanted, advise on the practicability of your ideas and the site, see that local council bye-laws and local planning requirements are met, conduct negotiations with builders, supervise construction, and generally look after all detail matters such as party walls and the rights of neighbouring owners. Initial details are usually settled on the basis of a sketch design, but once the final idea is agreed it is advisable, if the cost of building is not to be increased, to leave the final design well alone. Fees depend on the work done by the architect. For full service, covering everying from the initial instructions to certifying the final accounts of the builder, the minimum scale laid down by the Royal Institute of British Architects is:

Cost of Works	Fee %
Up to £2,500	10
£2,500 to £8,000	8·5
£8,000 to £14,000	7·5
£14,000 to £25,000	6·5
Over £25,000	6

Plus travelling and out-of-pocket expenses.

The minimum scale for extension and other work on existing houses is 13 per cent up to £2,500; 12·5 per cent, £2,500 to £8,000;

12 per cent, £8,000 to £14,000; 11 per cent, £14,000 to £25,000; and 10 per cent over £25,000.

A new development of recent years is the sale of flats. Although an established home-owning development in Scotland, where land laws are different, it is something relatively new in England and Wales. Because of legal complexities it calls for greater caution and better professional advice than does buying a house. The major factor is that two or more dwellings share common amenities such as the roof, land, main entrance, and public utility mains, plus perhaps lifts, porterage, and communal gardens. The rights of each flat owner must therefore be clearly defined and protected. There must also be simple means of ensuring that the whole property is maintained in good condition and appearance, and is adequately insured. One way of achieving these essential aims would be for all the flat owners to enter into covenants to carry out their share and provide the funds for preserving the mutual amenities. This could however lead to difficulties on a transference of ownership of any of the flats. Without going into the legal complexities, there might then be no means of adequately transferring the obligations to a new owner.

The first points to look into when buying a flat or maisonette are therefore (a) what exactly is offered, and (b) the arrangements for assuring and observing the common amenities, services, and obligations. Care is particularly essential if the property is an old house converted to flats – in addition to points of common concern, a structural survey covering the soundness of the walls and floors and fire-proofing is usually advisable. Contrary to the general rule with a house, a leasehold flat can be a better venture than a freehold one – it is much easier to look after the common interests and obligations of all owners and to transfer them to a subsequent purchaser. The ground landlord can in fact exercise considerable control, and where feasible can provide porterage and other common services on payment of the appropriate contributions to their cost. Sometimes owners form their own service company to run such essentials. The legal complexities involved can make it difficult to raise a mortgage on a flat; and this is a good reason for settling that side of the business at the earliest stage of the negotiations.

Buying or building a house usually calls for a substantial amount of money, which now means thousands of pounds. For many potential owners this means raising a loan or mortgage to fill the gap between what can or must be put down in cash and the total cost, including legal and other expenses; or because it is not feasible or profitable to realize investments to cover outright payment. The most widely-used means of filling such a gap are a loan from the bank or a mortgage from a building society, life insurance office, local council, or private source. Building societies are far and away the major source, providing around 75 per cent of house-purchase loan funds.

Except in special circumstances, only part of the purchase price or valuation, whichever is the lower, can normally be raised on mortgage. The proportion depends on the type, age, condition, and value of the house; the normal income, age, family commitments, and prospects of the purchaser; the amount which can be put down in cash; and lending conditions at the time of making the application. The current terms, advantages, and special points applicable to the methods of borrowing mentioned above can be summarized as follows:

Banks may lend up to say two-thirds – or more if additional security such as life assurances with surrender values, or stocks and shares, can be put up – to established and credit-worthy customers in a position to repay the loan over a period not exceeding in normal times up to say ten years. Interest at the current rate is payable on the daily balance outstanding. Costs of registering the charge over the deeds and any other security are negligible. A borrower benefits at once from any reduction in interest rates, though of course he is equally liable to pay more when increases occur. The possible snags are that the loan is liable to be called in at three to six months' notice, it has to be reduced at a fairly steady rate, and – as has happened several times in recent years – a credit squeeze or other Government action may prevent the bank from helping in this way, however good the security and speed of repayment. This method is particularly useful for financing the 'bridging operation' of selling one house and buying another, when a loan may be needed for no more than a few weeks.

Building societies (as shown in Chapter 4) are the major source of mortgage funds for private house-purchase. They are specialists who, provided funds are available, do their utmost to promote home-ownership. The normal maximum advance is 75 to 85 per cent on reasonably modern or new houses valued at not more than £7,000–£10,000 and up to say 66⅔ per cent on a higher-priced or oldish property. However, if additional security can be provided or an acceptable guarantee arranged, the maximum may be increased to 90–95 per cent. Insurance companies, incidentally, will provide such guarantees up to a limit of 10 to 15 per cent of the loan, at a single premium of not over 4–4½ per cent on the extra advance and which may be added to it. The advance may be repayable in a lump sum at an agreed date; be redeemable by means of an endowment assurance; or be re-payable partly by instalments and partly in a lump sum. *The bulk of building society mortgages are, however, redeemed by equal monthly instalments which cover interest and repayment of capital.* The outlay under this very workable system can be summarized as shown below:

BUILDING SOCIETY MORTGAGE REPAYMENTS
CALENDAR MONTH PER £1,000

Repayment	Interest Rate %						
term	9½	10	10½	11	11½	12	12½
Years	£p	£p	£p	£p	£p	£p	£p
10	13·28	13·57	13·86	14·16	14·45	14·75	15·06
15	10·65	10·96	11·28	11·59	11·92	12·24	12·57
20	9·46	9·79	10·13	10·47	10·81	11·16	11·51
25	8·83	9·19	9·54	9·90	10·26	10·63	11·00
30	8·48	8·84	9·22	9·59	9·97	10·35	10·74

Interest is generally subject to variation on the society giving three months' notice; which benefits the borrower when rates are falling but means increased monthly payments or an extension of the repayment period when they are rising. For the most part the maximum repayment term is twenty to twenty-five years, and it may also be expected that the loan will be cleared by the normal retirement age of sixty-five for a man and sixty for a woman borrower. The maximum advance will also be subject to the restriction that it does not exceed two to three times the borrower's normal gross annual income, or a figure on which repayments take no more than one-fifth to one-quarter of the latter. Most societies are prepared to take into account a wife's earnings when deciding the maximum advance, while some have schemes whereby young borrowers making their way in the world pay interest only in the first few years of the mortgage. Lump sums can be paid at any time, to speed up repayment, with an immediate or early saving in interest or a reduction in the monthly repayments – as rules vary between societies, it is advisable to find out the exact position before making such a reduction. Equally, subject to the security still being adequate, it may be possible to get an extra loan to help with payments for heavy repairs, improvements, or additions to the house.

The main advantages of borrowing from a building society are relative simplicity, greater flexibility, and (when interest rates are falling) reductions in cost. The normal type of reducing mortgage can be 'insured' (as shown in Chapter 5) by taking out a mortgage protection policy. The cost of the simplest type of assurance, which on death simply repays any balance owing, is exceptionally cheap and in the average case equals little more than the price of a packet of cigarettes a week. Payment of a larger premium will, however, provide a cash sum as well, again at a cost which can be little or nothing after allowing for tax reliefs on the premiums.

Life assurance offices (though not all of them) are ready to lend on mortgage up to some 75 to 80 per cent on modern-type houses. Repayment is by means of an endowment for the same amount as the loan, which means that until the policy matures at the agreed date, say twenty or twenty-five years ahead, or earlier death, the borrower pays interest on a fixed loan and premiums on the assurance. Interest may be fixed for the whole period of the loan, which means a benefit to the borrower if rates rise but a loss if they fall. Both interest and premiums are eligible for the usual tax reliefs. If the endowment is a with-profits assurance there is a cash sum to come on repayment of the loan; which can be useful in providing funds for major repairs, improvements, or for other purposes. As with a building society advance, limits apply according to age, income, and other individual circumstances. The main advantage of this method is the provision for automatic repayment in the event of death any time after payment of the first premium. Against this may have to be set the fact that there may not be the same flexibility should a larger loan later be required to pay for another and more expensive house, and that the offer of such facilities has proved to be susceptible to a credit squeeze – some offices tend to go right out of the market in such circumstances. A recent innovation is the *low-cost* endowment mortgage which, in effect, takes into account the bonuses which will accrue on the with-profits assurance – say the advance is £10,000, the sum assured is only £8,000, thus keeping down the premium cost, and over the years the bonuses will make up the difference.

Local authorities may, if they so wish, lend up to 100 per cent for the owner-occupation of a house of any value. In practice, however, most of them tend to stick to the same maxima as the building societies; some will not lend at all, and some suspend facilities during a credit squeeze or when funds are in short supply. Repayment, normally by equal monthly or quarterly instalments, may be spread over as many as thirty years in approved cases. Interest is mostly fixed for the whole period of the loan, and can be fractionally higher than the average building society rate. Otherwise, somewhat similar conditions apply, and the advance can be 'insured' by means of a mortgage protection assurance.

Private mortgages can sometimes be arranged through mortgage brokers, solicitors, or estate agents. The usual terms provide for repayment in a lump sum at the end of an agreed period of years, and for a fixed rate of interest which (depending on the nature of the security) may be as much as 3 to 5 per cent, or even more when loan money is very scarce, *above* normal building society rates. Provided a borrower is ready to pay for the facility, this type of advance can be useful when other sources fail, or – by arranging a second mortgage – to bridge the financial gap when not enough can be raised in the normal way. Second mortgages can carry an extra heavy rate of interest and may be repayable over a relatively short period. In fact, there has been a lot of exploitation in the second mortgage market in recent years with interest rates of up to 20 per cent and more being charged. One precaution is to find out the *real* interest rate – it may be stated to be, say, 10 per cent, but if this is calculated on an original loan repayable by monthly instalments the *annual* rate is nearer to 20 per cent!

Option mortgages were introduced in April 1968 as a means of simplifying tax relief on interest with the object, as officially stated, 'to help people with moderate incomes to buy their homes by giving benefits equivalent to those available to people with higher incomes'. In place of the normal tax relief the 'option' borrower gets an annual subsidy from the Government which is related to the basic income tax and mortgage interest rates. There have been several adjustments to the subsidy; and, as of 1 August 1974, examples based on 33 per cent base rate tax, give these reliefs on mortgages repayable by the annuity or fixed instalment methods:

Normal Interest %		Option
Exceeding	Not exceeding	Reduction %
8·8	9·4	3·0
9·4	10·0	3·2
10·0	10·6	3·4
10·6	11·2	3·6
11·2	11·8	3·8
11·8	—	4·0

If the mortgage is repayable by the endowment assurance methods the interest reduction is 0·25 ($\frac{1}{4}$) per cent below the above rates.

To qualify, the dwelling mortgaged must be occupied by the borrower, one of his children over sixteen years of age, or a parent. The Government pays the subsidy to the building society or other approved lender, which means that (a) the lender in effect reduces the interest by the appropriate rate; (b) monthly repayments are less; and (c) the capital debt is reduced more speedily in the early years than with the ordinary type of reducing mortgage. Under the original scheme there was no advantage to the borrower paying tax at the then standard rate of 8s. 3d. in the £. Now, however, there may be a small advantage for the average *base rate* tax payer. On the other hand, borrowers who are exempt from income tax get a definite advantage. It therefore pays to have the relevant figures available when raising a new mortgage – a building society, life assurance office or other reputable lender will be able to supply the essential data. While it is possible to switch, *after four years*, from an option mortgage to an ordinary mortgage, there will have to be special circumstances such as a substantial change in finances to make a reverse switch profitable. Under the latest rules, the option scheme is available only on loans up to £25,000.

Individual needs and circumstances *normally* decide the best way to borrow. But, as a result of the frantic rise in house prices and the uprush in interest rates in 1973, conditions have since been far from normal. For many would-be buyers it has been much more a case of where can enough money be raised than of picking and choosing.

In the early months of 1974 building societies were in the unhappy, and previously unknown, position of having a net outflow of investment funds and had to rely on repayments on existing mortgages to meet the needs of new borrowers; mortgages had to be sharply rationed. They could of course have rectified the position by raising interest rates to investors to competitive levels; which would have meant offering the equivalent, allowing for tax, of something like 12 to 15 per cent gross. In return, they would have had to demand much more than $9\frac{1}{2}$ to 10 per cent on mortgages. This alarmed the Government which, having already made a 'bridging grant' of £18 million to peg mortgage rates at around $9\frac{1}{2}$ per cent, searched frantically for other means of keeping the cost of home-ownership from soaring. The commercial banks were asked to limit their deposit interest to a maximum of $9\frac{1}{2}$ per cent on accounts under £10,000 and to exercise restraint in the rates offered on larger sums. This was in the hope that the building societies could compete more easily for investment funds. Like so many artificial expedients, it was only partially successful. By early 1974 the only way to avoid putting up both investment and mortgage interest was some form of government help, a means which the building societies did not favour. However, in the end, government advances of £100 million a month for a period of up to five months were accepted on the understanding that societies participating would hold mortgage rates at the 11 per cent then generally being charged on new business. Compared with rates asked by banks and other lenders that 11 per cent, though by far the highest ever known in the movement, was outstandingly cheap.

So, if similar conditions continue, the obvious first choice for most mortgage-seekers is a building society; and, in view of the shortage of funds, there is no demerit in trying several societies.

Local authorities vary considerably in their terms and facilities. Some will lend to owner-occupiers at lower interest than building societies, which means subsidization by ratepayers; others put relatively low ceilings on the maximum advance; and some are reluctant to lend at all.

Life assurance offices are an uncertain market, with policies changing with financial conditions generally and with a tendency as commercial undertakings to charge nearer to open market rates.

Banks can normally be a very good source for borrowers who can repay loans over a relatively shorter period; but of late they have had no option but to charge heavy interest – up to 15 per cent or more – and, because of credit restrictions, to turn away business.

Private mortgages have been costlier still with rates of up to 20 per cent and above.

It is appropriate here to consider the tax position of borrowers. Up to the 1974 Budget, relief against other income could be claimed on all interest paid, whoever the lender. Now, tax relief is restricted to the appropriate interest on up to only £25,000 loans. There is no relief on interest paid on loans above £25,000. For example, if the amount borrowed is exactly £25,000 at 11 per cent, relief is given on the whole interest of £2,750. But if the advance is £30,000, with interest costing £3,300, the amount taken into account is still only £2,750. However, in addition to getting up to the maximum deduction on one's own house, it is also possible to get similar relief on money borrowed to buy a house for a dependent relative. Two loans also qualify when one is a bridging advance raised to buy a new house while an existing one is being sold; tax inspectors have discretion to extend the period for relief to more than the 'statutory' limit of twelve months' interest.

Certain costs are payable in connection with a mortgage. They are generally the fees of the surveyor acting for the lender, and legal costs and out-of-pocket expenses on drawing up the mortgage deed. Building societies, life-assurance offices, and local authorities have set scales which do not vary much. Typical building-society costs of survey, for instance, are £5 on the first £2,000 plus 20p for each extra £100 up to a total price of £10,000, above which level the fee is negotiable. Where the work is simultaneous with the conveyance, legal charges on unregistered property, for example, are £14 on the first £2,000 of the advance plus 25p for each extra £50 up to a total of £7,000, at which level the fee is £39; and thereafter by arrangement. Where the same solicitor acts for both the purchaser and the society, fees for registered property are less and on, say, a £7,000 advance are £23·75. Travelling and other expenses may add a few pounds to the total. A good guide to the likely total of such expenses is to allow 2 to 2½ per cent on the purchase price.

A particular point to note in connection with the 'survey' made on behalf of a lender is that it may not be a complete survey. It is not therefore a guarantee of the soundness of the property; it is more an inspection to find out if the house offers adequate security for the loan required. Moreover, the fee is not returnable if the mortgage falls through. If there are doubts as to the soundness and value, the buyer (as already indicated) should have his own survey made.

It will be clear from these details of the different types of borrowing that the average home-buyer must have in hand a certain sum of money before venturing on such a substantial project. The amount needed naturally depends on circumstances, but for the average venture the minimum to cover the so-called 'deposit' and legal and other expenses should be up to 10 to 25 per cent on new or reasonably modern property and perhaps up to as much as $33\frac{1}{3}$ or 50 per cent on an old house or one costing much more than £13,000. A smaller starting capital will do if – as explained earlier – a guarantee or other security can be provided.

Buyers of old property without reasonable modern amenities such as a bathroom, hot and cold water supply, sink or water closet, or which can be put into good habitable condition by other work, can claim improvement grants through the local council. These can be up to £200 for standard amenities and £1,000 or more for major reconstruction work (or half the cost whichever is lower); and 50 per cent or up to £1,000 per unit of the cost of converting a larger house into flats. Building societies and local councils are usually ready to make advances to help meet the balance of improvement or conversion costs.

Whatever the cash position, it is advisable to draw up a *capital budget* before getting too far committed and certainly immediately after the first consultation with a solicitor who should be asked for an estimate of the legal fees and disbursements. The details will depend on whether you are buying an existing house or building one. The skeleton which follows allows for this:

CAPITAL BUDGET

Item	Buying	Building
Purchase Price:		
House	£	Nil
Land	Nil	£
Survey costs	£	£
Legal fees	£	£
Stamp duty	£	£
Architect's fees	Nil	£
Builder's costs	Nil	£
Repairs and improvements	£	Nil
Road charges	£	£
TOTAL ESTIMATED COST		

Spending, it should be remembered, may not end here. New furniture and furnishings may have to be bought, removal expenses paid, a garden laid out or redesigned, and other essentials provided, at a cost which calls for additional cash whether paid for outright or bought on hire purchase. A further *overall budget* is therefore needed, and its form should be as follows:

OVERALL BUDGET

	£
Expenditure	
House total cost	
Mortgage expenses	
Removal, garden, furniture, etc.	
	_____
OVERALL ESTIMATED COST	£
Less mortgage	
	_____
BALANCE TO FIND	
	_____

The main points to watch when buying a house or flat can now be summarized:

Make sure that the property is what is wanted and has the necessary amenities.

Make any agreement to buy 'subject to survey and contract'.

Have the property surveyed, if there are any doubts as to its soundness or value.

If buying an 'estate' house, find out if the builders are willing to let it be inspected under the National House Building Council scheme.

Consult your solicitor on all legal matters at the earliest possible stage.

Draw up a budget of the *whole* cost of purchase and settling in.

Ensure that all the money necessary can be raised. *If cash is likely to be short, discuss mortgage arrangements before signing any contract or agreeing to buy.*

Allow for the possibility that mortgage interest rates may rise, as they have done several times in recent years. For instance, in the short period November 1971 to September 1973, the B.S.A. recommended rate jumped from 8 per cent to 11 per cent. This meant that monthly repayments for £1,000 borrowed for a 25-year period rose from £7·81 to £9·90, an increase in outgoings of nearly 27 per cent!

If buying a flat make extra thorough inquiries as to its nature, the mutual covenants, soundness of structure, and the chances of getting a mortgage.

Finally, a note about selling a house. Solicitors' fees will have to be allowed for; and, if an estate agent is used, his fees will be a matter of negotiation – an old scale rate of 5 per cent on the first £500, 2½ per cent on the next £4,500 and 1½ per cent on the residue went out late in 1970 when agents became entitled to charge what they like and can agree with clients.

CHAPTER 7

Stock Exchange Investment

So far we have considered the traditionally safe, solid types of saving and investment, in which, following simple rules, every £1 put in always equals £1 and from which it is mostly possible to withdraw immediately or on giving relatively short notice. These are important, useful, and profitable sectors of our financial machine in which many thousands of millions of pounds are invested by a large proportion of savers. Now we come to another sector which, in terms of money and its particular functions, is much larger – the Stock Exchange.

Despite the spread of knowledge about the City, and its multifarious part in our economic affairs, the idea still persists that there is something mysterious about the Stock Exchange; that it is no place for the 'small' investor. The basic facts, whether they are understood or not, are that it plays a key part in the creation of employment and personal well-being; most of us have an interest in stocks and shares; and it is equally open to the man or woman with only a few hundred pounds to invest and to the big insurance company, bank, or other financial concern with assets of tens or hundreds of millions of pounds.

It is estimated that some $2\frac{1}{2}$ million individuals *directly* own shares. *Indirectly*, at least three out of four of us are concerned in securities quoted on the Stock Exchange. This large and important indirect interest comes through contributions to pension funds, payment of life insurance premiums, lodgement of savings in banks, building societies, and other forms of mutual investment, trade-union subscriptions, and other means. Surplus funds have to be put to profitable use. Life insurance offices and private pension funds alone have approaching £45 million a week to invest. Stocks and shares are a profitable source for a large proportion.

No one knows how or when the idea of a market for the purchase and sale of stocks and shares began. Like so many of our established institutions – and Topsy – 'it just grew'. As domestic and overseas trade blossomed under the stimulus of the Elizabethans, enterprises grew from one-man affairs to companies of venturers. Later, sovereigns began to raise money for the payment of wars and their other needs by means of loans. Both developments created a basic need. Not all the investors who put money into trading enterprises or Government loans were satisfied to hold them indefinitely. Funds might be wanted for other purposes, it might be thought that the venture was failing or the security diminishing, existing investors might want to increase their holdings, or new investors wish to participate. Amongst problems so varied were those of how and where to put sellers and buyers into touch with each other, to fix fair buying and selling prices, and to carry out the business as promptly as possible. These problems could be simplified, it was appreciated, by having a market place in which to buy and sell and by having intermediaries who would act as expert agents or be ready to buy or sell on their own account.

The obvious place for such a market was the centre of Britain's trading and financial world – the City of London. First stock jobbers dealing on their own account, and then stockbrokers acting as agents for investors, began to collect during the latter half of the seventeenth century in the old Royal Exchange, the City's principal market place. The volume and nature of their securities dealings grew with the expansion of trade and the opening up of vast new territories overseas. To seamen's tickets issued as I.O.U.s for pay, tontine and lottery tickets, Government stocks and Bank of England stock, were added the shares of an increasing number of companies, and in 1706 the first foreign loan, which was floated on behalf of the Emperor of Germany. Sound and unsound ventures were amongst the company-flotation boom that ballooned into the historic South Sea Bubble which brought enormous losses and a rude stocktaking when it burst in 1720. Then, and in the following more sober years, were floated concerns such as the Lustring Company, the Sword Blades Company, a company to manufacture square cannon balls, and – a powerful and flourishing survivor to this day – the Governor and Company of Adventurers of England Trading into Hudson's Bay, now known as the Hudson's Bay Company. When the noise of the stock market became too much for the staider City merchants, the jobbers and brokers moved across Cornhill to an open courtyard in Change Alley, from which, like the members of other City markets, they were driven in bad weather to nearby coffee houses, of which one, Jonathan's, became the centre.

After various attempts to find a place of its own, the vigorously expanding organization secured its first premises, and first used the name 'The Stock Exchange' in 1773. A tremendous increase in business during the Napoleonic Wars strained the accommodation. A fresh move at the start of the nineteenth century, to Capel Court, laid the foundations of the present Stock Exchange which now occupies a large part of a triangular site having the Bank of England close at hand on one side and bounded on another by Throgmorton Street, the narrow thoroughfare which bustles with activity during working hours but which is as deserted as a village street in the evening.

While the original 'House' was rebuilt in 1855 and a number of additions were made to it between then and 1904, the only major change in some fifty recent years was the construction of a Visitors' Gallery in 1953. Towards the end of 1961 the momentous decision was, however, taken that only a new Stock Exchange would meet modern requirements of trading and communications. Today, a great new structure has been erected on a site enlarged by the purchase of properties adjoining the old House. Astride the eastern end is a twenty-six-storey tower, 321 feet in height, which contains the Stock Exchange Council Offices, offices for renting to member firms, the Settling Room, reading, writing and other communal rooms, and other facilities. The western end, which is a much lower structure, includes the new trading floor of over 23,000 square feet; it is served by the most modern of communications systems of any market in the world and has 'boxes' (small offices) for brokers' own communications adjacent to the Floor. Contact direct from the Floor to members' offices, clients and other stock markets throughout Britain and the free world has been speeded up, which will make for greater efficiency and speedier dealings.

Three noteworthy systems inaugurated in this new era in rapid communications are: An inter-dialling system, which gives full intercommunication between all member firms, of a size which would be sufficient to serve a town of 40,000 inhabitants. A new personal paging system which can cope with 1,200 calls a minute and is the fastest and one of the largest currently in use in the world; it replaces the generations-old method of top-hatted 'waiters' calling members to receive messages and telephone calls, and is capable of expansion to 4,000 receivers. A market price display system which, through some 1,000 television receivers, provides in members' offices and to non-Stock Exchange subscribers 20 channels of prices of all leading securities, and news items such as company profit and dividend announcements, foreign exchange rates, commodity prices and other developments.

For many generations, London, although it is far and away the biggest, has not been the only securities market in Great Britain and Ireland. With histories going back into the eighteenth century, there are exchanges in other cities and towns. Until quite recently there were trading floors in another twenty-two centres and individual stockbrokers in a larger number of other towns. At one time, although they were linked by telephone, telegram and (later) teleprinter, they operated as independent markets. But modern needs and the development of distance-eliminating communications speeded up the processes of closer co-operation – and, eventually, of integration. The first step was the formation, in 1963, of the Federation of Stock Exchanges in Great Britain and Ireland, which did valuable work in closing the links.

The second step was the rationalization of exchanges outside London into single units. This began in January 1964, when Aberdeen, Dundee, Edinburgh and Glasgow combined to form the Scottish Stock Exchange which, including members in Paisley and Stirling, now does business on a single, modern floor in Glasgow. In August 1965, the nine stock exchanges in Bradford, Halifax, Huddersfield, Leeds, Liverpool, Manchester, Newcastle-upon-Tyne, Oldham and Sheffield joined together to form the Northern Stock Exchange based on Manchester and Liverpool. A third merger brought together Birmingham, Bristol, Cardiff, Nottingham and Swansea as the Midlands and Western Stock

Exchange. With headquarters in Dublin, the Irish Stock Exchange linked up all brokers in the Irish Republic. Belfast, because of its geographical situation, remained a single unit, while the Provincial Brokers Stock Exchange carried on representing its members in dozens of smaller centres throughout the U.K.

The third, and ultimately important, step was taken on 25 March 1973, when all these markets were welded into one organization called simply THE STOCK EXCHANGE. Now, although there are six 'floors' on which business is done personally between members, there are direct dealings – by telephone or teleprinter, or through representatives – between all the markets. Provincial firms have linked up with London firms or have opened their own offices in the City. London firms have opened branch offices in other cities and towns. By its very situation alone, London is however still the pivotal market where the great bulk of business is done. At the March 1974 count, 3,545 members belonged to the London unit, followed by 372 Northern, 213 Midlands and Western, 181 Scottish, 178 Provincial, 107 Irish and 29 Belfast members. One historic outcome of unification was that, although there had been women members in some provincial exchanges, London admitted women to membership for the first time in March 1973.

Our stock exchanges have for a very long time been more than domestic markets. The Stock Exchange is, in fact, a great international securities market. With London in the forefront, it carries on two-way business with recognized exchanges as near as Paris, Brussels, Amsterdam and other European centres and as far away as Wellington in New Zealand, Sydney, Melbourne, Singapore, Hong Kong, Calcutta, Johannesburg, Tokyo, New York, San Franscisco, Montreal, Calgary and elsewhere. Member firms also have overseas offices in eighteen countries, ranging from the Common Market territories to Australia, Hong Kong, Japan, Thailand, South Africa, the West Indies, Canada and the U.S.A. British investors can thus deal in securities quoted on foreign stock exchanges just as easily and speedily as in domestic stocks. Overseas investors have similar facilities in British securities.

The next step, towards which a lot of ground work has already been done, is to link up with Common Market bourses to form one big European Stock Exchange. Already London is providing an increasingly active market in Continental securities and when, in 1974, a strike closed the Paris Bourse a substantial volume of trading in French stocks was done in London. This growth in internationalization is reflected in the number of European and American companies which are getting their securities listed on The Stock Exchange.

The first feature of the new Floor of the London market which will strike anyone looking at it from the Visitors' Gallery will be the sixteen hexagonal stands spread around. The next noticeable fact will be that some of the men, and women, are standing or sitting outside and inside the stands; and others are moving about the floor. These features personify the unique way in which our Stock Exchange does its business and into which its membership is divided. Those at the stands, or 'pitches' as they are known, are *jobbers*. Those on the move are *brokers*.

Jobbers are dealers in particular groups of securities. Somewhat akin to wholesalers in any other market, they are principals who are ready to buy or sell the stocks and shares in which they deal, or 'make books'. Their profit or loss represents the difference between buying and selling prices, and depends to a considerable extent on their ability to judge market trends and demands. They quote two prices, the lower being the one at which they are ready to buy and the higher the one at which they are prepared to sell reasonable market quantities of their wares. Prices (as will be shown in a later chapter) are adjusted to meet supply and demand. In active securities they can vary minute by minute.

Positioning of jobbers at their own stands simplifies and speeds up business: brokers know exactly where to go when dealing in particular securities. The markets range from Gilt-edged (Government and similar stocks), Banks, and Insurance to Oil, Kaffirs (South African gold mines), and Rubber; and take in Breweries and Distilleries, Property, Tea, Water Works, a vast Commercial and Industrial sector, Copper and other Mines, Diamonds, Financial Trusts, Investment Trusts, and other groupings.

Brokers are agents who are paid for their services at definite minimum rates of commission. They buy and sell securities on behalf of the investing public, dealing mainly with their opposite numbers, the jobbers. They also look after all the paper work concerned in the transfer of securities from seller to buyer, give advice on existing or new investments, manage portfolios, and (as will be seen later) play an important part in the raising of new capital and the public flotation of companies.

What part do the 4,600 members of the Stock Exchange, together with the authorized and unauthorized clerks allowed into the House, and their office staffs, play in the financial and economic well-being of Britain? An important feature of any financial machine, as investors and borrowers have known for many generations, and as we have already noted, is a securities market where buyers and sellers can quickly come together. An indication of what this means is provided by a few facts. Between 1 April 1946 and 29 March 1974 the nominal value of the securities officially quoted in London increased from £23,021 million to £64,614 million. The market value, however, rose from £26,141 million to £176,898 million, or to an average approaching £3,200 per head of the population of the United Kingdom. The securities represented range from the loans of our own and other Commonwealth governments and corporations, the nationalized industries and public boards – the *gilt-edged* section, as it is called – to the stocks and shares of almost every conceivable kind of industrial, commercial, and financial enterprise. A summary of the number, nominal amount, and market value of the securities having official quotations at 29 March 1974 gives a good indication of the variety of choice (see overleaf).

Most of the concerns in the company section are British undertakings, many of which have ramifications in various parts of the rest of the free world. A number, such as most of the South African gold mines and American concerns, are however overseas companies, a fact which underlines another important feature of the London market. At the end of March 1974 as many as 395 foreign registered companies had their securities officially quoted. Of these, 147 were South African concerns, 90 American, 33 Canadian, 24 Australian and 12 Dutch. Market value, at £116,165 million, was over three times as large as the total of £38,404 million for the securities of the 3,479 U.K. and Irish registered companies with quotations. This was apart from a large amount for Government and other loans in foreign currencies.

STOCK EXCHANGE – SECURITIES QUOTED

Section	Number	Nominal amount £m.	Market value £m.
GILT-EDGED	1,076	31,545	20,051
FOREIGN GOVERNMENT, ETC.	416	2,978	2,278
TOTAL	1,492	£34,523	£22,329
COMPANIES			
Banks and Discount Companies	148	2,626	13,975
Breweries and Distilleries	275	1,268	2,756
Commercial, Industrial, etc.	4,719	15,327	93,408
Financial Trusts, Land, etc.	251	1,025	2,109
Insurance	66	491	2,885
Investment and Unit Trusts	1,003	2,381	4,612
Iron, Coal and Steel	63	539	1,388
Mines – Gold, Tin, Diamond, etc.	208	1,095	15,145
Oil	61	2,682	12,719
Property	369	1,257	1,738
Public Utilities	467	554	2,291
Railways	62	432	712
Rubber, Tea, etc.	171	123	369
Shipping	60	291	462
TOTAL COMPANIES	7,923	£30,091	£154,569
OVERALL TOTAL	9,415	£64,614	£176,898

Newcomers to share investment who do not know a broker can make the necessary contact by getting in touch with London or one of the other stock exchanges for a short list of names and addresses. Applications for names should be addressed to the respective Secretary:

LONDON: The Stock Exchange, London EC2N 1HP.

MIDLANDS AND WESTERN: The Stock Exchange, Margaret Street, Birmingham B3 3JL.

NORTHERN: The Stock Exchange, 4 Norfolk Street, Manchester M2 1DS.

SCOTTISH: The Stock Exchange, 69 St Georges Place, Glasgow G2 1BU.

BELFAST: The Stock Exchange, 10 High Street, Belfast BT1 2BP

IRISH: The Stock Exchange, Anglesea Street, Dublin 2, Eire.

PROVINCES: The Provincial Brokers Stock Exchange, 3 St Sampson's Square, York YO1 2RL.

Banks, solicitors and accountants provide agency facilities for buying and selling stocks and shares and obtaining advice for clients where no direct contact is, or can be, made with a stockbroker.

CHAPTER 8

Stocks and Shares

THERE is, as we have seen in the previous chapter, a wide range of choice in stock markets which offer investors the opportunity to participate in almost every kind of public and company enterprise. Within the broad general description 'stocks and shares' there are, however, different types of securities which it is important to distinguish. These can be divided into two broad classifications – fixed interest, or prior charge; and equity. Before considering the nature and particular features of the different types, it may be useful to define just what is meant by the terms 'stocks' and 'shares', two words which are used very loosely and which can cause confusion.

Stock, in its original sense, is created and quoted in units of £100 which may be the minimum that can be bought and sold. On the other hand, it may be bought and sold in units of £1 or some other fixed amount, or in the case of British Government securities in amounts as low as one penny. When a stock quotation is say £75, this is the price for £100 worth of the nominal, or face, value. A holding of £200 would thus be worth £150. Gilt-edged, foreign-government, and similar issues, together with the loan debt of companies, are issued and quoted in this form.

Shares always have a definite par or nominal value, which can be any figure, such as 10p; 25p; 50p; £1; £5; as little as 1p; 5p; or any other amount. However, a complication which has grown in recent years is for shares to be described as 'stock' or 'units of stock'. The main reason for this is to simplify the work of transfer from seller to buyer – stock does not have to have the serial numbers which used to be given to shares. Whatever the descriptive term used, however, shares or their equivalent of stock units are bought, sold, and transferred as one or more –

they cannot be divided, like the traditional stock, into units less than their par value. When shares are renamed stock, it is specified that they will be transferable in definite units, which may be 25p or £1 or 5p, and so on. American companies, incidentally, often adopt the useful compromise of referring to their capital as so many 'shares of stock'.

As already indicated, Governments, local authorities, the nationalized industries, and similar gilt-edged borrowers always issue the traditional form of stock. Companies can, however, arrange their capital structure in any one of a variety of combinations, ranging from a simple issue of one type of share to several types of shares and loans, the choice generally depending on the nature of their business and financial conditions at the time when new capital is issued.

Other distinctive features of Government and other fixed-interest securities are that they may or may not have repayment dates, and in some cases annual sinking funds may be provided for gradual repayment over a period of years or when the market price falls below a specified level. A few samples will show the position:

Three and a half per cent War Loan is described as redeemable '1952 or after'. This means that the Government has had the power since 1952 of repaying the £1,900 million of this First World War debt at its par value of 100. It does not, however, *have* to take any action, and until monetary conditions are good enough to replace the entire loan with another stock carrying a lower rate of interest nothing need be done. War Loan for all practical purposes is therefore an *irredeemable*, or *undated*, stock.

Nine per cent Treasury stock is described as repayable 15 March 1978. Whatever happens the Government is committed to redeeming the entire issue of £600 million on that date. Buyers thus know that they will get £100 for each £100 stock in mid-March 1978.

Five per cent Exchequer Loan is described as repayable 26 September 1976/8. This means that the Government can give notice to repay the whole issue at par any time on or after 26 September 1976 and in any event not later than the end of September 1978. Holders thus know that they will get repayment at £100 by September 1978 at the latest, and have a chance (if monetary conditions improve sufficiently) of being paid off earlier.

As detailed elsewhere, $3\frac{1}{2}$ per cent Conversion Loan is being redeemed half-yearly by means of a sinking fund which operates when the market price over six-monthly periods averages less than £90 per £100 of stock; which it has done since 1952.

It is worth noting at this point that irredeemable and very long-dated stocks fluctuate most in market value, particularly when interest rates generally are moving up and down or when there is a political, economic, or international crisis. They must, as some violent movements in recent years have shown, fall into the highly speculative category. On the other hand, they have attractions for investors who wish to 'buy' a definite annual income for a long period ahead. Subject to the chance of repayment, they produce an assured income year by year.

Companies have an *authorized* and an *issued* share capital. They may also be able to raise loan capital, up to a stipulated limit which can be related to the issued share capital. The issued amount of shares or loans may be in one class or several classes – some companies have one class of shares only, while others have a mixture of up to half a dozen or more. An important point, however, is that, before the authorized limit of any class can be exceeded, the shareholders, and in the appropriate instances the loan-holders, usually have to approve the increase, at specially convened meetings. The various ways in which companies are supplied with capital are as follows:

Debentures rank first in the capital line. They are mostly, as with a mortgage, secured on part or all of the fixed assets such as property, plant, and machinery and perhaps also on the floating assets such as investments, stocks, and book debts. Interest is paid at a fixed rate on specified dates, generally half-yearly. Unless described as income debentures, the interest is payable whether the company earns sufficient profits or not. If there is not enough profit or cash to meet the interest, or the company in some other way defaults on the terms on which the issue was made, debenture-holders can foreclose, put in a receiver, or take other action to protect their interests. Responsible bodies or individuals generally act as trustees for the issue and take such steps when necessary. Debentures may be *irredeemable*, which means that the capital is not repaid until the company goes into liquidation; or, the more usual form, are *redeemable* at a speci- fied date or dates or over a stated number of years either at par or at a premium which might be say £105 for each £100 worth. Investors thus know that (as with a 'dated' gilt-edged security) they can look forward to redemption of their stock at some future time or times. If they have bought below the par, or redemption value, there will be a capital profit. Some issues have a sinking fund which provides that a certain annual amount must be set aside, usually out of profits, for repayment of stock; in other words redemption is carried out over a period which may be the full life of the loan or the later part of it. Sinking-fund operations, which may be by drawings at par or at a premium or by purchases in the market, can help to sustain the price of redeemable stock.

Loan stocks are another more recent form of loan capital. Interest is generally fixed, repayment is at a specified date or dates any- thing up to say ten or thirty years from issue, and – while often not secured specifically on fixed or other assets – the loan ranks before share capital for repayment and interest. A variation which can make such issues more attractive and give holders the best of the fixed interest and equity worlds is the **convertible loan stock.** In addition to the above features, holders have the option at certain times, or over a stated period, of converting into ordinary shares. Such a right might for instance be to convert £100 of stock into a hundred 50p ordinary shares at the end of year one; into ninety shares at the end of year two; and into eighty shares at the end of years three and four. To make the conversion profitable, the price of the ordinary shares must be over 100p at the first year end, over 111p at the second, and over 125p at the remaining conversion dates. If a holder does not convert, because the price of the shares is not favourable or it is thought better to stay in a fixed interest security, the stock is repaid at the fixed maturity date. One thing which can occur during the conversion period is for the price of the loan stock to keep in line with that of the ordinary shares when the latter rise above the normal corresponding price of the stock. If, say, the shares rise to 150p before the second conversion date, the loan stock will be quoted in the region of £135 per £100 or the equivalent of ninety shares worth 150p in the market. Naturally, if the company is making good progress it pays to convert at the first suitable opportunity. On the other hand, in uncertain times like those of 1974, it could be more profitable to stick to the loan stock until a later conversion date, particularly if the terms are the same and the interest yield is more than the equivalent which the ordinary shares would give. It can, in fact, pay to forgo a little 'equity jam' in return for the greater security of the loan stock.

A recent variation from the conversion option is to attach subscription rights to take up ordinary shares at a stated time or times at a definite price or variety of prices. This me ins that loan stock-holders can move into the equity if, at the appropriate time or times, the ordinary shares stand at a price which makes subscription attractive; and continue to hold the loan stock as a fixed interest investment or to sell it. The subscription rights can be in the form of 'detachable' warrants which can be bought and sold separately. There can also be cases of a loan stock having a mixture of subscription *and* conversion rights.

Mortgages may be raised on the security of their property by some companies. Such finance is not marketable in the usual way. It is important, however, to know whether or not such finance is being used, for the simple reason that the mortgagee will have the right to seize assets if interest or repayments are not met.

Bank loans and similar shorter term borrowings which may be secured on part or all of the assets need to be carefully noted. Recent developments in the property, secondary banking and conglomerate company spheres have shown the trouble that can ensue when lenders call in their loans, or refuse to renew them, and the assets pledged as security have to be sold, quite probably on a weak market. A single company or a whole empire of companies can collapse, with substantial or total loss to investors, in such circumstances.

Preference shares, as their name implies, are first in the second line of capital. They come before other types of share capital for dividends and repayment, but after debentures and loan stocks. Dividends are paid only out of profits. If these are not earned, shareholders go dividendless, or receive part only of the amount due. Most issues have a form of protection in that dividends are *cumulative*; if profits are insufficient to pay the whole or part of the dividend, the balance is carried forward for payment out of any future profits. Otherwise, dividends are generally paid half-yearly on fixed dates. Some, though not many, preference shares are *participating* – after their fixed dividend they receive a specified portion of surplus profits, or additional payments which are in proportion to dividends paid on the ordinary shares, together with a share of the surplus assets over and above redemption at par if the company goes into liquidation. Other issues are *redeemable* at par or at a premium such as 110p per £1 share at a stated date or dates, at the option of the directors or by annual drawings or purchases in the same way as with a debenture sinking fund. Preference shareholders, although they are part-proprietors of a company, do not often have much legal say in its affairs. Few such issues have full voting rights. Most, in fact, have votes only if the dividend is six or twelve months in arrears or if any change in the company's constitution is proposed which affects their rights, such as an increase in borrowing powers, the creation of additional preference capital, or a change in the dividend rate. Investors in these securities are therefore mostly in the position of being in receipt of a fixed income which is one degree less certain than that payable on any debenture or loan stock capital. Another description, which can mean the same thing, is **preferred shares.**

Ordinary shares represent the *equity*, or what is left after other classes of capital have had their portions of profits and assets. They are the risk capital, taking the major share of any cream if things go well, and shouldering all or the bulk of the loss if they go badly. Some companies, as already indicated, have loan capital and/or one or more classes of preference shares ranking before the ordinary. Others, and these are often the more speculative ventures like mining, tea, rubber, and oil exploration companies, whose fortunes depend on striking it rich or on fluctuations in commodity prices, have only the one class – everything belongs to the equity holders. Where there are prior charges, these take the first slice of the profits, the ordinary shareholders standing to get a dividend only if anything is left over. In practice, most companies retain part of their surplus profits to provide a buffer against bad times or to finance expansion or modernization, to the ultimate benefit of the equity. Although such retentions naturally vary, the average British industrial and manufacturing company pays out in ordinary dividends only a part of the available profits. The practice has, however, grown of distributing portions of these retentions in the form of 'free' share issues, which are variously described as *scrip* or *capitalization issues*. Another practice which has grown in recent years is the division of the equity capital into two classes – the ordinary, which has full voting rights; and the voteless or only partially-voting ordinary, which, by custom and nothing else, is usually given the distinguishing mark 'A'. Such shares are often the outcome of scrip issues. Sometimes, however, they are issued on the conversion of a business into a public company, in order to leave control in the hands of the smaller and voting portion of the equity capital. The general aim is usually to achieve the object of limiting the amount of capital with the dominant voice; which can be a beneficial or a harmful state of affairs. Opposition to voteless equity shares has been growing in recent years and some of the big institutional investors such as insurance companies, pension funds and investment trusts have registered their views by refusing to buy them or by pressing for a change to one class of voting shares.

Deferred shares are mostly a relic of earlier forms of concentrating voting control in or giving a greater proportionate share of profits to a portion of the equity. Where such issues still exist, the ordinary shares may be entitled say to priority for dividends of up to 10 per cent and then to a share with the deferred in specified proportions of the surplus. Occasionally – the well-known Peninsular & Oriental Steam Navigation Company is an example – the entire equity is so described.

Accumulating Ordinary shares are a very new form of equity capital which came into being in 1973. Holders of the 'normal' type of ordinary can elect to take their dividends in shares; though, to maintain trustee status, a small fraction such as 0·1p a share is paid in cash each year. The 'elected' part of the dividend is distributed in accumulating ordinary shares, the price of which is calculated on the average middle market price of the ordinary shares for a period of, say, five days before announcement of the dividend. The benefits of taking accumulating shares are that, under existing legislation, the dividend is not liable to income tax at the higher rates and there is a compound growth in the shareholding. There is, however, liability to capital gains tax on any profit from selling the shares. Naturally, such shares are not so attractive to investors who need cash dividends as to those who can do without. Although the idea was slow to catch on, and only a few companies such as Trafalgar House Investments and Rio Tinto-Zinc were amongst the innovators, their number is now growing rapidly.

Warrants are in effect a form of potential capital to the company issuing them. As already mentioned, they may be part of a loan stock, or equity or preference share, issue given free as a sweetener or as a deferred means of taking an enlarged equity stake at some date ahead. There is a specific price (or prices) at which the warrants can be exercised and a date (or dates) when they expire. In other words, they are options given to holders, who can take them up if it is profitable to do so or can tear them up if there is no benefit. The issuing company does not, of course, benefit until warrants are exercised and it gets the appropriate cash for the shares issued in exchange.

An illustration will show how a company might arrange its capital structure, and how, described in the simplest way, the various classes of holders would share in the profits (see overleaf).

SHARE CAPITAL

Authorized £		Issued £
500,000	7% £1 Cumulative Preference Shares	500,000
750,000	6% £1 Cumulative Redeemable Preference Shares, 1975–80	500,000
3,750,000	25p Ordinary Shares	3,000,000
£5,000,000		£4,000,000

LOAN CAPITAL

£		£
1,000,000	6½% Debenture Stock, 1982–7	1,000,000
500,000	6% Convertible Loan Stock, 1975	500,000

This hypothetical company has issued up to the authorized limit of its loan capital and 7 per cent preference shares, but has in hand for further issue £250,000 of the 6 per cent redeemable preference shares and £750,000 of its ordinary capital. As the 6 per cent loan stock can be converted into 25p ordinary shares at the rate of two for every £1 of stock, £250,000 of the ordinary has to be kept in hand for any such exchanges. Otherwise, the directors can issue up to a further £500,000 of ordinary shares and £250,000 of the redeemable preference. Equally, by getting the approval of shareholders, they could change the nature of this £750,000 of 'reserve' capital. They could, for instance, turn the unissued preference into ordinary shares, or create a new class of preference share from either or both sources.

Interest and dividends on the prior charge capital require the following gross annual sums:

	£
Debentures	65,000
Loan stock	30,000
Total interest	95,000
7% Preference	35,000
6% Preference	30,000
TOTAL	£160,000

For the sake of simplicity, the figures are gross amounts *before* taxation (tax has become an increasingly complicated element in such calculations) and are designed to give a straightforward picture of what is involved.

Yearly profits before taxation thus have to reach £95,000 to cover debenture and loan interest. The 7 per cent preference shares do not qualify for full dividend until profits total £130,000, and the second issue of 6 per cent preference capital until they reach £160,000 – if profits fall short of these amounts, part or all of the dividends cannot be met and must be carried forward until profits are sufficient to catch up with the accumulated arrears. Similarly, the ordinary shares do not begin to share in profits until they exceed £160,000. If, however, the sum earned is say £460,000, the amount available for the ordinary is £300,000 or enough to pay 10 per cent; and if it is £760,000 the equivalent rises to 20 per cent. This is a straightforward example.

In normal circumstances, i.e. unlike those which hit the investment world so harshly and in such a traumatic way in late 1973, the salient points about the various types of Stock Exchange securities can now be summarized:

Fixed-interest and prior-charge stocks are the safest way of buying an assured income. Unless gilt-edged have definite repayment dates, however, they can be speculative, and a well-secured *redeemable* debenture of a sound progressive company can be a more stable investment.

If safety is required but interest income is not the most important factor, useful profits which are exempt from income tax but are liable in certain cases to capital gains tax can be made from buying short or medium dated stocks below their repayment price. These are good investments where capital will be wanted at a known date ahead.

Preference shares are not as safe as debentures or loan stocks, and therefore usually give a higher yield on the money invested. Issues of sound, established companies are, however, good investments for those wanting to 'buy income'. Because preference dividends are not treated as a charge against profits for corporation tax, which thus increases their cost to the company paying them, it is likely that this form of finance will be rarely used in the future. In fact, where legally and financially possible, the tendency now is to repay such capital or to offer conversion into a loan or debenture stock, the interest on which is allowed as a charge against profits for corporation tax.

Equity shares, as the risk capital, are only suitable for investors who appreciate the factors involved. By and large, such shares can, however, be profitable investments over a period of years. They have the advantage that unlike fixed-interest stocks they can provide protection against inflation – progressive companies can be expected to increase their profits over the years, and so be able to raise equity dividends in line with rises in the cost of living, or even faster.

Convertible loan stocks are a good choice for those wanting to: maximize income while reducing the risk of investing directly in equities; minimize the risk of loss in times of industrial, financial and political uncertainty; or get the best out of two investment worlds.

Succeeding chapters deal more fully with these investment factors.

CHAPTER 9

Buying and Selling Stocks and Shares

THE Stock Exchange, as we have already seen, has its own particular way of dealing. It is skilled business calling for something more than the actual operation of buying or selling. The best way of explaining the procedure is to follow through a transaction from start to finish – from contacting a broker to receiving the share certificate which is the evidence of ownership.

The initial step for the newcomer is to get in touch with a stockbroker, preferably direct, or through the agency of a bank. Failing a personal introduction, application can be made to the London Stock Exchange or one of the other stock exchanges for a list of names and addresses (as shown in Chapter 7). You may have your own ideas about the stocks or shares you want bought, have received a 'tip' from a friend, or have seen suitable recommendations in the City columns of a newspaper or periodical. Alternatively, you may have no specific or general ideas. Whatever the position, a broker will advise on the merits of your selections, or will make his own recommendations. Firstly, however, he should know something about you: whether you can or should take reasonable risk, how much you have saved or come into, whether income is more important than capital growth, what provision has to be made for the education of children and retirement, and whether you are already retired or will be giving up work fairly soon.

The next step is the selection of the most suitable investments. Part of a broker's services is to be well informed on stock market conditions, economic trends, developments in individual industries, and the progress and standing of individual companies and other securities. He has first-hand knowledge of the affairs of particular companies, and has sources of information on the others whose securities are dealt in.

When the selections are finally settled, the broker should be given clear instructions orally, by telephone or telegram, or in writing, as to exactly what he should buy. If an order is given orally or by telephone it should be checked back – a misunderstanding can mean the purchase of too much or too little of a selected security, or the wrong stock, and the possible loss of money trying to correct the error.

Let us assume that you decide to buy 500 of the 25p ordinary shares of the A.K.Z. Engineering Company Ltd (a hypothetical concern). If the broker has not had an up-to-the-minute price from the market he will probably: first, if A.K.Z. are amongst the many hundreds of share prices quoted as changes take place, switch to the appropriate channel of the Market Price Display Service T.V. in his office; second, get an indication from the previous day's Stock Exchange Daily Official List, which gives the prices of all quoted securities and prices at which bargains (not all, because marking is voluntary) were done; or, third, put in a telephone call to his dealer on the floor of the House through the paging systems, and get a quote.

Under decimalization prices below £10 are quoted in new pence and fractions of pence – $\frac{1}{4}$, $\frac{1}{2}$, etc. – and £10 and over in pounds and fractions of £1 – $\frac{1}{8}$, $\frac{1}{4}$, $\frac{1}{2}$, $\frac{3}{4}$, etc.

While the Daily List does not record all the business done in any security it does give what may be useful information. For instance, data for our dummy company may record these facts for a day:

	Price	Business done			
A.K.Z. Engineering	68–73	70	68ɸ	69$\frac{1}{2}$	73
		69‡	72	70§	
		72$\frac{1}{2}$△			

Although the number of marks indicates that business in the shares was fairly active, the prices do not tell which were purchases and which sales or the number of shares changing hands. The marks also are not necessarily in the order of execution, and represent deals only up to 2.15 p.m. The code signs distinguish bargains which were not normal ones. These are as follows:

‡ Bargains done at special prices, which may be small lots of

shares for which less than the normal price is received and on which, for very small numbers, the seller may have to pay the Government stamp duty and the registration fee. Such a mark may also represent a purchase or sale for 'new time', which means a bargain done on the last two days of a Stock Exchange account for the next account – the buyer or seller, as will be explained later, will not have to settle the transaction until the end of the succeeding account.

ϕ Bargains done on the previous day, either after the close of the marking lists at 2.15 p.m. or not marked by that time.

Δ This is mainly a domestic recording of bargains done by a member of the London Stock Exchange with a non-member, or between non-members.

§ Bargains done with members of another recognized Stock Exchange.

♣ Bargains done for delayed delivery or which the buyer agrees he will not press for delivery. Such deals may cover sales of, say, South African securities, which may take some time to ship to London.

Advantages of marking are that the daily totals give an indication of the market activity as a whole, in particular sections and in specific securities; they help brokers to get the 'feel of the market' in particular securities; and they are a useful check on the astuteness or otherwise of deals.

With or without these preliminaries, the broker will make for the particular part of the House where the jobbers in engineering shares forgather. He will look at the lists which jobbers display on boards above or alongside their 'pitches'. This will give an indication of the up-to-the-minute price and whether it is moving up or down – rises are recorded in blue pencil; falls in red. As A.K.Z. Engineering is a fairly large company with a good turnover, several jobbers 'make books' in the shares and so ensure competition for business.

Approaching the jobber listing what appears to be the best price, the broker will ask 'What are A.K.Z.s?' or, more tersely, 'A.K.Z.s?' He gives no indication as to whether he is a buyer or seller and, by custom, the jobber does not ask – it is part of his skill to try to 'read which way' the broker is. Briefly he may reply '69–71.' Taking the view that he might get a better price elsewhere, the broker goes to a second jobber, who quotes '68–70'. Not satisfied, he tries a third jobber, who gives him '69½–71½'.

As jobber number two's 70p is the best buying price, the broker goes back to him, saying simply 'Buy 500 A.K.Z.s at 70p'. Equally laconic, the jobber replies 'Sell 500 at 70'. If the broker had been a seller, he would have done business at 69½p with jobber number three. Broker and jobber then make pencilled notes, nothing more, in their dealing books and go about their next business. It is a tradition of the Stock Exchange that (as its motto indicates) 'My Word is My Bond'. Oral bargains are as binding as the tightest legal document. In order to pick up any mistakes or misunderstandings made during the rush of business bargains are checked on the following day. It is rare that the relatively few errors which arise are not settled amicably and without affecting the client.

The differences in prices between jobbers emphasize an important basic fact of stock markets. Prices are fluid. They rise and fall in accordance with supply and demand. If there are more buyers than sellers, jobbers will automatically raise their prices until sellers are attracted. Similarly, if sellers predominate they will lower their quotations until buyers come in at the lower and presumably more attractive levels. Changes in active shares are often almost second-to-second. When a broker quotes a price to his client it is therefore the price ruling at the time he gets it from the market; it will not necessarily stand good a minute or a day later. But if turnover in a particular security is infrequent, the price may remain fairly static and change only on the passing of business. In fact, in some of the out-of-the-way stocks trading may be a matter of negotiation – if stock is on offer or there is a buyer about, jobbers will know of it and be ready to make a price which they hope will suit both parties. The general position in the great bulk of securities, however, is that jobbers are always ready to deal in marketable quantities.

This perfectly natural tendency for quotations to alter quickly can give rise to misunderstanding between client and broker. Although it may be possible to buy or sell at or very close to the closing prices given in the daily newspapers, there can be no guarantee of doing so. *The quotation that matters is the one ruling at the time the broker deals*; and, as already shown, he will check round to get the best price.

What then does a client do when giving an order? The price can be left to the discretion of the broker. He can be instructed to buy or sell 'at best'. Or he can be given limits which may be very close to the latest quotations, or may be some way out, and which he keeps on until executed or cancelled – it is advisable to check unexecuted limits at fairly frequent intervals. The course taken will depend on individual circumstances. A good price may be missed by holding out for a better one. Against this may be set the fact that if a fair price is decided on it can sometimes pay to be patient and wait for it to materialize. The average investor would however be wise, if he particularly wants to buy or sell, to leave it to his broker to make the decision. This is especially desirable if the security in mind is being actively traded. If however it is a share in which dealings are infrequent, it may pay to set a limit.

Decimalization has made no difference to the long usage of the Stock Exchange of quoting in fractions of a pound. The lowest fraction is $\frac{1}{64}$ (or approximately $1\frac{1}{2}$ new pence) and others are $\frac{1}{32}$ (about 3p), $\frac{1}{16}$, $\frac{1}{8}$, $\frac{1}{4}$, $\frac{1}{2}$ and so on. A price of $94\frac{5}{8}$ for a stock would thus be £94·625. As already shown, the fractions for share prices below £10 are parts of a new penny. A share price of $20\frac{1}{2}$p would be 20·5p. Various terms are used in the market. The 'big figure' is rarely given, it being taken for granted that in the example above the broker would know that it was £94. The price mentioned would therefore be no more than '$\frac{5}{8}$'.

Back in his office, the broker's clerks set in motion a chain of paper work which eventually, some weeks or months later, produces the document which is the evidence of ownership – the share certificate. The first document sent to a buyer – or seller – is a *contract note*. This sets out the necessary details of the transaction and is evidence of the purchase or sale. For our example it would give the following details:

CONTRACT NOTE   *14 November 1974*

      Bought by order of ....

A	500 A.K.Z. Engineering Company Ltd	
	25p Ordinary shares @ 70p	£350·00
B	Transfer stamp	7·00
C	Other expenses	Nil
D	Contract stamp	0·10
E	Commission @ 1¼%	4·37
F	Value Added Tax	0·35
G	TOTAL	£361·82

H   Settlement date 3 December 1974

The same items will be set out *across* the contract note if the broker uses a mechanical system of book-keeping. The effect is exactly the same. The meaning of the different items should be known. They are:

(A) **Consideration** of £350 is the cost of buying the 500 shares at the price of 70p at which the jobber sold them.

(B) **Transfer stamp** is the duty which is levied by the Government on the purchase of most shares. The only securities that escape this impost are bearer securities, which pass from hand to hand without the necessity of completing transfer forms and of which there are not many; the shares and stocks of American, Canadian, and other foreign-domiciled companies; allotment letters issued on a new capital offer or a scrip issue; and British Government, Nationalized Industries, Local Authority, Commonwealth Government, and City and similar stocks – all of these are transferable free of stamp duty. For a number of years the duty was 1 per cent on the consideration money. The 1974 Budget doubled it, however, to 2 per cent, but left the rate at 1 per cent for non-residents of the U.K. Duty is broken down into steps, which means that the real cost can sometimes be slightly more. For example, the steps are small up to £100 consideration, but thereafter they widen to 40p for each £20, or part thereof, up to £300; and from then onwards to £1 for every

£50 or part of £50. This means that, whereas the 'stamp' on £300 consideration is £6, or exactly 2 per cent, it is £7 on, say, £302.

(C) **Other expenses** are the rare cases where a company charges a registration fee (normally 12½p) or surrender of 25 per cent of the investment premium which is discussed later.

(D) **Contract stamp** is another stamp duty levied by the Government on every bought or sold transaction. The scale of this impost is:

Where the price:	Stamp
exceeds £100 but not £500	10p
exceeds £500 but not £1,500	30p
exceeds £1,500	60p

(E) **Commission** is payable to the broker on most bought and sold transactions at minimum rates laid down by the Council of the Stock Exchange. The main rates are as follows:

(a) British Government, Local Authority, Public Boards, Commonwealth Government and most other gilt-edged stocks:

(1) With no final redemption date within ten years:

> *Bargains up to £50,000 consideration*
> 0·5% on the first   £2,000 consideration
> 0·2% on the next £12,000 consideration
> 0·1% on the next £36,000 consideration
>
> *Bargains over £50,000 consideration*
> 0·14% on the first £250,000 consideration
> 0·125% on the excess.

(2) New Issues:

> *Bargains up to £50,000 consideration*
> 0·5%   on the first   £2,000 consideration
> 0·1%   on the next   £2,000 consideration
> 0·05% on the next £46,000 consideration
>
> *Bargains over £50,000 consideration*
> 0·07%   on the first £250,000 consideration
> 0·0625% on the excess.

147

(3) Having ten years or less to final redemption:

> *Bargains up to £50,000 consideration*
> 0·5%   on the first   £2,000 consideration
> 0·1%   on the next   £2,000 consideration
> 0·05% on the next £46,000 consideration
>
> *Bargains over £50,000 consideration*
> 0·07%   on the first £250,000 consideration
> 0·0625% on the excess.

Note: Reduced rates apply to deals over £1,000,000 consideration in these three categories.

(4) Having five years or less to final redemption and not in default:

> At discretion.

(b) Debentures, bonds, loan stocks and notes other than in (a):

(1) Registered

> 0·75%   on the first   £5,000 consideration
> 0·375% on the next   £15,000 consideration
> Nil   on the next   £5,000 consideration
> 0·375% on the next   £25,000 consideration
> 0·325% on the next   £50,000 consideration
> 0·3%   on the next   £150,000 consideration
> 0·25%   on the next   £500,000 consideration
> 0·2%   on the next £1,000,000 consideration
> 0·125% on the excess.

(2) Bearer

> 0·5%   on the first   £5,000 consideration
> 0·25% on the next £15,000 consideration
> Nil   on the next   £5,000 consideration
> 0·25% on the excess.

(c) Stocks and shares other than those in (a), (b) and (d):

> 1·25%   on the first   £5,000 consideration
> 0·625% on the next   £15,000 consideration
> Nil   on the next   £5,000 consideration
> 0·625% on the next   £25,000 consideration
> 0·5%   on the next   £50,000 consideration
> 0·4%   on the next   £150,000 consideration
> 0·3%   on the next   £500,000 consideration
> 0·2%   on the next £1,000,000 consideration
> 0·125% on the excess.

(d) American and Canadian shares not deliverable by transfer:

> 0·75 % on the first £5,000 consideration
> 0·375 % on the next £15,000 consideration
> Nil on the next £5,000 consideration
> 0·375 % on the excess.

(e) Short-dated securities having five years or less to final redemption:

> At discretion.

Minimum commissions apply to *small bargains* in the different sections of securities, as under:

	Section (a)	Other sections
Minimum charge	£2	£4
except in case of:		
Transactions on which commission may be	at discretion	at discretion
Transactions less than £100	£1	£2
Transactions under £10	at discretion	at discretion

Because of the steep rise in expenses in recent years some brokers have their own minimum commission charges, such as £7 to £10, or £12 per bargain.

If securities are bought and sold in the same Stock Exchange account only one commission may be payable – at the appropriate rate on the highest consideration of the two bargains.

(F) **Value Added Tax,** currently 8 per cent, is payable on the stockbroker's commission.

(G) **The total** of the contract is the amount payable to the broker. It is the figure which matters when calculating the **all-in** cost of the shares. This is not 70p but 72·4, after rightly taking into account the transfer stamp, brokerage, and other expenses amounting to £11·82. Before the shares show a profit, the selling price must therefore rise to about 72½p. In fact, allowing for commission on a sale, they would have to rise to a little over 73½p just to break even.

(H) **Settlement date** is the day on which the broker should receive payment. In order to avoid the settlement of too many bargains, the Stock Exchange divides its year into **accounts,** the majority

of which run for a fortnight, from a Monday to a Friday. A few
accounts, covering Christmas and other holidays, may extend
to three weeks. Settlement Day, or Account Day, is normally
eleven days after the end of the account. In our specimen
transaction, the last day of the account was 22 November and
settlement was due by 3 December, as shown on the contracts.

Most transactions in shares and other company securities are
for settlement on the appropriate account day. *The great bulk of
Government and other gilt-edged stocks and allotments of certain
issues of new shares are, however, for* CASH *settlement: payment is
due the day after purchase.* Contract notes always show the position.
Payment for sales of securities is also made on Settlement Day,
always providing the seller has completed his part of the transfer
arrangements. A broker is fully justified in withholding settlement
until all the completed documents are in his hands. This is one very
good reason why a seller should sign and return transfer and other
documents without delay.

*An important point to note here is that because of the minimum
expenses involved in most transactions the least sum which should
be put into any one security is about £320.* The minimum can be
higher if, as is the case with some stockbrokers, there is a minimum
brokerage charge of £7 or £8 to £12 a bargain. It is of course true
that any smaller sum, down to £1 or less, can be invested, but in
most cases small transactions are not practicable. The best way
of putting small sums into shares is through a unit trust, as we shall
see in a later chapter.

The documentary work of transferring the shares from seller (or
sellers) to buyer has been considerably simplified since October
1963. Instead of both buyer and seller having to sign and have
witnessed a transfer form, the general rule now is that the seller
only signs and no witness is needed. (The exception concerns
almost entirely securities of overseas-registered companies whose
articles still insist on the older method of signatures, duly witnessed,
of both parties.) Operations begin at the selling end. Immediately
a bargain is done the seller's broker sends his client for signature a
blank transfer form (white in colour) which sets out the name of

the company, the type of its security sold, and the number of its shares or amount of its stock concerned. The selling broker asks for the prompt return of the transfer together with the relevant share or stock certificate(s). The name of the buyer or other details of the deal do not appear on the form.

So far so good – and simple. But how do the essential details of the buyer get through to the selling broker or jobber? Well-tried Stock Exchange machinery takes care of this part of the operation. Immediately after the end of the Account the buying broker makes out a *name ticket* which gives (a) the name of the company, and (b) the class and number of shares or amount of stock bought by his client – it is not essential to add the full names and address of the buyer. This 'invoice', as it may be termed, goes to the jobber who sold the shares, or through the Clearing Department of the Stock Exchange to the broker or jobber who has to deliver them. One of the major tasks of the Clearing Department is to reduce the work of unnecessary transfers in active stocks by 'matching up', or eliminating complementary deals, with the result that only the ultimate sellers and buyers are brought together. Our broker may not therefore get delivery of the A.K.Z. Engineering shares direct from the jobber from whom they were bought. They may come through another jobber or broker. They may also come from more than one seller – when a fairly large number of shares is bought there may be anything up to a dozen or more sellers. The name ticket may therefore have to be 'split' one or more times on its journey. All that concerns the buyer is that there is efficient machinery which ensures that he will sooner or later get delivery of all the shares to which he is entitled.

On receipt of the 'invoice' the selling broker finally gets to know the number of transfer forms needed to cover the sale by his client. Should one 'invoice' cover the entire sale all he has to do is to deliver the original (white) transfer with the covering certificate of shares or stock to the buyer's broker. The shares may, however, have been bought by more than one investor. The selling broker deals simply with this situation by splitting the white, or 'master', transfer into the necessary number of what are called *Broker's transfer forms* which, to distinguish them from the original, are printed on green or blue green paper; and inserting in each the essential facts from the information reaching him through the name tickets. Brokers' transfers have to be certified by the company's registrars or by the Share and Loan Department of the Stock Exchange to the effect that a certificate covering the required number of shares or amount of stock has been safely lodged for transfer. Where applicable, transfers are stamped with the appropriate Government duty of two per cent.

Means of simplifying, speeding up and reducing the cost of transfer work have been under investigation by the Stock Exchange for some years. Data-processing and computerization have speeded the inquiries and it is likely that a centralized system will be in use before long.

After completion of the formalities under the age-long system still in use at the time of writing, and when the buying broker has seen that the full names and address of the purchaser are entered on the transfer reaching him, the form goes to the *registration* department of the company. The seller's share certificate – if it has not already been lodged – is also sent. The job of the registration department is the important one of keeping the records of shareholdings. Each investor has his own account in which are recorded purchases and sales and the balance owned. On receipt of a transfer, the account of the seller is debited with the number of shares shown as sold and a new or existing account of the buyer is credited. The old share certificate is then cancelled, and a new one is made out in the name of the buyer. If the seller has sold part only of his holding, a new certificate covering the balance is also made out in his name. The new certificates are sent to the respective brokers, or to whoever else has lodged the transfer, to be passed on to their clients.

The registration of transfers and preparation of share certificates takes time, the amount depending on the efficiency of the department, the volume of turnover in the particular shares, and the policy of individual companies. Until recent times it was necessary for a meeting of directors to approve and often sign certificates before their issue. Increasing numbers of companies are now taking powers to issue certificates without going through such formalities. The result is that, although some companies still take several weeks to complete the work, others – including some very large concerns – get everything through within a few days, or as little as twenty-four or forty-eight hours. Under new requirements, the Stock Exchange asks for certificates to be ready within 14 days of the lodgement of transfers.

The share registers are the records from which are prepared dividend payments and other distributions to shareholders. When a distribution is to be made, notice is given that the registers will be closed between specified dates covering anything up to a week or more. This enables the registrar to calculate what is due to each shareholder from the balances extracted, and to prepare the necessary documents. In the case of an interim dividend and a rights offer, the cheques or other papers may be posted within a few days. But with the final dividend, or any other operation which needs the approval of shareholders, posting does not take place until after the necessary resolutions have been passed at the annual general meeting or a special meeting. One or more of several things may thus happen between the date of buying shares and being put on the register as a shareholder, and while the seller is still registered as the owner of the shares.

Does the new shareholder suffer as a result of these unavoidable time gaps? The answer is a definite NO. The Stock Exchange has machinery to deal with these situations. Before explaining them, a vital factor must be noted. When buying – and selling – securities it should be seen whether the price is 'ex' or not. Soon after a dividend is declared, the price will be quoted '*ex dividend*', which means that although it may not be paid for some weeks the seller – not the buyer – is entitled to the distribution; only future dividends will belong to the buyer. Theoretically, the price is adjusted to allow for the net dividend. For instance, if the price before the declaration was 78p–80p and the net dividend is worth 2p per share, the price will become 76p–78p ex div., or simply X.D. Similar adjustments are made for scrip issues, rights offers, and any other distributions having a bearing on the market price, the appropriate abbreviations being 'ex capital' and 'ex rights', or simply 'ex.c.' and 'ex.r.'

Unless a price is specifically quoted 'ex', it can generally be taken that it is 'cum' and that all subsequent declarations or rights belong to the buyer. Because of this tacit understanding, it is rare for a price to be specifically quoted 'cum dividend' or 'cum' anything else.

It follows that if shares are 'cum' when bought, but are not registered in time for a new holder to receive any distribution direct, it is necessary to claim from the seller. This is done by the buying broker claiming from the selling broker, who in turn recovers from his client. An investor who sells shares or stock which are not 'ex' must therefore hand over any dividend, bonus shares, or right to subscribe for new shares, should they go direct to him after he has sold.

Must an investor wait for the share certificate before he can sell? This is another important question. The answer again is NO. Securities, once bought, can be sold at any time, which may be a minute, a day, a week, or many years after purchase. If sold within the account, the two bargains cancel out, no share certificate is required, and the investor pays or receives the difference in the two considerations. He is rightly credited on the sale contract with the transfer duty and, as previously stated, he pays only one commission on the two transactions. If, however, the shares are not sold until the next or a subsequent account, all the transfer formalities must be completed, both buying and selling. The Stock Exchange has all the facilities to deal with the paper work and sort out balances between buyers, sellers, and intermediaries.

A specimen selling transaction shows what happens. Suppose that the 500 A.K.Z. Engineering shares bought earlier at an all-in price of around 72½p are sold about a year later at 85p ex a final dividend of 10 per cent declared some days before. The contract note would show the details of the transaction as set out on page 155.

The net price realized was thus just over 83¾p and the profit was £419·16 less £361·82, or £57·34, and the equivalent of nearly 11½p per share. The investor would also get the 10 per cent final dividend. Providing the transfer was completed and the share certificate lodged with his broker in time, he would be paid £419·16 on 2

CONTRACT NOTE   *18 November 1975*
Sold by order of...
500 A.K.Z. Engineering Company Ltd.
  25p Ordinary Shares @ 85p ex. div.   £425·00
Less Contract stamp   0·10
       Commission @ 1¼%   £5·31
       Value Added Tax @ 8%   0·43
                                               ———
                                                              5·84

TOTAL   £419·16
                                                              ———

Settlement date 2 December 1975

December, the settlement day. Capital gains tax would of course
take away some of the profit.

Unnecessary delays and misunderstanding can be avoided by
following some simple rules when buying or selling securities:

1. Give clear instructions to your broker. Have telephone orders
repeated.

2. Be quite sure of the security in which you want to deal. Some
names are very similar. Also, if there are two kinds of share, such
as ordinary and A ordinary, be quite clear which are to be bought
or (if you hold them) sold.

3. Before giving a selling order, check the number of shares held.
Scrip issues, rights issues, or the splitting of shares can radically
alter an original holding.

4. When selling send the share certificate with the order, or as
soon as possible after giving it, to the broker. This can save time
and correspondence and ensure prompt payment.

5. Keep certificates in a safe place, preferably at the bank. They
are the evidence of ownership and are troublesome to replace if
lost.

6. Sign and return all documents promptly.

7. If in doubt ask your broker or bank. Money can be lost by
failure to deal correctly and promptly with allotment letters and
similar documents.

8. If securities are not 'ex' when sold, be prepared to hand over
a dividend or other distribution received subsequently.

There is a simple way of calculating costs for the average size deal by the average investor. Based on 2 per cent transfer duty, current minimum brokerage rates and 8 per cent V.A.T., allow for *shares*:

Buying: 3·4 per cent, say 3½p in the £.

Selling: 1·4 per cent, say 1½p in the £.

For *debenture and loan stocks*, at the lower brokerage rates, allow:

Buying: £2·8 per £100.

Selling: 80p per £100.

CHAPTER 10

Weighing Up the Merits: Gilt-Edged Stocks and Foreign Bonds

STOCKS and shares, it will have been gathered, should not be bought haphazard. They have to be chosen to meet particular needs. What may be suitable for a young man or woman may be the wrong thing for a retired couple who want a secure income. Within particular categories discrimination is also essential – while the shares of say one chemical company may be an attractive long-term investment, those of another may be very much of a gamble. And once a policy is decided general and specific factors have to be assessed.

General factors which influence security prices as a whole are political, international, economic, and the market position. To these, as shown later, have to be added in the public company sector, trade trends, financial facts, and management. Specific factors cover the present standing and future possibilities of a particular stock or share or of groups of securities. It is important therefore to assess the present position and to try to read the portents before making a purchase or sale.

Political developments such as a general election, a crisis within the Government, or the promotion of generally unpopular legislation can affect gilt-edged securities or markets as a whole, temporarily or for a relatively long period. As the stock market collapse in 1973/4 showed in such costly ways, the political factor can be the most disastrous and harmful. It can be the direct cause of economic and financial slumps, with dangerous repercussions throughout the entire nation.

International developments such as the outbreak of war or threat of war, changes in foreign Governments or demands for self-government, or other happenings in other countries can affect specific sections or our entire market. Recent examples include the recurring disturbances in Israel and Egypt and the reactions of the Arab oil-producers.

Economic factors have been major influences in recent years. Domestically, a watchful eye has had to be kept on inflation, the trend of industrial production, the rise in wages, and the result of these last two items – productivity, or output per man. Linked with the attempts to control or boost such factors are credit squeezes – affecting some industries like those for cars, domestic equipment, and other consumer goods more than others – and changes in interest rates which result in dear or cheap money. Externally, the nightmare has been the balance of payments, which is mainly governed by whether we are spending too much on imports or not earning sufficient foreign currencies from exports, and which has as its side-effects the inflow or outflow of the 'hot' money that rushes about the free world seeking the highest interest rates; and gyrations in the all too meagre gold and dollar reserves essential for settling the trading balances of the greater part of the Commonwealth as well as of the U.K. These latter factors, as has been all too unpleasantly evident in recent times, can affect the value of our currency and the currencies of other countries. Devaluation of the pound, or the up-valuation of other countries' currencies, makes for weakness in Government stocks, strength in gold and other mining shares, and plus or minus impacts on different groups of industrial and commercial shares. Another more direct external consideration is the buying or selling of British securities by American and other foreign investors – persistent one-way business, which can happen fairly frequently in particular stocks or groups of stocks, can have a marked effect on prices.

A final factor applying to straightforward investment is the *yield* or return which can be expected from the money invested. This depends on the all-in price paid and the rate of interest or dividend. The method of calculating the yield is to multiply the interest or dividend by the par value and to divide by the all-in price. For instance if £100 of a 6 per cent fixed-interest stock is bought at an all-in price of £60, the yield on the interest alone is:

$$\frac{100 \times 6}{60} = £10 \text{ per cent.}$$

158

Similarly, the yield on a 25p ordinary share on which the last annual dividend was 15 per cent, bought at 50p, is:

$$\frac{25 \times 15}{50} = £7 \cdot 50 \text{ per cent.}$$

In the case of fixed-interest stocks repayable at definite dates, yields can be *flat* or *running*, and *redemption*. The first is calculated, as shown above, on the ratio of the price paid to the par value and interest rate. The latter takes into account the profit which accrues (as seen later) when a stock bought below par is repaid. While such a profit is normally free of income tax to an individual, part or all of it may be liable to capital gains tax, an impost dealt with in Chapter 20.

With these general considerations in mind, we can now look at the specific points to consider carefully when purchasing different types of securities. For this purpose the market can be divided into three broad groups – gilt-edged, foreign bonds, and company securities.

GILT-EDGED

The gilt-edged market, as already shown, comprises loans issued by the Government to the tune (at 29 March 1974) of £26,732 million; nationalization, trade facilities, guaranteed, Northern Ireland, and other stocks totalling £1,040 million; Irish Government stocks of £807 million; corporation and county stocks of £2,066 million; public board and similar loans of £366 million; and £535 million of Commonwealth government and corporation loans.

Public debt cannot be assessed in the same way as company and other securities. Taking the National Debt, which is made up of the above-mentioned quoted stocks and a further £13,400 million of unquoted securities in the form of Savings Certificates, Savings and similar Bonds, Premium Bonds, Treasury Bills, debts due to American, Canadian and other foreign governments, and other loans, the total of over £40,000 million is only partly represented by assets. Soaring interest rates have made Government borrowing very costly in recent years. No longer can the 'soundest' borrower get money at 3 per cent to 6 or 7 per cent. It is hard for those who lived in cheap money days to think in terms of double-figure interest; yet, by May 1974, 12¾ per cent had to be offered on a Treasury Loan repayable in 1995 which, moreover, was issued at £94·50 per £100 of stock – a discount of 5·5 per cent. What a change from 1946, when a *2½ per cent* Treasury stock was successfully floated! Up to then most of the debt had been 'blown into the air' financing two world and earlier wars. The security for investors was almost entirely the continuing ability of successive administrations to raise sufficient taxes to pay the interest, to meet any sinking-fund requirements, and to repay loans as they fell due.

Since the late 1940s there has, however, been an important change, of which too little notice has been taken. Successive governments have taken it on their shoulders to provide a large proportion of the finance needed for capital development by local authorities, the nationalized industries, the Post Office and a few commercial enterprises; and for overseas development, for housing associations and for Britain's participation in such world bodies as the International Monetary Fund. All these loans are repayable in various ways. So, with the exception of any 'bad debts' which may have to be written off loans to nationalized industries which run into the red, they represent sound financial assets.

Between March 1951 and March 1974 such assets multiplied more than six times to some £26,000 million. Yet, *a key factor*, Government debt increased during the twenty-three years at a very much slower rate from just over £26,000 million to around £40,000 million, a rise of little more than 50 per cent. True, political mismanagement of the economy has meant, and may continue to mean, writing off some of the debt due from nationalized industries. But, despite this, the great bulk of these assets is good and, if ever national finances return to normal, their total could grow at a faster pace than the National Debt. Not included in the assets are nationally-owned shares in British Petroleum, Suez Finance, and other companies worth at least £600 million, and many properties and other assets owned by Government departments.

While it is true that the recent upsurge in assets is due to the large Budget surpluses of a number of recent years, continuation of the recent policy of encouraging nationalized industries and Local Authorities to raise funds directly through U.K. and international money markets, and of using Budget surpluses for debt repayment, would make a noticeable difference to the gilt-edged market. Assuming that there would continue to be surpluses on future Budgets, there would be a growing repayment of Government stocks; which would help to keep up market prices. The stage could in fact be reached where a 'date' could be put on the undated stocks like 3½ per cent War Loan, or they could be bought in through the market, with a resultant improvement in their prices as the amount outstanding was reduced. There is actually a good precept for action. When the average daily price in any half year is below 90 a sinking fund operates to repay 3½ per cent Conversion Loan – one per cent of the amount outstanding is applied to market purchases, with the result that the original amount of £935 million will have been reduced to below £300 million by April 1975; about £200 million of stock has been bought in over the past ten years alone. This stock, War Loan and the other currently discredited undated stocks could be attractive speculations over the next few years.

Nationalization stocks are backed by the assets of the electricity, railway, gas, and other industries concerned – for what they are worth – and, of greater importance, by the guarantee of the Government. Corporation and similar loans, having been raised to finance housing and other public works, have substantial asset backing, which is supported by the fact that their service is a charge on the rates levied. Most of the Commonwealth and colonial loans have been issued to finance public works providing tangible security, to which must be added the power to levy taxes to meet commitments.

Most gilt-edged stocks are repayable on a definite date or dates: an investor knows that in due course he will be repaid, usually at the par value. Some loans do not, however, have any specified repayment date, or if they have one it is purely at the option of the borrower to repay then or at some subsequent but unspecified time. These important distinctions have a direct bearing on investment rating, market prices and fluctuations, yields, and tax considerations. Taking the extremes of a 3 per cent loan repayable in one year and a 3 per cent undated issue, the former will be priced very close to its par value, because a buyer knows he will be paid £100 in twelve months' time. The second issue will, however, stand at only a small fraction of its face value (say, 20 to 25 per cent), because it is at the whim of various financial winds, of which the most potent is the general level of interest rates. If investors expect a yield of, say, 12 per cent to 15 per cent, as has been the case of late, on top-grade fixed-interest securities, the general level of yields will be adjusted accordingly, with the greatest impact falling on the longer and undated issues. We thus have a second class of groupings within gilt-edged which fall broadly into four categories – short-dated, medium-dated, long-dated, and undated or irredeemable.

Short-dated, or 'shorts', have a life of up to five years and because of the certainty of repayment by a known date are the type of 'money' stocks that appeal to the banks, discount houses, and other financial institutions. They like to have a substantial part of their investment funds in securities which it is reasonably sure (a) can be realized speedily with little or no loss; (b) if bought below their repayment price will show a profit on redemption; and (c) will give a fair return on the investment. Shorts, of which there are never many issues, are bought and sold in a special way. A buyer, in addition to paying the market price, also has to 'buy' the interest accrued to the date of purchase, or if the stock is 'ex dividend' to receive the amount accruing from the ex-dividend date to the date of payment. In other words, the interest is calculated on a day-to-day basis as between buyer and seller. A 5 per cent stock repayable at 100 approximately four years and six weeks ahead is bought, say, on 6 August at $82\frac{1}{4}$. As 134 days' interest has accrued the buyer pays an extra £1·836 for such accumulated income. The flat (or running) yield is £6·08 per cent. Allowing, however, for the tax-free capital gain on repayment at par in about 4 years and $1\frac{1}{2}$ months time the gross redemption yield is £10·376 per cent; or, allowing for income tax on the interest at 33 per cent, the net redemption yield is £8·328 per cent.

Medium-dated stocks are those with a life of 5 to 15 years, which means that their market prices are more at the whim of financial and economic winds. Against this, they generally offer greater tax-free redemption profits, particularly stocks carrying a low rate of interest.

Long-dated stocks are those with lives of more than fifteen years. At the time of writing there are a few stocks which have repayment dates early in the next century, and one of the longest is $7\frac{3}{4}$ per cent Treasury Loan 2012–15. This group is even more at the mercy of changing interest levels and other influences.

Undated stocks are those relatively few issues which have no repayment date or are repayable on *or after* a specified date. The borrower is the sole arbiter, and can repay or not as inclined. This means that repayment will take place on the first redemption date, or later, only if the general level of interest rates is such that the entire issue can be replaced by a new loan carrying a lower rate of interest, or at least the equivalent rate. One example is $3\frac{1}{2}$ per cent War Loan, a relic of the First World War. Since December 1952 the Government has had powers to repay it on giving three months' notice. But it is unlikely to do so until a loan of equal size can be issued at say 3 per cent. Other Government stocks of the same kind include $2\frac{1}{2}$ per cent Consolidated stock, known as 'Consols'; $2\frac{1}{2}$ per cent Treasury Stock, 1975 or after, known as 'Daltons' because they were issued when the late Dr (later Lord) Dalton was Chancellor of the Exchequer, during the cheap-money era of the post-war Labour Governments; and 4 per cent Consolidated Loan. Another stock in this group is the already-mentioned $3\frac{1}{2}$ per cent Conversion Loan.

Undated or irredeemable issues are subject to the widest fluctuations. They have no redemption 'floor' to stop falls when interest rates are rising or there is a crisis of one kind or another. Against this must be set the fact that they offer greater scope for recovery when conditions are favourable. They are also of interest for investors who want to 'buy' an assured income for a long period ahead. For example, a purchase of $3\frac{1}{2}$ per cent Conversion Loan at, say, £25 for £1000 of stock would give a yield of 14 per cent, or an annual gross income of £14 for every £100 invested. By and large, however, such issues are more suited to investors who are ready to speculate on a fall in interest rates, a strongly improving economy, or some other development which might lead to a lower yield basis and price recovery.

Some examples from the medium, long, and undated sectors of gilt-edged stocks show how running and redemption yields operate. (See the table opposite.)

The running yield, or interest, is liable to income tax, but any redemption profit on stocks held for more than one year is exempt from capital gains tax. The second yield column shows the gross yield plus the gross redemption profit; it is the running yield plus the average annual redemption profit calculated to the latest repayment date where options exist. The third yield column shows the net redemption yield after allowing for income tax at the 1974/5 base rate of 33 per cent. This representative sample provides some wide variations in flat yields and some narrower ones in redemption yields. On the other hand, there is a noticeable closeness in the net redemption yields, which tend to keep pretty well in line in relation to the length of time the various stocks have to run to their latest repayment dates. There is therefore a useful choice for investors who want the maximum income yield and for those who, because of high income tax liability, prefer capital appreciation.

Tax-conscious buyers of Government stocks should, where possible, consider timing. While the length varies somewhat, most issues go 'ex-dividend' five to six weeks before the half yearly interest is due; which means that the interest goes to the seller with the buyer having to wait six months *plus* the five–six weeks before his turn comes along. It is possible to anticipate the ex-

Stock	Interest due	Redemption dates	Price	Yield Flat* £%	Redemption £%	Redemption Net yield† £%
Treasury 6½%	15 Feb. & 15 Aug.	Aug. 1976	92¾ X.D.	7·008	10·555	8·335
Exchequer 5%	26 Mar. & 26 Sept.	Sept. 1976/78	82¼	6·079	10·376	8·328
Treasury 3½%	15 June & 15 Dec.	June 1977/80	73⅞	4·771	9·540	8·112
Treasury 12%	17 Mar. & 17 Sept.	Mar. 1983	96½	13·053	13·613	9·155
Funding 6½%	1 May & 1 Nov.	May 1985/87	61⅛	10·946	13·154	9·976
Transport 3%	1 Jan. & 1 July	July 1978/88	40½	7·463	11·902	10·092
Funding 5¾%	5 Apr. & 5 Oct.	April 1987/91	51	11·724	13·510	10·186
Treasury 9%	17 May & 17 Nov.	Nov. 1994	65	14·291	14·782	10·344
Treasury 9%	15 Mar. & 15 Sept.	Mar. 1992/96	65½	14·534	14·954	10·327
Treasury 9½%	15 Jan. & 15 July	Jan. 1999	65¼	14·694	14·930	10·331
Treasury 5½%	10 Mar. & 10 Sept.	Sept. 2008/12	37¼ X.D.	14·565	14·683	10·197
War Loan 3½%	1 June & 1 Dec.	1952 or after	24⅛	14·905	—	—
Conversion 3½%	1 Apr. & 1 Oct.	1961 or after	24⅝	14·959	—	—
Consols 2½%	5 Jan., 5 Apr., 5 July, 5 Oct.	1923 or after	16⅝	15·245	—	—

* Flat yield takes account of accrued interest in price of stock.

† After allowing for income tax at 33 per cent on interest.

dividend date by 21 days – a jobber will sell the stock up to three weeks before it is officially so quoted on such a basis. This means that an investor can hold the stock for more than the year necessary to be exempt from capital gains tax and receive only one half year's interest liable to income tax. Hence, if the price goes up, he gets a tax-free capital profit and pays income tax on only one-half of a full year's interest. An example of the effect on the buying price is that if $3\frac{1}{2}$ per cent Conversion Loan is quoted normally at, say, 26 the special ex-dividend price will be $24\frac{1}{4}$ – 26 *less* six months' interest at $1\frac{3}{4}$ per cent.

A useful point to note about British Government stocks is that most of them can be bought and sold through the National Savings Bank, and the Trustee Savings Banks. Although not more than £5,000 nominal of any particular stock can be bought at one time, there is nothing to stop anyone accumulating as much as he or she likes by lots of not more than £5,000 worth a day. The main advantage of this method of purchase is that as the stock goes on to what are called the National Savings Stock Register or the Trustee Savings Bank Registers income tax is not deducted from the interest. This does not mean that such interest is tax-free; it is liable in the appropriate cases. But it does mean that small investors who are not liable to tax do not have to bother making repayment claims. Payment can be made by a debit to a Savings Bank account; by money deposited in such an account for the specific purpose; or by cash, money order, or cheque remitted with the order to buy. Purchases and sales are made at prices current when the transactions take place. The Department for National Savings (through which business from the National Savings Bank is done) or a Trustee Savings Bank cannot therefore undertake to buy or sell at any specified price or on any particular day, as may be possible when buying in the normal way through the Stock Exchange. Commission is small, the rates being, for example, 25p per £100 of stock with an additional charge of 5p for each £50 of stock above £100. There is of course no limit to the nominal amount of stock which can be sold at any one time. Stock bought directly on the Stock Exchange is put on to the Bank of England Register. It is possible, however, subject to a £5,000 a year limit, to have stock transferred from the latter to the National Savings Stock Register or the Trustee Savings Bank Registers.

Interest on most Government stocks will be paid free of income tax to residents abroad who make the necessary application. These, at the time of writing, include 5 per cent Exchequer Stock 1976–8; $5\frac{1}{4}$ per cent Funding Loan 1978–80; $5\frac{1}{2}$ per cent Funding Loan 1982–4; 4 per cent Funding Loan 1960+90; $5\frac{3}{4}$ per cent Funding Loan 1987–91; $5\frac{1}{2}$ per cent Treasury Stock 2008–12; and $3\frac{1}{2}$ per cent War Loan.

FOREIGN BONDS

Because of defaults on interest and redemption obligations foreign government and municipal stocks, with a few exceptions, are in a special category of their own. At one extreme are the bonds of the pre-Revolution Russian government and other Iron Curtain countries, which sometimes can be bought for less than £1 per £100 worth, but which can rise sharply on talk of recognition of liability by the respective present governments. At the other extreme are stocks of some of the West European countries such as the Federal Republic of Germany, and of Japan, which are comparable to gilt-edged and are priced accordingly. In between are issues of South American states and cities which have undergone reorganization or funding, or which are partially or entirely in default.

Generally speaking, this is a highly specialized market and one in which the speculative element predominates. Most foreign bonds are only suitable for those who know something of economic conditions in the countries concerned and who can time purchases when there has been a sharp set-back. One practical advantage is that most issues are in the form of bearer bonds which are physically passed from seller to buyer. There is thus no 2 per cent transfer duty to pay.

Another feature which is common to all bearer securities is that, as there can be no register of holders (as with registered securities), interest or dividend payments have to be collected by presentation of a coupon. Each bond therefore has attached to it some numbered coupons. On announcement of a distribution, the holder has to cut off the coupon and present it, direct or through the agency of his or her bank, to what is known as the paying bank. When the coupons run out, a fresh set is issued on presentation of the necessary evidence of ownership. As our foreign exchange regulations provide that bearer securities must be left in the care of 'authorized depositaries' such as banks, merchant banks, brokers, and other approved agents, this work, together with that of safe custody, is left to such concerns.

International currency problems, of which there has been a surfeit in recent times, have served to develop a new and spectacularly growing financial market. Loosely called the *Eurobond* market, it has proved to be a useful way for U.K., U.S., French and other borrowers to raise loans on what, in the case of Britain, have proved to be cheap rates of interest. Merchant bankers and brokers in London were amongst the first to realize the potentialities of channelling an increasing part of the thousands of millions of Eurodollars floating around Europe into bond issues running for periods of from five to twenty years. (A Eurodollar has been described by the Bank for International Settlements as 'a dollar that has been acquired by a bank outside the United States and used directly or after conversion into another currency for lending to a non-bank customer . . .')

Although the term 'Euro-' can be applied to a large part of the loans raised during the past few years in this market, it is noteworthy that other loans have been floated by non-resident borrowers in Germany, Switzerland and other 'strong currency' countries. The basis of the 'fund' has been, however, the flow of U.S. dollars to the rest of the world resulting from deficits on the American balance of payments. Tapping it was stimulated by U.S. Government restrictions on foreign borrowings. Today, it is a common feature of the London financial world to see Euro and similar loans being raised for American as well as other borrowers by City houses in conjunction with Continental, American and other foreign bankers and brokers. More recently, and reflecting the great upsurge in their income from oil, the Arab states have been stepping up the supply of funds to this ever-hungry market.

But, as U.K. residents have to pay a premium to buy 'investment dollars' for subscription to such loans, it is not surprising that their appeal has been mostly to overseas investors who do not have the same problem. While at one time the dollar premium was only a few per cent it has been well over seventy per cent in more recent troublous days – a somewhat hefty deterrent!

CHAPTER 11

Weighing Up the Merits: Company Securities

ASSESSMENT of the merits of company stocks and shares demands, in addition to an understanding of the universal factors that apply to all securities set out in the previous chapter, consideration of the standing of each concern in its particular industry, its record, quality of management, and prospects. More specific points can be summarized as follows:

Financial facts include the profit record and trend; indications as to the current trading position and prospects; the strength or weakness of the finances; the possibility that new capital will have to be raised, and the chances of getting it; the asset value of the equity shares as shown by the balance sheet in relation to the market price; the possibility of a scrip issue; and the chances of a take-over bid, or of the company itself trying to absorb other concerns.

Trade and economic facts cover the outlook for the trade or industry and the company; the ownership or lack of ownership of profitable and valuable patents, processes, or products; the effect which new processes or developments might have on future output and sales; the ability and skill of the management; reliance on raw materials, particularly those which fluctuate widely in price or are subject to shortages; the amount of export trade; whether home market sales can be affected by credit squeezes or other Government measures to restrict consumer spending; labour conditions; whether demand for the company's products is rising or falling; the degree of competition within the industry; and the modernity of the factories, methods of production, and distribution facilities. Two potent, and sometimes damaging, factors which have troubled most industries and companies in recent times have been the increased pace of inflation and the disruptive tactics of shop stewards and some of the trade unions; it has been very difficult, if not impossible, to foresee their impact. Projections based on normal criteria can thus be upset by uncontrollable, and unpredictable, happenings with serious effects on trading and profits.

Political considerations have unfortunately become far too much of an influence, and a bad one, in the last few years. As discussed in the earlier part of this edition, even the most astute and able businessmen cannot be expected to anticipate the uncommercial and fallacious policies of governments which, whatever their political creed, create situations in which it is impossible to plan ahead and to keep a check on production costs. There can be no doubt that the politicians, together with many of the trade unions, have made business management and forecasting hazardous occupations. While there is political uncertainty and mistrust on the scale of 1973 and 1974 it is impossible to apply normal, sane rules to the assessment of company securities.

Management is normally the key of all keys. A company can have all or most of the other advantages but it will not get far if it is badly or inefficiently managed. Far too many are the examples of first-class assets and possibilities being frittered away by people who do not know how to exploit them. On the other hand, there are also many cases where the introduction of keen, dynamic management has transformed an ailing or almost dead company into a prosperous, go-ahead concern.

Market facts to consider are the present price of the shares in relation to the high and low points of recent months and years; the extent of recent movements; the freedom or otherwise of dealings; the closeness or wideness of jobbers' prices; the state of the market; and whether it is subject to sudden bursts of activity or keeps on a fairly even keel. Particular markets, it is essential to note, can be in or out of fashion, the two governing factors being the state of trade in particular industries and the mood of investors – or of the financial pundits in Throgmorton Street or Fleet Street.

Yield, though it may have to be assessed with different objects in view in relation to the type of security, has to be considered. There can be no yield on the ordinary shares of a company in the course of opening up a new gold mine until it starts to make profits, or on those of one which is striving to recover from a run of losses. On

171

the other hand, it can be high on the equity of a company which is liable to sharp fluctuations in profits or is operating in a dying industry. Two good general rules are: first, the higher the yield the greater the risk; and secondly, the greater the profits and assets cover, the lower may be the yield.

The balance sheet and profit record of the hypothetical company referred to in Chapter 8 will serve to demonstrate and elaborate the points to watch. The latest balance sheet shows the following financial position:

	Assets	£	£
FIXED:	Land, plant, machinery, etc.	6,500,000	
	Less Depreciation	3,500,000	
			3,000,000
ASSOCIATED COMPANIES – Investments in			500,000
CURRENT ASSETS			
	Stock	2,250,000	
	Debtors	1,750,000	
	Investments at market value	500,000	
	Cash at bank	750,000	
	TOTAL	5,250,000	
Less Current liabilities		1,750,000	
			3,500,000
	TOTAL NET ASSETS		7,000,000
	Represented by:		
LOAN CAPITAL:	6½% Debentures	1,000,000	
	6% Loan stock	500,000	
			1,500,000
SHARE CAPITAL:	7% Preference	500,000	
	6% Redeemable preference	500,000	
			1,000,000
	Ordinary		3,000,000
RESERVES AND UNDISTRIBUTED PROFITS			1,500,000
	TOTAL		7,000,000

This shows that the company is in a healthy financial position. Its manufacturing or fixed assets appear to have been written down

172

at a rate well in line with that at which they consume themselves in producing goods and profits. Its trading assets – in the form of stocks, debtors, and liquid resources, less what it owes to suppliers, for taxes, dividends, and other liabilities – are strong. And it carries in the balance sheet no intangible assets such as goodwill, patents, or other items which have no concrete form and which would therefore be difficult to value. The result is that the net assets attributable to the various classes of capital can be taken to be worth the figure of £7,000,000 shown on the balance sheet. This means that on a *cumulative* basis the assets cover for the various prior charges is:

$6\frac{1}{2}$% Debentures	7 times
$6\frac{1}{2}$% Debentures + 6% loan stock	
–£7,000,000 ÷ £1,500,000	$4\frac{3}{4}$ times
Above plus 7% preference	$3\frac{1}{2}$ times
Above plus 6% Red. preference	
–£7,000,000 ÷ £2,500,000	2·8 times

The final calculation concerns the twelve million 25p ordinary shares. After deducting the £2,500,000 of loan and preference capital, there is £4,500,000 left – the issued ordinary capital of £3,000,000 and the £1,500,000 of reserves and profits ploughed back. Each 25p share is thus covered one and a half times. Put in the more usual way, their *net asset* value is $37\frac{1}{2}$p each.

The introduction of the 'corporation' method of taxing company profits, followed by the imputation system, has complicated the important financial exercise of calculating the *cover* available for interest and dividends on the various classes of a company's capital. As will be shown later, even if there is only one class (equity), the result depends on dividend policy. A class distinction is, however, made between interest on loan capital and dividends on preference and equity shares. The former is an allowable deduction from profits and can therefore be charged gross; the latter are not and are therefore, in effect, 'chargeable' net, that is after deduction of income tax at the basic rate.

If tax life were simple, with corporation tax at 50 per cent (actually it is 52 per cent for the current tax year) and our company made a profit of £1,595,000 before tax and paid 15 per cent dividend on the ordinary shares its profit and loss account would show:

		£
Profit		1,595,000
Less Debenture interest (gross)	£65,000	
Loan stock interest (gross)	30,000	
		95,000
Balance		1,500,000
Less Corporation tax		750,000
Leaving for dividends		750,000
Allocation:		
Preference dividend (gross)	£65,000	
Ordinary dividend (gross)	450,000	
		515,000
Balance (surplus)		235,000

Two ways of calculating interest and dividend cover can be used. The first is the *number of times* the individual cash needs are covered by the profits available for each payment. The second, and much more widely used, method, is the *priority percentage* system which breaks down the amount required for payments on each class of capital into cumulative ranges of the profit.

Starting with the net profit of £750,000, we have to add back the *net* debenture interest of £32,500 (£65,000 less 50 per cent tax) and *net* loan stock interest of £15,000 (£30,000 less £15,000) to give an available total of £797,500. Priorities are then:

Class of capital	Cost £	Priority %
6½% Debentures	32,500*	0–4
6% Loan stock	15,000*	4–6
7% Preference	35,000	6–10½
6% Preference	30,000	10½–14
Ordinary – 15%	450,000	14–70½
Balance, to Reserves	235,000	70½–100

* Gross, less 50 per cent corporation tax.

Interest on the 6½ per cent debentures thus takes only about 4 per cent of the available profit, while requirements of the entire loan and preference capital are only some 14 per cent, or less than one-seventh of the sum in hand. About 56½ per cent is absorbed by the gross cost of the ordinary dividend and 29½ per cent is left for reserves.

The next calculation is the amount *earned* on the 12,000,000 ordinary shares. As seen, the 15 per cent dividend costs £450,000 and £235,000 is retained in the business. Leaving out of account tax complications considered later, £685,000 is attributable to the ordinary shareholders and could have been paid to them on a full distribution of profits. Earnings could then be calculated as below:

$$\frac{£685,000 \times 100}{£3,000,000} = 22 \cdot 83 \text{ per cent.}$$

This is made up of the 15 per cent dividend and 7·83 per cent put to reserves. In effect, the payment was covered just over 1½ times by available profits.

A newer, and in its way more easily understood, method now generally used is pence per share earnings. Our earnings of £685,000 are therefore divided by 12,000,000 to give 5·71p, or almost 5¾p, per share, from which the 15 per cent divided equals 3¾p, to leave a surplus of nearly 2p. The figures would be shown as:

Earned per share	5·71p
Paid per share	3·75p

Now we come to an important contingent consideration. Earnings have so far been calculated on the capital structure at the date of the latest balance sheet. No account has been taken of what would happen if holders of loan capital or preference shares with conversion rights exercised these and switched, as they might do, into ordinary shares. Equally, the earnings rate would be altered when any special class of equity not entitled to dividends until a specified date, or a certain happening, began to take its share of the profits. Prudence dictates that in such cases account should be taken of the *diluted earnings*. Taking a simple example let us assume that a company's capital structure is:

175

£3,000,000 in 12,000,000 25p ordinary shares.
£2,000,000 in 7½ per cent loan stock of which
each £100 nominal can be converted into
ordinary shares as under:
  1975 150 shares
  1976 140 shares
  1977 130 shares

and that results for 1974 were:

	£
Profit before interest and tax	1,750,000
Less Loan stock interest	150,000
	1,600,000
Less Corporation tax @ 50 per cent	800,000
Profit after tax	800,000
Earnings per share	6·66p

To get the diluted earnings it is assumed that conversion of the loan stock takes place entirely in 1975; £2,000,000 stock would then become 3,000,000 ordinary shares, to make a total of 15,000,000. The fully diluted earnings would then be:

		£
Profit as before		800,000
Plus Loan stock interest	£150,000	
Less Corporation tax	75,000	
		75,000
Adjusted earnings		£875,000

Fully diluted earnings per 25p share
  £875,000 ÷ 15,000,000 = 5·83p

Similarly, if instead of the loan stock being convertible, there were 3,000,000 deferred shares entitled to dividends only after conversion into ordinary shares, the fully diluted earnings would be:

$$\frac{£800,000 \text{ Profit}}{15,000,000 \text{ Shares}} = 5·33p$$

Adjustments of like nature would be necessary for capitalization issues, share exchanges, rights issues at less than market price and issues at full market price.

From April 1973 companies have been taxed by an *imputation system*. Corporation tax (currently 52 per cent, but liable to change with future budget policies) is charged on profits, whether retained or distributed. Profits paid out in dividends are, however, treated as if they had borne income tax at the basic rate (33 per cent for 1974/75) and an imputation credit for the appropriate amount is given against the corporation tax paid.

Shareholders are treated as though each £67 of dividend had suffered tax of £33; and, though the method of showing the appropriate amounts in annual returns seems odd, the gross income taken into account for assessment to higher rates of tax – and for repayment claims – is a gross amount of £100. One exception is preference shares. When imputation began (and the tax rate was 30 per cent) many companies changed the gross dividend rate to a net rate – a 5 per cent preference share became a 3·5 per cent share. Now that the base tax rate is 33 per cent, shareholders are still paid 3·5 per cent; but their tax credit is increased from the 30 per cent to the 33 per cent level.

Problems begin with the calculation of earnings on the ordinary shares. They depend on the amount of available profit paid out in dividends. As already mentioned, the income tax equivalent on the net dividend is allowed as a set-off against corporation tax. This tax is due as an advance payment of corporation tax and is generally known therefore as A.C.T. It is currently equal to thirty-three sixty-sevenths of the dividend paid to shareholders. The position therefore becomes that the company is due to pay 52 per cent corporation tax on its profit but gets back an A.C.T. credit of 33 per cent. The after-tax earnings on the ordinary shares thus depend on the amount of net available profit paid out in dividends. Three methods of calculation are open:

Nil distribution, which assumes that all earnings are kept in hand and no credit is taken for A.C.T.

Net distribution, which takes into account the actual dividends paid and allows for the A.C.T. paid.

Maximum distribution, which assumes that all earnings are paid out and the maximum A.C.T. accrues.

A simple example shows how the three methods work. Assume that a company with £4,000,000 issued capital, all in ordinary shares, makes £1,000,000 pre-tax profit and that the tax rates are: Corporation 52 per cent and income 33 per cent. Dividends are: nil; 10 per cent; and maximum distribution. Here are the results:

		Nil		10%		Maximum
	£	£	£	£	£	£
Pre-tax profit		1,000,000		1,000,000		1,000,000
Less Corporation tax		520,000		520,000		520,000
		480,000		480,000		480,000
Dividend: Gross	Nil		400,000		716,418	
A.C.T.	Nil		132,000		236,418	
		Nil		268,000		480,000
Retained		480,000		212,000		Nil
Earnings yield		12%		15·3%		17·9%

Dividend Distribution Rate

Investment and accountancy experts are sharply divided on the method which shows the fairest and most informative result. There is therefore a tendency to give two figures – *nil* and *maximum* – though some investment analysts, and the Institute of Chartered Accountants, favour the *net* basis. Further complications, particularly when comparing one year with others, or the performance of a group of companies in similar lines of business, arise through the actual tax liability, which can deviate quite materially from the norm. A company may, for instance, get substantial capital reliefs; or it may not get sufficient set-off for foreign taxes paid because its U.K. profits are not enough to attract at least equivalent A.C.T. Which means that performance calculations based on after-tax profits are a somewhat dicey operation. *The surest and simplest bases of comparison are profits before taxation.*

Another vital consideration is the ratio of profits to the net assets employed in the business. Is the ratio rising, falling, or merely keeping pace with the growth? Again, it can be calculated on profits before or after tax. For the reasons given above, and because of changing tax rates, the pre-tax figures are the more reliable and consistent. Take a company which made £1,500,000 profit before tax on net assets of £7,000,000. Its profit/asset ratio was 21·4 per cent. If, in the following year, it made the same £1,500,000 but its assets had grown to £7,250,000 because of ploughing back some of its surplus, the ratio would drop to 20·7 per cent. This could mean a decline in efficiency, a fall in turnover, a rise in production costs, cuts in selling prices to meet competition, a Government-imposed restraint on profit margins or selling prices, or some other factor of concern to shareholders. On the other hand, if the profit rose to £1,750,000, the ratio of 24·1 per cent would indicate expansion of one kind or another, improved efficiency, a rise in selling prices, a reduction in competition or some other favourable impact.

A further indicator of progress, or regression, is the ratio of profits (once more pre-tax) to turnover. Sticking to the above theoretical company, if the turnover in year 1 were £15,000,000 the pre-tax profit of £1,500,000 would equal 10 per cent. Moving to year 2, if the turnover were exactly the same and the profit fell to £1,250,000 the ratio would be only 8·33 per cent; but if the profit rose to £1,750,000 on an unchanged turnover the ratio would improve to 11·67 per cent, and if the turnover increased to £17,500,000 the return would be unaltered at 10 per cent. The causes of change could be any one or more of the factors which can affect profit ratios. Turnover, incidentally, demands a cautionary note. Increases in monetary value may be entirely, or largely, due to inflation in selling prices – the volume of *real* turnover, or units of production, may be unchanged, or actually fall. It is just another of those things which inflation plays havoc with, making it more difficult to get true comparisons and trends.

We can now turn from the general to the particular as it concerns the selection of the different types of company securities. In all cases it is assumed that the general tests of management, financial and profits standing, and future prospects have been applied.

Debenture and loan stocks should be assessed by the following measuring-rods:

Flat yield, and how it compares with the general average on similar securities.

Repayment provisions; and, if there is a sinking fund, whether it gives the company the option of meeting annual requirements by purchases in the market or is restricted to drawings at par or at a premium. The latter can provide a useful buffer against heavy falls in price, or a capital profit for a holder who has stock drawn for repayment at a price above that paid for it. In times of 'tight' or 'dear' money, or credit squeezes, it is well to note the maturity dates of loan capital. A well spread out series of maturities is safer than a tightly bunched block of repayments.

Interest cover or priority percentage. While this naturally varies with the type of company – a property-owning concern offers more tangible security than an oil company – it should generally be a minimum of say three to four times.

Capital cover again depends on the type of concern and the make-up of its net assets. A property company might for instance raise one-half or more of its capital on debentures and/or mortgages. The minimum for the average industrial or commercial company should, however, be an assets cover of say two or three times.

Conversion terms if the issue is convertible into ordinary shares; or subscription terms if there are rights to subscribe for ordinary shares. These are the date or dates or period over which such rights can be exercised and their bases. The price of such stocks tends to keep in line with the corresponding value of the ordinary shares.

Preference shares need to be assessed on these criteria:

Yield, dividend, and capital cover. Whether the dividend is cumulative (which is generally the case).

Whether there are any participation rights to a share in surplus profits after meeting the fixed dividend.

Are there any voting rights? Preference shares with full or partial voting rights can have a special value in a take-over bid –

their votes can play an important part in a battle for control, as has happened in several tense fights of recent years.

The terms of repayment, if they are a redeemable issue. There may be an annual sinking fund for redemption at par or at a premium; repayment may be at the option of the directors; or the entire issue may have to be redeemed on a specified date or dates. Any powers to repay have gained importance since the coming of corporation tax, which, as previously mentioned, does not allow preference dividends as a charge against profits and thus makes it profitable to eliminate such capital by repayment or, where feasible, by conversion into a loan stock, the interest on which is allowable for tax.

Ordinary shares, as the equity or risk capital taking what is left, require a somewhat different assessment, which can be summarized as follows:

Profit and dividend trends – up, down, or static.

Whether the profit/net assets and profit/turnover ratios are rising, falling, or showing no change.

Earnings and earnings yield, calculated on the market price.

A newer method of assessment is the Price–Earnings Ratio: as its description implies, it is the number of times the market price of the shares bears to its earnings; or, put another way, it is the number of years needed for earnings to equal price. For example, if £1,000,000 profit is available for dividends on a company's issued ordinary capital of £5,000,000 in 25p shares, earnings will equal 20 per cent or 5p per share; so, if the market price is 50p, the P/E Ratio is 10; or $\frac{50p}{5p}$ to 1. Hence, on the assumption that profits and capital remain stable, it will take ten years for the company to earn the market price of 50p. As already indicated, the new imputation system of company taxation brings problems of calculating dividend cover and earnings, and these affect P/E ratios. Both *nil* and *maximum* bases should be used.

Dividend yield, which in the case of a 'growth' company with scope for expansion can be substantially less than on fixed interest securities or the equities of companies with little immediate chance of increasing their profits. Yields of 1 or 2 per cent may be justified on an ordinary share with dynamic prospects, whereas 5 to 8 per cent may be the average on non-growth concerns.

Risk element such as – in the case of rubber and other producers of raw materials – dependence on fluctuations in selling prices or on the maintenance of the sources of supply.

Net asset value gives an indication of the balance-sheet worth. It is not, however, an absolute valuation. Shares can only be worth their break-up value if the company goes into liquidation, with the assets realizing their book values and the liabilities not exceeding the amounts stated. Clearly, whereas the factories, plant, and machinery of a company may be worth their balance-sheet valuation or more while it is a going concern, they may be worth very much less if put on the market for sale, particularly if they are highly specialized in nature. On the other hand, it may be revealed when the directors of a company are fighting a take-over bid that balance sheets considerably understate both book and realizable values of assets such as land, commercial buildings, and trade investments. Property, in particular, has risen in value since 1945, and some companies carry such an asset at pre-war cost or much less after allowing for depreciation. Despite the guess-work, there has been too much tendency, particularly in times of booming stock markets, to brush aside net asset values and to over-concentrate on projections of future profits. The 1973/4 débâcle in equities has done something to restore this once effective measuring-rod to its essential place in the assessment of share values. Never forget it.

Since the drastic stiffening of the capital gains tax in the 1965 Budget, many companies have had their property and other fixed assets revalued, often with a striking surplus on book values. Some have written the new values into their balance sheets; and in some cases part or all of the surpluses have been distributed in scrip issues to equity shareholders. Others, however, have been content simply to let shareholders know the new valuations and have not written up the assets. Directors are now expected to give some indication of the market value of properties in annual reports.

The need for regular, up-to-date valuations of fixed assets, particularly land and premises in city areas, has been rammed home by the breathtaking rises – and the slumps – in values over the last few years. Apart from the asset value to shareholders, many companies are now faced with the increasingly pressing problem of 'inflation accounting' – replacement cost, especially of plant and machinery, has to be provided for at a rapidly accelerating scale of depreciation. This problem is exercising the minds of the accountancy profession which, amongst other things, is striving to find ways of bringing realism into company balance sheets and profit and loss accounts.

CHAPTER 12

Investment or Speculation?

Apart from updating some figures and facts, this chapter has been left largely unaltered from earlier editions; even though the stock market collapse of 1973/4 came as a shock to basic thinking. There is always a chance of recovery and, with it, a return to rational investment policies.

THE answer to the question of where investment stops and speculation begins would have been comparatively easy to give in the days before the Second World War. There was then a fairly clear dividing line, making it much easier to classify groups of securities and individual shares. Investment life was that much simpler. Although there were such problems as the changing value of money and international politics, the basic problem was more one of deflation than of inflation. It could be reckoned that stock markets would move in accordance with certain clearly defined rules, and in cycles. A rise in interest rates, and therefore in yields, would be succeeded sooner or later by falls, when the market process would be reversed. There was thus a certain amount of averaging-out over the years: the swings alternated with the roundabouts. A key factor was, however, that £1 worth of investment income would always equal more or less 20s. worth of purchasing power.

Fixed-interest securities, not surprisingly, had an impregnability that was hard to shake, which resulted in the long-term investor (as opposed to the speculator) putting the bulk of his or her funds into such stocks. It was not unusual to find investment portfolios consisting entirely or almost entirely of gilt-edged stocks, debentures, and preference shares. Where ordinary shares were included, the proportion judged to be sound policy might be no more than one quarter of the fund. The line was clear-cut. Prime fixed-interest securities were sound, safe investments – for widow, orphan, and everyone else. Equities, even the best, were speculative.

A very different situation has ruled with increasing force in recent years. The position has to a considerable extent been reversed. Fixed-interest securities, particularly undated stocks and preference shares, are now nearer to being the speculations, and equities are much more the investments. This is mainly because creeping inflation has been steadily eroding the purchasing value of money: the pound today buys far less than one-half of what it bought in 1946. An investor who bought £1,000 of 3½ per cent stock at par at the end of the war still draws £35 a year gross interest; but this £35 now buys him only a few pounds worth of food, rent, travel, and other essentials. Apart therefore from the other key factor of the general level of interest rates, which is much higher than in the immediate post-war years, a greater yield is expected from fixed-interest stocks in order to counter this loss of purchasing power and, equally important, any further diminution which might occur in the future. During recent financial crises yields on Government stocks have approached, first, 10 per cent and, later, 14 to 17 per cent and over, while big, substantial industrial companies have had to pay still higher rates on issues of new loan stocks. Income and capital both diminish in *real* value as inflation spreads its corrosive poison.

On the other hand, the 'cult of the equity' has developed to the point where ordinary shares are treated in more normal economic and political times as the sound investments. The main argument in their favour is that progressively-managed companies will expand their profits and thereby be able to pay out an increasing amount in dividends on their ordinary capital. Providing the increases in dividends keep pace with inflation, the equity investor will be able to maintain the purchasing value of his pound of income. For example, if a company has raised its dividend rate from 15 per cent to 20 per cent, and the cost of living has risen by 15 per cent, the rise of 33⅓ per cent in investment income has more than counterbalanced the fall in the *real* value of money.

Other beneficial effects of investing in growth shares are that (a) free shares may be distributed from the reserves which all progressive companies build up out of profits; (b) if expansion is particularly rapid, fresh capital may be raised from shareholders on bonus terms; and (c) there will be a tendency to discount future expansion by accepting a low immediate yield in the hope of securing bigger returns in the future – the shares may be priced to yield only 1 to 3 per cent compared with the 5 or 7 per cent offered on the equities of 'static' companies. All the successful equity investor needs is to pick the right companies at the right time. But this is far from easy, and calls for shrewd inquiry and sometimes a good deal of courage and tenacity.

Some examples show the changes in these investment winds. The *Financial Times* has for many years published daily indices of prices for four main categories of Stock Exchange wares – Government Securities, Fixed Interest, Industrial Ordinary, and Gold Mines. These indices, while supplemented in recent years by more widely-based daily indicators such as the FT-Actuaries and those of *The Times*, are the traditional measuring rods for assessing the day-to-day picture of market trends. In 1949 the Government Securities index touched a high level of 114; the cheap-money policy of the Labour Government was still going strong. By 1969 the same index had dropped to a low point of 64·21, while in the first eleven months of 1974 it fluctuated between a high of 60·80 and a low of 50·91. Corresponding movements for the Fixed Interest index were from a high point of 134·2 to a lowest ever point of 51·34 in November 1974 and a top level for the first eleven months of 1974 of 60·38. But the Industrial Ordinary share index climbed – with considerable ups and downs – from just under 100 in 1949 to a record 543·6 in May 1972 before slipping off and fluctuating widely on a down-trend until mid-1973, when the flood gates burst open and the year-end index was almost 200 points off the all-time peak at 344·0. Further collapses followed down to a low for more than fifteen years of 164·6 in November 1974. Unhappily, investors have had to become inured to *daily* falls of 10 to 15 points, even to as much as 24 points on a particularly bad day; and, reverse-wise, few days with rises of more than a few points.

Much wider changes are to be found amongst individual securities. War Loan, the now notorious stock on which hundreds of thousands of investors of all sizes have large paper losses, was selling at over its par value for some time after the last war – it touched a peak of 109⅛ and yielded only 3·2 per cent in 1946. It stood so high in investment esteem that it was in fact an almost automatic choice for trust funds and other top-rate portfolios. In more recent times War Loan has been down to as little as 20⅛, or barely one fifth of its par value, to yield almost 17½ per cent! Yet in the equity sector cases can be found of shares which have multiplied not twice or thrice in price but ten, twenty, or more times.

Many examples of spectacular increases – and some of decreases – in the market value of 'growth' company equity shares could be given. Within a few years those of Western Mining, the Australian nickel and other metal mining company, jumped something like fifty times after allowing for the various rights issues of new shares; another Australian nickel share soared within a few weeks in 1969 from a few shillings to over £100; it did not take many years for £100 put into Great Universal Stores to grow to over £2,300; De Beers, the diamond giant, has given some of its lucky shareholders ten, fifteen times and more growth in their investment within recent times. Equally, some of the popular high-fliers have slumped to only small fractions of their peak prices, while a few, like Rolls Razor, have brought shareholders complete loss.

An excellent annual picture of long-term trends in equities and fixed-interest stocks is provided by de Zoete & Bevan, the London stockbrokers. Taking a base date of 1 January 1919, their studies are based on the ordinary shares of a cross-section of thirty well-known companies and 2½ per cent Consolidated Stock (Consols) which have been the bell-wether of irredeemable gilt-edged for several generations. A bird's-eye view of the 55 years to January 1974 shows that equity share values, after rising over 13 times by the beginning of 1973, were about 9⅓ up, while Consols had dropped to little more than one-third of their price. It was not, however, all one-way traffic. Within the period, fixed-interest stocks outpaced or kept level with equities in 22 out of the 55 years. Put another way, if grandfather had invested £1,000 a year in both equities and Consols, by the beginning of 1974 his £56,000 in the former would have been worth £202,600 and his £56,000 in the latter only £22,190. The long-term superiority of equity investment is demonstrated by relating income with changes in the cost of living, which multiplied 4 times over the period. Equity dividends multiplied 7·8 times, to give a *real* increase of about twice in income. On the other hand, income from a 1919 investment in Consols had a purchasing value of less than one-tenth.

Spectacular performances are not confined to growth stocks. Another group worth watching is *recovery* shares. Most companies at some time or times in their careers strike a difficult patch, which may be the result of mismanagement, changes of fashion, excessive competition, a general slump, losses on raw materials or stocks, or some other factor. Some companies go to the wall in such circumstances. Others struggle along as shadows of their former glorious selves. And some – as a result of the turn of the trade cycle, reorganization, a change of control, or the infusion of new enterprise or products – recover fairly quickly, or after an uphill grind. A good example is the Rank Organization, which after being successively hit by heavy losses on film production, and a big decline in cinema-going, boldly met its problems by reorganization and expansion into electronics, light engineering, the money-spinning Xerox copying system, and hotels and catering. On appreciation of the recovery taking place and the future potential of the greatly diversified interests, the 25p ordinary shares came out of the Stock Exchange 'dog-house' to become a long-term popular investment at many times the price to which they had dropped when few financial experts had a good word for them.

Gold shares demonstrate the effect of factors over which individual companies and entire industries have no control. From 1935 to early 1972 the *official* price of the metal was pegged at $35 an ounce, due to the obstinate policy of successive United States governments which opposed all attempts to bring it into line with the general rise in prices and with the market value of other metals. It was only when the once almighty dollar was under pressure and funds were draining out of the U.S. that the Americans agreed to what was no more than a token rise to $38. From 1968 a 'two-tiered' system of allowing sales at free market prices has however operated. Though such sales were relatively small at first, virtually all newly-mined gold coming on to the market is now sold at the 'free' price, which leapt in a few weeks during the first half of 1972 from a low of $44·30 an ounce to over $70 and has since been well over $185. Gold shares, for many years with few friends, burst into fashion again and in a very short time the leaders doubled, and more than doubled, in price. In the six months to the end of 1972 the F.T. Gold Mines index more than doubled from its near all-time low of 46·4 to 97·3 and then, with inevitable fluctuations largely in line with changes in the price of the metal, soared to a record 425·4, or just 4¼ times its 1955 base of 100. While many staid stockbrokers and investors will not touch gold, and other mining, shares with the proverbial barge-pole, this performance demonstrates the costliness of adhering to hide-bound investment rules.

Price movements in the stock market as a whole, or among individual sections or currently popular stocks, are not always one-way. Although it may appear that prices will continue indefinitely up and up – or down and down – sooner or later something happens to halt or reverse the movement. A political or economic crisis may intervene; a speculative bubble which has started as a genuine investment move may be punctured by the pin of realism; or one of a dozen or more factors which can affect sentiment may begin to operate. While markets may carry optimism or pessimism to extremes, they have a knack of anticipating the red or green light.

Timing of investment transactions is therefore important. Purchases of fixed-interest stocks before an almost certain rise in interest rates, for instance, would not be particularly wise; while on the other hand sales in advance of an almost certain reduction might be costly. To jump on the band wagon of a bull market after it has been in progress for some time may call for thought: although individual equity shares or groups of shares may still look reasonably priced on the prospects which started the upward move, it may be wise to await a reaction before buying. There are always investors, or speculators, who overdo the optimism or pessimism.

This is a good reason to be guided on investment timing by an expert – your stockbroker or portfolio manager.

Framing the right investment policy in present conditions is not easy. The first major point to decide is whether the emphasis must be put on (a) immediate income or (b) capital growth. Retired people, or those nearing retirement, may have little choice but to opt for income. Younger investors who are not dependent on income from savings may, however, prefer to spread their holdings in ways which could add to the capital value and so enlarge their self-generated pension fund. Other important points to take into account are the amount to be invested, or saved, and the risks which can or should be taken – all equities do not improve in value over the years; a quite high proportion lose ground. Capital gains tax is also a factor.

Despite the attractions of a 100 per cent equity investment programme it may therefore pay to follow the older policy of having part of one's funds in fixed-interest stocks. The proportion will depend on individual needs, circumstances, and amount of capital. Whereas, for instance, 10–25 per cent might be enough where the emphasis is on growth, 50 per cent or more might be essential for those heavily dependent on investment income. A point which could be of profitable significance is that monetary and economic fears which have been such a recurringly alarming feature in recent years may disappear, or be reduced in effect, in times to come. We might then see more settled conditions in fixed-interest securities with a lowering of rates from levels at which first-class industrial and water company loan and preference stocks stand at prices yielding substantially less than recent rates of 12 to 16 per cent, even 18 to 20 per cent. Any long-term downtrend in interest rates would mean higher prices for fixed-interest securities.

Whatever the basic plan adopted, it is a good idea to take account of the following investment rules:

1. Spread the risk, particularly in equity shares, so that if one company or industry strikes a bad patch it does not affect the whole portfolio.

2. Be ready to switch. Never look on a portfolio as static. Even if it means selling at a loss, it is a sound policy to switch from an investment which is declining or static to one which is dynamic.

3. Study all the relevant facts (as outlined in Chapter 11) before making an investment. Avoid industries in decline or which are likely to be superseded by new processes. The retail trades consistently do well, while the capital goods industries have fluctuating fortunes.

4. Keep some capital – say, 5 to 10 per cent, depending on the total – in readily realizable form, to meet financial emergencies without being forced to sell good investments, for taking up 'rights' issues, or for a promising new purchase. Building societies, bank deposits, and short dated gilt-edged stock are profitable ways of investing such reserves.

5. There are times when it is worthwhile to be 'liquid', when it can be profitable to sell even the best investments and to hold cash for repurchasing them at lower levels.

6. It can be good policy to sell part of an investment holding which has had a big rise. This reduces the cost of the shares kept. If, for instance, the price of 300 shares bought at 100p rises to 300p the sale of 100 will reduce the net cost of the remaining 200 to nil.

7. Keep an eye on interest and dividend payment dates. It is helpful, if investment income has to be relied on, to have it flowing in fairly evenly over the year. But do not be put off a good investment simply because the dividend dates do not fit in with an income pattern.

8. Watch an investment portfolio, however large or small. Make a monthly, quarterly, half-yearly, or annual valuation, and weigh up the merits of each holding in the light of current conditions and the outlook.

9. Bear in mind the latest tax impost – capital gains tax. It cannot, as explained in Chapter 20, be escaped. The rate is 30 per cent at the time of writing. To clear say 100 per cent net profit the *gross* rise has to be nearly 143 per cent!

10. Do not be afraid to cut a loss. It can pay to sell at less than cost and, if there is hope of recovery, to buy back at still lower prices.

CHAPTER 13

Speculation

ALTHOUGH, as we saw in the last chapter, it is today impossible to draw a clear line between investment and speculation, it is possible to distinguish between speculation as an unavoidable element of investment and as a deliberate policy. There is no denying the fact that many people, particularly those entering the stock market for the first time, really want to speculate and not to invest. Their itch for easy money has been stimulated by newspaper stories of fortunes large and small made from sudden rises in particular shares or from the marketing of shares in a business which catches the popular fancy. How often a stockbroker or investment adviser is asked to 'recommend something safe which will double in price'! Equally common is the appeal to 'pick a share which will guarantee a profit before it has to be paid for'. Such profits can be made; but rarely, and only with a considerable amount of luck or intelligent anticipation.

Speculation must be a matter of deliberate policy, entered into with eyes wide open to the risks involved and the knowledge that it is easier to lose than to win. It is not for the small investor with only a few hundred pounds of hard-won savings behind him. Even the experienced and hardy veteran will not venture more than one-half of a substantial capital in this way.

The basic principle is never to get out of one's financial depth. Never buy more shares than can be readily paid for. Although it is possible to make profits buying and selling within a Stock Exchange account, there can be no guarantee of this – it may take weeks, months, or even years for the profits to mature. Thus, while it is possible (as we shall see later) to carry over transactions from one account to another, the average speculator should have the money in the bank before starting operations.

The key to success is, of course, to pick shares which are undervalued or which, because of a take-over bid or some other development, will rise in price. This may be easy in theory, but is extremely difficult in practice. It is one of the irritations of speculation and investment that, although a share may look very much under-valued according to all the accepted yardsticks, it will not go up until buyers appear; and they will not come in until it is clear that a bargain is going begging. In fact, the price of what otherwise measures up as an obvious winner may continue to dwindle away – simply because sellers outnumber buyers.

One way to operate is to get a tip. Tips can be good, bad, or harmless. What matters as much as or more than the name of a likely share is the source of the information. The City has some apt sayings, and one of the wisest is 'there's never a tip without a tap'. When the word is passed round to buy a share, it may be that the information is perfectly sound and that it is genuinely undervalued. There may, however, be a big line for sale; and one way of getting the market going is to create a demand. In a perfectly genuine operation, this may be a good thing, but it equally may mean that the buyer is being asked to 'take over someone else's baby'. We come back to reliance on the source of information. If there is any doubt, check with your stockbroker before rushing in. When markets are active, tips – some good, some bad – can be picked up by the dozen, without the asking. It is no more than human nature after buying shares to 'talk them up'.

Some general rules can be given at this stage:

1. Beware of tips or 'inside information', particularly gratuitous ones. It is surprising how many people who do not know a stock from a share know of a 'sure thing' in markets.

2. Don't rush in. Find out all you can about a share before buying it. Check on the standing of the company, its management, profit record, possibilities of growth or a take-over. Compare the present price with the high and low points for the past two or three years.

3. Check on the 'market' in the shares. Is it a narrow one which might make it difficult to buy – or sell – a reasonable number of shares? Do jobbers quote a wide price such as say 50p–62½p, or a narrow one like 55p–57p? Has there been much recent activity?

And is there any indication that a line of shares is on offer or that a 'tap' may develop? City cynics say: 'When a pal whispers to you, "Buy a share", sell it quick.'

4. Be ready to cut a loss if things do not work out. More money has been lost by holding on to a stumer than by any other form of speculation.

5. Don't be greedy. It is a rare and lucky chance to get in at the bottom and out at the top. Leave something for the next man – he must have something to go for.

6. Don't spread the net too wide. Some of the most successful speculators stick to a few companies or a particular industry or industries and keep a close watch on developments.

7. Never invest up to the limit. Keep some cash in reserve in order to have funds for further purchases. Getting out of depth may mean having to sell just at the wrong time.

8. It can pay to stick to shares with a free market when speculating in a particular group. They are the best and most widely selected choice. Money can, however, be made in second or third rate or low-priced shares with a less free market providing it is understood that they may be difficult to sell on a reversal of speculative sentiment.

9. Scratch around on your own: do some original research. Not all the shares on the scrap heap, or without any apparent friends, are worthless or near-worthless. Though it may need a lot of patience, bargains can be found which will turn pence into pounds.

A general point about speculation (and for that matter long-term investment) on which there are sharply divided opinions is that of *averaging*. Opinion is fairly unanimous that it can pay to average *up* when the price is rising, but is mostly against averaging *down* when it is falling. Before discussing the pros and cons, it is as well to see how such operations work. Suppose that a favourable view is taken of a particular share, in the reasonably certain knowledge that some weeks or months may elapse before the expected rise actually occurs.

The first lot of 500 shares is bought at an all-in cost of 100p. The price moves up, and – backing one's fancy – a further 250 shares are bought at 110p. The position then is that 750 shares are held at a total cost of £775 and an average of some 103p, which is below the current market price. The rise goes on; continuing the averaging-up operation, another 250 are bought at 120p; the position at this stage is then:

500 shares @ 100p	£500
250 shares @ 110p	275
250 shares @ 120p	300
1,000 TOTALS	£1,075

The holding has been doubled and the average price for the 1,000 shares is 107½p, or comfortably below the current quotation. *Averaging-up beats the market so long as the price is rising.*

Assume, however, that after buying the first lot of 500 shares the price falls and another 250 are bought at 90p and a further 250 at 80p. The position will then be:

500 shares @ 100p	£500
250 shares @ 90p	225
250 shares @ 80p	200
1,000 TOTALS	£925

The average price of the doubled holding is 92½p or well above the latest quotation. *Averaging down while the market is falling increases the overall loss.* It must therefore be an act of faith. If it is justified, the eventual profit can be much greater. Say the shares are sold eventually at 150p, to realize £1,500 net, the profit on an *averaging-up transaction* would be £425, but as much as £575 on an *averaging-down* operation. Seasoned market operators claim that as 'the first loss is the smallest' it pays to cut a speculation which goes the wrong way. Against this advice can be set the fact that averaging-down can pay if the shares really have in them what must make for recovery. Each purchase or sale must be judged entirely on its own merits and in the light of conditions at the particular time.

Another problem which must arise when a speculation is going well is when to sell. With one exception, no speculator, whatever the expectations and knowledge, can definitely decide when the top is reached. The exception is a *cash* take-over bid; it allows no argument about the top price.

No one, the Stock Exchange rightly asserts, can lose money by taking a profit. It is also said that the basis of the vast Rothschild fortune was 'selling too soon'. Although each investor's policy must depend on his individual circumstances, the speculator who is operating partly in the dark should start taking profits after a good rise. *Selling on the rise reduces the net cost of the balance.* Another example shows the effect. Assume that 1,000 shares have been bought at 100p all-in. If 200 are sold on a rise to 125p, to produce £250, the net cost of the 800 left is £750, or an average of 93¾p. Should the price go bounding up, and 200 shares be sold on each further rise of 25p, the position would work out like this:

Original purchase 1,000 @ 100p	£1,000
Sale of	200 @ 125p	250
Balance	800 @ 93¾p	750
Sale of	200 @ 150p	300
Balance	600 @ 75p	450
Sale of	200 @ 175p	350
Balance	400 @ 25p	£100

The fourth sale of 200 at 200p yields £400, to give *before gains tax* a profit of £300 and leave 200 shares standing in at *nothing*. This is of course a somewhat extreme case, but it does show how a speculative position can be consolidated.

Jobbing is another useful variation which if successful reduces the net cost of a speculative holding. It is only feasible in shares which fluctuate fairly widely in price over relatively short intervals. Sticking to our 1,000 shares bought at 100p, we will assume that 500 are sold at 125p and bought back at an all-in cost of 110p. The position will be as shown at the top of page 197. These calculations demonstrate that, if fortunate in the timing of purchases and sales, the operations can go on until the speculation is ended or the original shares are left in at a low net cost or even nothing.

1,000 bought	@ 100p	£1,000
500 sold	@ 125p	625
500 left	@ 75p	375
500 bought	@ 110p	550
1,000 left	@ 92½p	£925

Speculation is not confined to buying for a rise, or as the Stock Exchange terms it 'going a bull'. It is possible to be a 'bear', or a speculator who sells shares not owned, in the hope that before delivery is due they can be bought back at a lower price. Success thus depends on being able to sell and buy back within the Stock Exchange account, or if this is impossible, to carry over the sale to the next account by borrowing the shares from someone who is willing to lend or who does not wish to take up a corresponding purchase. The main danger with a short or bear sale is that there is no limit for buying back; there is no floor, as with a bull purchase. When bears are 'squeezed' they may have to pay two, three, or more times to get back their shares. Selling short is therefore only advisable for the experienced speculator with strong nerves, a long purse, or very certain information, or for the professional. Used judiciously, bear sales by jobbers can have a steadying effect on markets – they put a brake on what might otherwise be a wild run up in prices, and repurchases in due course help to steady prices on the reaction.

Mention has been made of carrying over a bull or bear transaction from one account to the next. Continuation, or carrying over, is a double transaction – the closing of a purchase or sale for the current account, and its reopening for the next one. With the exception of bearer securities, which can be financed in most cases more easily than registered stocks, the total of a particular security carried over must match 'both ways'. This is because of the nature of the two classes of operators seeking facilities. They are:

Buyers who are ready to pay a rate of interest, or contango, for the privilege of postponing settlement for stock bought to the next account. They are termed 'givers' or 'givers-on', as they generally give the contango rate to . . .

Sellers who wish to postpone delivery of stock and who, as they usually take the rate, are called 'takers' or 'takers-in'.

It follows that givers and takers in each stock must match in the totals if it is wished to carry over or continue, and the market has machinery for sorting them out. If there is a balance either way, the unlucky bulls or bears who have been 'thrown out' must make other arrangements to complete their bargains – by sales, purchases, or borrowing funds or stock. As the carry-over is not completed until the afternoon of the last day of the account, little time is available to close a bargain which cannot be continued. The unlucky speculator without facilities to settle otherwise must therefore try to close his position for 'cash' on the morning of the first day of the new account; as stamp duty and other factors have to be taken into account, this means accepting less than the normal market price on a sale and paying more on a purchase.

Successful carry-over transactions are made-up each account at 'making-up' prices, which are officially fixed at 3.30 p.m. on the last day of the account or for securities with no official make-up are generally the middle prices at 3.30 p.m. When a carry-over is successful, the broker sends his client a contract note setting out the two sides of the bargain. For a giver this is the sale and repurchase and for a taker the purchase and resale, both at the making-up price.

The note, which is liable to the usual contract duty, states the rate of interest payable or receivable. This depends on (a) the general level of interest rates; (b) the demand either way for carry-over facilities in the particular stock; and (c) its market rating. The rate on investment stocks is usually less than that on speculative shares such as oils and mines, on which the rate is mostly about one per cent higher. Brokers generally take payment for their services by adding or deducting a percentage from the contango rate, which is calculated on an annual basis. They may also charge a commission for the facility.

The client also gets a statement showing the balance due to or by him after taking into account the carried-over securities at their making-up price. If the latter is less than the purchase price (after crediting the appropriate transfer duty and registration fee) on a buying transaction, the difference is due on settlement day. Payment of the difference is similarly due on a selling or bear transaction if the making-up price is higher than the selling price. Differences continue to be paid by or to the client after each account, until the transaction is closed. Dividends falling due while stocks are open are credited to givers and debited to takers at their net amounts after deducting tax.

Many brokers will not execute carry-over business, while those who extend the facilities to approved clients may insist on a margin of anything up to 40 to 50 per cent being put down and maintained. Such transactions are mostly restricted to principals in business on their own account. Before an employee can carry over, his employer must give written permission to the broker. Like other things in life, carry-overs can be a useful factor when judiciously used and costly or disastrous affairs when used unwisely or indiscriminately. Interest paid, it should be noted, is not eligible for tax relief, for the simple reason that it is not interest in the true sense of the term. Capital gains tax can, however, come into the picture, in respect of profits made by both the giver and the taker of the shares. Incidentally, takers-in include 'protected' or 'covered' bears, who are sellers of stock they actually own but which they do not want to deliver because (a) they hope to get it back at a lower price and to save stamp duty on repurchasing, or (b) they do not wish to re-invest the proceeds, and by taking in until they want to deliver they earn interest on otherwise idle money.

A type of transaction which is an alternative to a carry-over, and which is sometimes confused with it, is to '*sell for cash and buy for new*'. This means closing the transaction for the current account and simultaneously buying or selling for the next account. It can be a costly business, particularly when extended over a number of accounts. Three items of cost are involved – some 'turn' between buying and selling prices, payment to the jobber of something extra for the facility, and the usual brokers' commission. This is how the cost can mount. Shares are first bought at 100p each, or 101¼p after adding brokerage at 1¼ per cent – as they will not be taken up, stamp duty is ignored. When 'put through' at the end of the account, the price is 96p–98p; the jobber asks 100p, or 2p a share more, for the sale for the new account. The loss on the cash sale is $5\frac{1}{4}$p – $101\frac{1}{4}$p less 96p. To this must be added 2p a share for the facility charged by the jobber, and another $1\frac{1}{4}$p brokerage. The cost has risen at one swoop by $8\frac{1}{2}$p a share. Repeat this over a few accounts, and the shares have to rise pretty substantially before it is possible to break even, let alone make a profit.

Options are another and specialized form of Stock Exchange transaction, which – depending on circumstances – can be an insurance against a rise or fall, a means of limiting the cost of 'taking a view', or simply a bet on a stock or share going up or down. An option gives the right to buy or sell at a stated price within a specified period, which is generally one, two, or three months. It can be a *single option* under which the buyer/giver pays/gives money to the seller/taker for the right to buy/call or sell/put securities at an agreed price over an agreed period. Or it can be a double option (put and call) giving the right to buy *or* sell. Bargains are done at what is called the striking price, which is the price at which the security can be bought or sold at the forward date. The normal striking price is market price at the time the option is arranged, plus an interest charge to cover carry-over facilities during the period of the option. Brokerage is calculated on the striking price.

The advantage of options is that over the period they are open they limit the cost of 'taking a view'. If, for example, it is thought that certain shares will rise substantially during the next three months, it may be profitable instead of buying them outright to give something per share for the right to take them up, or call them. Should they rise to more than the striking price plus the option money and the brokerage and other expenses, a profit can then be taken. But if they do not rise at all, or they fall, by the option declaration date, the transaction can be abandoned with the loss limited to the option money and expenses. Alternatively, if it is thought the shares will fall, money can be given for the put, or the right to sell them at the striking price. Again the loss is limited to the costs. A double option, which usually costs twice as much as a single one, allows for operating either way. It is possible to job in and out of the shares during the period of a single or double option.

Option rates depend on the security concerned, its price at the time of entering into the bargain, and the period to be covered. Competition amongst option dealers is keen, and for a three months' put or call the rate may be anything from 5–7 per cent to 12 per cent. Although, as already shown, options have their uses, they are rarely suitable for the small investor. Getting the maximum benefit from them calls for skill and patience in dealing in the securities during the period the options are open.

Mr Punch must have the final word in this chapter. His advice to those about to marry applies equally to those who cannot afford to lose money speculating: DON'T! What goes up can come down even faster, as witness the Rolls Razor débâcle of 1964. Within some eight months the price of the shares crashed from 47s. 9d. to barely sixpence!

CHAPTER 14

Investment Trusts and Unit Trusts

SHARE investment, to be successful, calls for careful selection and supervision. There are always times when it pays to be in or out of particular securities or industries. The investor may have the ability and time to make his own inquiries and decisions. He may perforce have, as many individuals do, to rely on the advice of a stockbroker or other investment expert. Or he may hand over the whole responsibility to professional investors, by buying shares in two forms of mutual investment – an investment trust or a unit trust.

INVESTMENT TRUSTS

Investment trusts were the creation of Scottish promoters who in the latter half of the nineteenth century saw the advantages of a mutual pooling of resources for investment under expert management. Today, despite reductions resulting from mergers and amalgamations, there are some 300 such companies whose securities are quoted on the Stock Exchange and whose combined assets are in the region of £4,000 million. Some count their resources in hundreds of thousands of pounds, others in tens of millions. Basic methods of operation are, however, (a) to spread the risk both sectionally and geographically; and (b) by trying to assess future trends, to change investments when it appears profitable to do so. The average investment trust thus gives a spread over some hundreds of securities whose nature may be fairly constantly changing. Whereas in pre-inflationary days most trusts included a substantial proportion of debentures, preference shares, and other fixed-interest stocks in their portfolios, post-1945 policy has been to have the bulk of funds in equities. This policy has been profitable, both in income and in capital growth.

By and large, despite the heavy falls in 1973/4, shares of most of the old-established investment trusts have done reasonably well for holders of long standing. Capital appreciation in most companies has been greater than individual investors could have expected by direct investment in leading industrial equities. The key measuring rod for performance is the *asset value* per ordinary share. This naturally varies between investment trusts; but taking one well-known and sizeable example – The Mercantile Investment Trust – figures per 25p ordinary share for the ten years to 31 January 1974 were: 1965, 39p; 1966, 43p; 1967, 41p; 1968, 57p; 1969, 78p; 1970, 59p; 1971, 52½p; 1972, 70¼p; 1973, 74½p; 1974, 57p.

A good indication of the investment spread, by industry and geographically, is given by the same company, whose net assets at the end of January 1974 totalled £118·75 million. Details, together with comparative totals for the previous year, are shown on pages 204–5.

Other features which can enhance the attraction of buying investment trust equities are:

Gearing: Most of them have part of their capital in the form of debentures and preference stocks, on which – in cases where such money was raised in less inflationary times – a relatively low rate of interest is paid. It follows that, as the bulk of this capital is invested in equity shares on which increasing dividends are probably being received, there is an extra margin for ordinary shareholders. A simple illustration shows the effect. If the profit in one year is £450,000, and interest and dividends on the prior charge capital take £100,000, the amount left for ordinary shareholders is £350,000. If however the profit for the next year increases to £500,000, the prior charges will still take only their £100,000 and the amount available for the ordinary will be £50,000 greater, at £400,000. So the process goes on – until there is a setback in profits. Another factor is that, unless the prior charge stock is convertible into ordinary shares, equity shareholders enjoy all the capital appreciation on the portfolio, just of course as they suffer the losses. The ordinary capital is described

THE MERCANTILE INVESTMENT TRUST LIMITED

Distribution of Investments – Geographical and Industrial

Total 1973 %	Total 1974 %	EQUITIES AND CONVERTIBLE STOCKS	U.K. %	U.S.A. & Canada %	South Africa %	Other countries %
		CAPITAL GOODS				
3·3	2·8	Building	1·8	0·6	—	0·4
1·1	1·0	Electrical Equipment	0·6	0·2	—	0·2
2·3	4·8	Engineering	1·2	3·1	0·4	0·1
0·7	0·2	Motors and Components	0·2	—	—	—
0·4	0·1	Steel	—	0·1	—	—
0·2	0·1	Miscellaneous	0·1	—	—	—
8·0	*9·0*		*3·9*	*4·0*	*0·4*	*0·7*
		CONSUMER GOODS AND SERVICES				
3·3	2·4	Breweries and Distilleries	1·8	—	0·6	—
2·3	2·5	Chemicals and Drugs	1·4	1·1	—	—
2·3	1·4	Electrical Equipment	1·3	0·1	—	—
1·5	1·1	Entertainment	1·0	0·1	—	—
1·7	1·2	Food	0·5	0·6	—	0·1
0·3	0·1	Hotels and Catering	—	0·1	—	—
1·2	0·9	Household Goods and Textiles	0·7	0·2	—	—
1·2	1·2	Newspapers and Publishing	1·2	—	—	—
1·7	1·6	Office Equipment	0·4	1·2	—	—
0·8	1·0	Paper and Packaging	0·7	0·3	—	—
5·9	4·5	Retail Trade	2·6	1·3	0·4	0·2

					1974	1973
Rubber Manufacturing	0·1	—	—	—	0·1	0·1
Service Companies	0·1	0·9	—	—	1·0	2·3
Tobacco	1·7	—	—	—	1·7	2·8
Transport	2·6	0·2	0·2	—	3·0	4·2
Miscellaneous	1·9	0·3	—	0·3	2·5	1·8
	18·0	6·4	1·2	0·6	26·2	33·4
FINANCIAL						
Banks	1·1	0·2	0·8	0·4	2·4	2·4
Finance	3·7	1·3	—	0·1	5·1	8·0
Insurance	4·5	0·7	0·3	0·1	5·6	6·2
Investment Trusts	0·4	—	—	0·3	0·7	1·4
Offshore Funds	0·3	2·2	—	—	2·5	3·6
Property	4·5	3·9	0·1	1·3	9·8	9·0
	14·5	8·3	1·2	2·2	26·2	30·6
COMMODITIES						
Mines and Metals	0·8	0·6	7·1	0·7	9·2	10·3
Oil and Gas	3·7	6·4	—	1·1	11·2	5·7
	4·5	7·0	7·1	1·8	20·4	16·0
EQUITIES AND CONVERTIBLE STOCKS	40·9	25·7	9·9	5·3	81·8	88·0
FIXED INTEREST – NON-CONVERTIBLE	2·8	0·3	—	—	3·1	3·2
RECIPROCAL STERLING LOANS	10·4	—	—	—	4·7	4·7
NET CURRENT ASSETS	0·7	3·1	0·1	0·8	1·9	1·9
FULMER SECURITIES LTD.	—	—	—	—	2·2	—
TOTALS 1974	54·8	29·1	10·0	6·1	100·0	
1973	56·9	23·7	11·0	8·4		100·0

as low-geared when the equity is large in relation to the prior charge capital, and high-geared when its proportion is small.

Net asset value: The main asset, the investment portfolio, has two values. These are first the book value, which is usually the actual cost price of each investment, or the cost less anything written off and less capital reserves built up from profits on sales; and second the market value at the date of the balance sheet – general practice today is to show investments in the balance sheet at market value with the surplus over book cost being credited to a capital investment reserve which naturally fluctuates with year-end changes in value. Most managements have been successful enough, even in really bad stock markets, to ensure a surplus over book cost. Another valuable feature is that the market price of investment trust shares themselves is almost always below the break-up value. They can therefore be bought at what can be a discount of anything up to 30 per cent or more on their break-up worth. An increasing number of trusts are now publishing periodical valuations monthly or quarterly and thus showing their up-to-date net asset worth; which is a useful factor in assessing the ability of individual managements and comparing portfolio worth with market prices of the shares.

Diversification: The policy of spreading the portfolio over different securities as well as a variety of industries and countries provides a means of diversification for large and small investors. Some managements have shown considerable foresight in getting out of markets which have exhausted their possibilities and into others which have dynamic opportunities of growth. Equal expertise has been shown in geographic diversification. Most companies have anything up to 20 to 40 per cent (more in a few cases) in North America, while the U.K. entry into the Common Market has stimulated purchases of European company shares. Japan and other Far Eastern countries have also received attention. The spectacular rise in the price of the metal encouraged some of the more adventurous managements to switch from U.K. industrials to South African gold shares – mostly with highly profitable results. Many managements have increased their participation in U.S. and Canadian stocks by raising dollar loans in America. This special 'gearing' has the particular benefit that the dollar premium which would be payable on indirect investment from the U.K., and which has been well over 70 per cent at times, does not have to be paid and equally that one quarter of it does not have to be surrendered on resales.

Dividends on investment trust equities enjoy a useful cushion. Although, until the new capital gains tax made it necessary for at least 85 per cent of investment income to be distributed for a company to qualify as an investment trust, the general policy is to plough back some revenue. Also, as the average company in which most of the funds are invested pays out only about two-thirds of available profits, there is an additional indirect cushion.

Capital gains realized by investment trusts are taxed at sharply reduced rates and investors get a credit which can mean payment of lower rates (or nothing at all) if they sell their shares at a profit.

Underwriting new issues of capital, in which investment trusts actively participate, may bring double benefits. The commission can be a useful, even if a relatively small, addition to revenue. Where it is desired to hold securities underwritten as investments, the commission if so applied reduces the net cost.

An unfavourable feature of investment trust shares may be *marketability*. It can be difficult to buy or sell largish blocks of the shares of the smaller companies, because the issued equity capital is relatively small and the bulk of it is firmly held by investors who appreciate the long-term merits. This problem of marketability is however being met by amalgamations – it is not unusual to find two or more companies under similar management – and by splitting the stock or shares into smaller units, usually of 25p. Distribution of scrip issues is also helping this process.

A new development came in 1965 with the introduction of the split-level, or *dual*, investment trust company. Its capital is divided into two share classes – income and capital – which may have in front of them preference shares and debentures or loan stock. The life is usually fixed at say fifteen or twenty years or longer, and during it all or most of the income accruing to the equity is paid in dividends to the income shareholders. At the end of the specified life the company will be liquidated and after repaying the income shares at a prearranged price (par, or par plus a specified premium) the balance of the assets will go to the capital shareholders. If these trusts enjoy substantial capital growth it is clear that the capital shares will show proportionately larger profits but that the income shares will benefit from increases in the dividend income of the trust.

Another development followed in 1967 with the innovation of a special type of capital share, usually known as 'B', which has equal rights with the ordinary shares but with an important exception. The 'B' shares usually receive instead of normal cash dividends scrip issues equivalent to their gross amounts which can be converted into ordinary shares. As the scrip issues are not taxable as income they are attractive to investors paying high tax rates. They are also a useful means for automatic re-investment of dividends. Later innovations have been issues of convertible debentures, sometimes at a nominal rate of interest; and warrants to subscribe shares on specified terms.

While it is an unhappy fact that investment trusts generally have taken a heavy pounding in recent times their ordinary shares are one of the best ways to take a view on recovery in stock markets. They provide, as already explained, a way to buy a portfolio at a discount which can be quite substantial. But, in view of the political risks which may face Britain for some time ahead, it is well to pick a company which has *at least 30 to 40 per cent of its portfolio in North American and other overseas shares*; which has an active management; and in which there is a reasonably free market in its shares.

UNIT TRUSTS

Unit trusts are a much newer form of mutual investment under expert management, which began life in the United States and spread to Britain in 1931. One of the main differences from investment trusts is that they do not issue shares in the accepted way.

Their fund of investments is divided into equal units, which belong to holders in proportion to the cash they subscribe. Another basic distinction is that the units are not quoted in the same way as other securities. The daily quotations, calculated according to a formula laid down by Department of Trade and Industry rules, reflect the market value of the stocks and shares in the fund. Subject to necessary allowances for expenses, the buying and selling prices are directly based on current break-up values.

The earliest ventures were known as fixed trusts. Funds were invested in a panel of previously-selected securities, in specified proportions. A buyer of units thus knew that however small the fractions, his money represented specific interests in the shares of some dozens of companies. When it became apparent that fixity created handicaps, the managers acquired powers to switch to a list of alternative investments. From this it was a relatively short step to complete flexibility. The modern unit trust can therefore spread its net as widely or as narrowly as the managers consider desirable, although it is usual on launching a new venture to set out a list of securities from which the bulk of the choice will be made. The success of this type of investment is proved by the fact that the value of their funds, although subject to fluctuations in line with stock market ups and downs, has grown between four- and five-fold from £429 million at the end of 1964. The peak was reached in December 1972, when funds totalled over £2,600 million. By the end of 1973 the heavy fall in stock markets had reduced the value to £2,060 million, and there have been further falls since. Gratifyingly, however, investors have largely maintained faith in this type of investment and sales continue to exceed repurchases. It is estimated that around 1,250,000 people save and invest through unit trusts – many have holdings in more than one fund.

Unit trusts differ in nature. Some put the emphasis on immediate dividend income and invest part of their funds in fixed-interest securities, while others concentrate on growth through a 100 per cent equity policy. Some spread their net widely over all classes of ordinary shares and hold 300 or so different securities. A few, however, specialize in particular fields such as bank, insurance, or investment-trust shares, or put a high proportion of their money into say the metal and mining industries. Several have schemes which link endowment assurance with unit trust shares and thus give some protection against inflation. Some (unlike their brethren, who distribute their net dividend income to unit-holders) re-invest all income. All, however, have the common feature that although continuation may be subsequently agreed they have a life limited to twenty years or some other period, at the end of which the investments – or underlying securities, as they are called – are technically distributable to investors. Other important features are that shareholders' interests are protected by the compulsory vesting of all securities in the safekeeping of trustees, who are usually one of the banks or insurance companies; the Department of Trade and Industry, which alone authorizes the setting up of a unit trust, lays down strict rules of practice which go far to curb any attempt at dishonesty; and the management companies are mostly composed of people with a high reputation in the City and with considerable investment expertise.

D.T.I. regulations already mentioned rightly aim to safeguard the interests of investors and to regulate day-to-day operations. The trust deed therefore sets out the basis of calculating buying and selling prices, and the yield; the need for the trustees to approve all advertisements; the setting-up of a fund to cover operating expenses; audit of the trust and management accounts; and the issue of share certificates. Management expenses, which are restricted to a total of $13\frac{1}{4}$ per cent over a twenty-year period, are provided in two ways. First there is an initial service charge, usually between 3 and 5 per cent, which is included in the selling price of new units. Secondly there is a half-yearly service charge, calculated on the value of the fund at an annual rate of say between 35p and 50p per £100 and usually taken out of dividend income.

Income, after deduction of the appropriate proportion for expenses, is distributed in the form of half-yearly dividends of so much per unit; following the common practice, income tax is deducted at the standard rate. The income from which payments are made is of course flowing in throughout the half-year. Investors buying units between distribution dates are thus entitled to share only in dividends received after purchase of their units. Their first half-yearly dividend is therefore made up of (a) their relative proportion of income, and (b) a balancing payment equal to the income received in the earlier part of the six months, which is treated as capital and allowed for in the price of the units. Managers usually provide facilities for the re-investment of dividends in the purchase of further shares, which is a useful means of building up a fund at what is in effect compound interest.

Yields on units are calculated according to a somewhat complicated Board of Trade formula. Broadly, however, they represent the annual income, less expenses, expressed as a gross amount on the investment of £100. A yield of say £3·85 per cent is the gross income which £100 would produce from investment in units bought at the offered price on the day of calculation. Naturally, the yield varies with changes in the offered price at which units can be bought. It also varies widely between trusts, the general range being from less than 1 per cent to as much as 17 per cent.

Two prices are quoted for units, the higher being the offered price at which units can be bought and the lower the bid price or figure at which they can be sold back. Managers are always ready to buy back units at the bid price ruling at the time of sale. The difference in the two prices represents stamp duty, brokerage, management profit, and other expenses. It can be varied up to limits laid down by the Department of Trade and Industry, and can be as much as 12½ per cent. But the usual figure is in practice only about 5 to 6 per cent, sometimes less.

Units are sold in various ways. First by creation of new units as they are sold. Secondly by the resale of old units sold back to the managers, which they have not liquidated by realization of the appropriate underlying investments. Thirdly by the block offer, which is advertised widely and makes available for a specified period a minimum number of units at a fixed price or the current daily price, whichever is the lower. Fourthly by the re-investment of dividends as already mentioned. Fifthly by savings schemes for the regular investment of monthly sums.

Units can be bought and sold through stockbrokers, banks, solicitors, accountants, and the managers. It is also possible to buy up to specified quantities of units of a few of the unit trusts which have close links with banks over the counter of such banks. Initial investments must be for at least a specified minimum number of units, which is now generally not less than £50 or £100 worth. At the other end of the scale trusts which want to keep management costs to a minimum will not accept initial investments of less than £1,500, £2,500 or even larger sums; and there are some which reduce the management charges in proportion to the increasing size of individual holdings of units.

Choice of a unit trust requires thought. The major consideration must always be to select one or more which meet particular needs. Some, as previously mentioned, go mostly for immediate income and are therefore the type for investors who must have the maximum return on their capital. Some have a speculative touch, through investments in metal mining and commodity shares. Some of the more recent newcomers are 'performance' or 'go-go' funds which put the emphasis on capital growth through active dealings in stock markets, or which strive to pick out recovery shares. And the latest type is the 'Offshore' fund which is based abroad, say in the Bahamas, and which concentrates on American, Continental, Australian and other foreign shares. There has also been some expansion in trusts which invest directly in property. But the bulk, whether general or specialized, lean heavily towards growth combined with a reasonable dividend return. One measuring-rod sometimes used is the comparative prices of different units. It should, however, be a very secondary factor. Prices, as shown earlier, are based on the proportionate share of each unit in the whole fund. The considerations which really matter are the nature of the trust, its record, the standing of the managers, and the type of investment – growth or otherwise – required.

A few trusts have exchange arrangements under which they will accept approved shares instead of cash subscriptions. This can mean a saving in brokerage and other expenses, and provision of a wider spread of investment.

Some managements have Gift Plans for children which give the choice of lump sum investments or regular savings, or a combination of both, and which provide for handing over to the child at any age between 18 and 25 years. Others have Withdrawal Plans which are somewhat like annuities and are suitable for retired people or those wanting a regular income; the investor decides how much net income is required and this is paid half-yearly out of the income of the trust and from capital – the withdrawal rate can be anything between say 5 and 10 per cent a year. If the fund appreciates in market value the income withdrawn can be matched, or more than covered, by appreciation in the capital value. But, and once more a reflection of the 1973/4 stock market slump, such schemes can be very costly – as prices fall, more units have to be sold to maintain withdrawals. Considerable care is therefore necessary (a) in deciding on such a scheme; (b) fixing the withdrawal rate; and (c) *in suspending an existing scheme when share prices are falling*.

The growth record of unit trusts varies, with the performance depending largely on the date of launching. During the better part of 1971 and the early days of 1972 some spectacular performances were achieved, mainly as a result of the general upsurge in stock market prices and partly from the investment skill of the managers. Rises in values of 40 to 50 per cent over twelve months were comparatively common, and all but a small handful of trusts showed less than 20 per cent appreciation. Some almost doubled in value in 1971! But the story has differed in more recent times. A useful overall picture of performance is provided by the Unitholder Index compiled by Fundex Limited, publishers of the very useful *Unit Trust Year Book*. Taking end-December 1963 as 1,000, the average performance of all trusts at subsequent year ends was: 1964, 930; 1965, 1,020; 1966, 941; 1967, 1,202; 1968, 1,636; 1969, 1,390; 1970, 1,279; 1971, 1,784; 1972, 2,144; and 1973, 1,561. These indices went against 437 at end-1955; 542 at 1958; 760 at 1960 and 883 at 1962. By mid-1974 the index was down to around 1,300, and dropped further in later months.

Common aims of managements are to outclass rivals and to beat stock-market indices such as the F.T. 30-share and the F.T.-Actuaries. Some have universally beaten the latter in most of recent years while others which have had the courage to buy gold and other mining shares have actually shown useful appreciation.

These are of course historical examples which do not necessarily apply to all trusts. They are moreover no guarantee of similar performances in the future, though it may be assumed that given reasonably good stock-market conditions the growth will continue at a satisfactory pace. Regular monthly investments, it is worth noting, help to iron out price fluctuations – when markets are flat, units are acquired more cheaply than when they are booming, which helps towards a better average price. This is called *pound averaging*.

The most important points to keep in mind when investing in unit trusts are:

1. They are simpler to buy and sell than shares in investment trusts, which makes them more suitable for the very small investor.

2. They are a good way to begin investment in shares: the wide spread of their portfolios helps to cushion the risk inherent in equity share investment.

3. Although some managements will accept minimum initial investments of a lesser sum, my view is that, unless starting a regular saving plan, the least to put into one unit trust is say £100 to £200. Receipt of small dividend cheques and any consequent claims for tax repayments are hardly worth the trouble.

4. Unless a cash income is essential, re-invest all dividends in the purchase of further units. The effect is then similar to the useful way in which Savings Certificates grow in value over the years.

5. Like other Stock Exchange securities, the prices can fluctuate. Account must also be taken of the differences between buying and selling prices. Unit trusts are not therefore ideal for short-term investment – building societies or bank deposits are the better choice.

6. They should be regarded more as long-term holdings which offer prospects of capital growth and increasing dividends over a period of years.

7. Like other investments, shares of unit trusts sold at a profit are now liable to capital gains tax. Since April 1972 it has, however, been limited, as outlined on page 278. It is most important

therefore to keep safely and ready to hand contract notes and other records of purchases.

8. As explained in Chapter 5, life assurance linked with unit trust investment can be a profitable means of regular saving which has some useful tax advantages. Most of the unit trust managements now have such schemes.

9. Like the dual, or split-level, capital and income type of investment trust, a similar idea is provided by some unit trust managements. Income and capital shares are issued and quoted on the Stock Exchange. The net funds are invested, however, in a particular unit trust or trusts, with the income shareholders taking all the net income and the capital shareholders getting all the growth or, if the fund depreciates, standing the brunt of the portfolio losses.

10. If a fair sum is to be invested it may be better to consider investment trusts in preference to unit trusts. As pointed out earlier, the former can be bought at useful discounts on their net asset values while there is no such advantage with unit trusts which, however, can sometimes be more readily sold at much closer to their current worth.

11. Lastly, as with investment trusts, it makes good sense in our existing political climates to give preference to unit trusts which have a fair proportion of their funds invested in North American and other overseas companies.

CHAPTER 15

A Look at Some Specialized Share Markets

SOME sections of the market, because of the specialized nature of the companies whose shares are included, call for additions to the normal rules of assessment. They are most North American and Western European securities, and speculative stocks such as those of gold and other mining and raw material suppliers. This chapter will attempt to summarize the particular aspects which have to be considered.

American and Canadian stocks, in which there is a substantial two-way business between London and trans-Atlantic markets, were until recently quoted over here in 'dummy' dollars, of which there were five to the £. Now however they are quoted in £'s and pence in the same way as U.K. shares – in pence up to £10 and in £'s and fractions of £'s thereover. Sterling prices include what is known as the dollar premium, which U.K. residents may have to pay in order to get sufficient 'security' dollars out of the common pool which has to be kept while there are restrictions on the export of dollars.

If a share is quoted in New York at say $100 and the premium is 30 per cent the equivalent London price (in dollars) would be $130. Assuming for simplicity that the exchange rate was $2·50 to £1 the London price would be:

$$\frac{\$130}{\$2·5} = £52$$

No stamp duty on transfer is payable, however – virtually none of the companies concerned have registration offices in the U.K., while many of the shares are in bearer form or its equivalent. Also, as shown in Chapter 9, brokerage starting at 0·75 per cent is less than on U.K. shares. From 7 April 1965, one-quarter of the proceeds of sales in dollars (or other foreign currencies) must be exchanged into sterling at the normal rate. This means that (a) the dollar premium is now received on only three-quarters of the gross amount and (b) as sales take place there is a chance that the pool of security dollars will be reduced, so forcing up the premium. Whereas it was no more than 10–15 per cent a few years ago, it has been over 70 per cent at times and has shown considerable fluctuations in line with currency fears, and changes in sentiment towards dollar stocks. In practice there are two premium rates. One is based on a 'dummy' dollar ratio of $2·60 to £1, the other, and older one, on the actual dollar rate which fluctuates daily. There is of course no ultimate difference in the amount payable or receivable.

Overseas Sterling Area securities dealt in by U.K. residents are also liable, since June 1972, to pay an investment currency premium in the same way as for dollar securities. Until the March 1974 Budget, there was however no surrender of part of the premium. Now there is; and investors selling South African, Australian and other O.S.A. shares have to give up 25 per cent of the premium.

Western European shares have increased considerably in popularity since Britain began to toy with the idea of joining the Common Market. Some of the leading West German, Dutch, Belgian, Italian, and French companies are now known amongst U.K. investors. Such shares, however, can suffer from a major handicap. Company laws on the Continent are not so insistent as ours on the minimum information which must be given to shareholders. As a result, although a few concerns which are anxious to attract British and American investors, or which have come up against the strict requirements of the London Stock Exchange, do publish a great deal of information, many European companies produce annual accounts and reports which tell shareholders virtually nothing. It can be argued that it is a good thing to understate assets and profits, to keep something in hand, and not to give information to rivals. But such policies do not offer much scope for the outsider to weigh up the merits of specific shares. Another important consideration is that Continental investors tend to buy equities not on immediate or fairly near yield considerations, but on projections of earnings well into the future. Many such shares therefore give negligible yields. The prime consideration is capital growth. Hence, while many of these shares are probably good long-term investments, assessment of their merits may have to be left to financial experts who have close knowledge of the progress of the particular companies. Direct investment should thus be approached with caution and be based on thoroughly reliable advice. Much the better way for the average investor to take an interest in the Continental side of the Common Market is through one of the European-based investment trusts, of which there are a number with able managements and good records, whose shares are officially quoted on the Stock Exchange or can be bought through it. It is significant of the standing of the U.K. Stock Exchange that an increasing number of leading European companies are obtaining official quotations, which means that they have to give a lot of information.

Japanese shares have also been in increasing demand, largely on the strength of the Nipponese economy and the growth prospects of leading companies. Again, this is a specialized market, with a few brokerage companies dominating the Tokyo and other local stock exchanges. Most U.K. investment trusts and some unit trusts have, however, been putting money into Japanese shares, while there are a few which concentrate entirely, or almost entirely, on this market.

Gold-mining shares fall into a special category of their own. A gold mine is a suitable investment or speculation only so long as the metal can be profitably taken out of it. Once it no longer pays to work the mine, it becomes little more than a hole in the ground, and the only value attaching to the shares is the sum which will be repaid on them from the realization of the plant and machinery, rights in the land, and other saleable assets. The chief measuring-rods are the grade of ore, which is measured now in grams per metric ton; the width over which the gold veins run; the estimated tonnage of workable ore opened up in the mine, and whether these reserves, as they are called, are increasing or decreasing; the amount of gold being produced; the working costs and profit per ton; the prospects of opening up further profitable ground; and the estimated life, or the number of years the mine is likely to continue working at a profit. Until a mine is opened up for working, which generally entails considerable expenditure of money and time on sinking shafts and other work, its future rests on sampling the ground by means of bore holes that may go down many thousands of feet. During this period the shares are very much in the speculative category, and sharp fluctuations occur as the drilling results are published. Once a mine is operating, however, there is a steady flow of information, especially from South African companies. Details of the tonnage of ore treated, kilograms of gold extracted, yield, costs, profits per ton, and working profit are given in quarterly reports that supplement this information with details of development work on opening up fresh ground, amounts spent on capital account, and other data. Still more facts are contained in the annual report, which gives the estimated tonnage of ore in reserve and possibly an indication of future prospects. The South African mines which also produce uranium add the relevant facts concerning this side of their operations. Far and away the greatest interest is in South African companies, though the shares of concerns operating in Canada, Australia, and other countries are quoted on the Stock Exchange.

From being looked on as very speculative ventures, gold shares have come into the limelight since the Americans had to drop their obstinate refusal to let the metal find its real market level instead of trying to peg the price at the totally unrealistic figure of $38 an ounce. The price has recently been well above the $180 level and, as individuals lose faith in other investment media, it could easily go over the $200 mark – and stay there. As most of the current production is sold on the open market, South African and other gold-mining companies are, despite sharp rises in labour and other costs, making much greater profits while, where practicable, digging out lower grade ores and so extending their working lives. Although the prices of many shares have multiplied many times since it was suggested in the sixth edition of this book that they should be in portfolios, the same advice can still apply. Investors who want to spread their money – and the risk – can do so by concentration on the shares of the well-known and powerful mining finance companies, most of which have widespread interests in base metals, oil and other industries as well as in gold mines.

Base metal mining companies have to be assessed by rather similar standards – grade of ore, reserves, life, cost of production, and profitability. However, the selling price of the metal or metals mined is a direct factor which must also be watched. Although attempts may be made to achieve some degree of stability by output restriction schemes, prices for copper, tin, lead, zinc, and other base metals fluctuate in response to supply and demand. To this extent there is some degree of fluidity in revenue per ton of ore treated. The investor must therefore study the trend of metal prices and attempt to guess how they will move in the immediate future. The political risk is particularly strong in copper – some of the leading shares dealt in are of companies operating in Zambia Republic and other parts of Africa. The bulk of the world's tin supplies comes from Malaya, where – after some scares – political tension is easier. The London market in tin shares can be strongly influenced by buying or selling from the Far East. Although there has been a tendency for some governments such as the Australian and the Canadian to try to take a much larger slice of profits through excessive sales and profits taxes, most of the established base-metal mining companies in the advanced countries should be good speculations. As with gold and other commodities, 1973 and 1974 saw some sharp increases in prices; and, providing there is no world slump in trade, demand is sure to expand. U.S. copper, lead and zinc companies are likely to be the safest political and taxation bets, followed by Canadian ventures. But again, some of the risks can be ironed out by investment in mining-finance shares such as Charter Consolidated, Rio Tinto-Zinc, Anglo-American Corporation of South Africa, Minerals and Resources Corporation and Consolidated Gold Fields, which bring great expertise to bear on developing new mines and which give a wide spread over various kinds of mining.

A Look at Some Specialized Share Markets

Rubber is produced mostly in the Far East, with Malaya, Ceylon, and Indonesia the largest sources. At one time there were many dozens of small and large companies. More recently there has been a strong tendency towards amalgamation, which has resulted in the building up of some very large units. The factors to take into account when weighing-up the shares of a rubber company are the extent of the estates, the area planted, the area under mature rubber, the extent of replanting in order to improve the output by modern methods of growing, the crop in pounds per acre, the average selling price, the amount of output sold in advance and the average price, and whether other commodities such as tea, palm oil, or coconuts are also grown. Most companies have been actively replanting since the war; as a result the average crop per acre has been rising, with a consequent increase in profits. Fluctuations in the price of raw rubber are vital considerations. It usually pays to buy shares when the price has been flat for some time. Recurrent scares that synthetic rubber will displace the natural product are a perennial feature. The blunt fact is that so long as the price of the latter does not rise too steeply both types can live profitably together.

Tea shares are similar to rubber shares in that they should be assessed by similar standards. Although popular amongst investors in pre-war days, they are now very much of a speculative market. As virtually all companies operate in India, Ceylon, Indonesia, and Central Africa there is a heavy political risk. On the other hand, some of the companies maintain large liquid resources in the U.K., with the result that the market price of their shares can represent largely cash or its equivalent and leave a relatively small fraction to cover the risk element tied up in estates and other assets abroad. A study of tea company balance sheets is specially important.

Oil shares fall into three broad categories – the integrated companies which have their own production, refining, distribution, and chemical interests; similar companies whose major interests are subject to foreign political factors; and the smaller producers and exploration ventures. Shares of the big international companies are more or less on a par with those of big industrial concerns, and increasing importance attaches to their rapidly broadening interests in chemicals as by-products of oil production and refining. In the second group are concerns whose main sources of crude oil supplies are in the Middle East, India, Venezuela, and those other countries where local politics can play havoc with orderly production planning and profits; and, as the Arab oil embargo of 1973 so drastically taught the free world, producers can throw nasty spanners into the economic works. Third in the oil and natural gas productive spheres are the North Sea and other off-shore areas round the U.K. on which such high hopes rest and in which a wide variety of giants and small operators of various nationalities are interested. The fourth group, so far as British interest is concerned, comprises dozens of Canadian companies of varying size – which are still at the exploration stage, are relatively small producers of oil and natural gas, or are pipe line operators – together with a number of Australian exploration companies, most of whose assets are merely dry holes in the ground or simply hopes of one day 'striking it rich', and whose shares are subject to periodic and hectic bouts of speculation. While it is possible to find a highly profitable winner amongst the smaller exploration companies, the surest investment policy is to stick to the big or established groups, of which there is a good choice in Britain, Canada and the U.S.A.

Premium note: The machinery of the investment premium has already been explained. A factor of great importance is the impact when shares liable to the surrender levy are sold. For instance, if the premium is 40 per cent at the time of a sale, the net receivable is not at the rate of $1·40 but only $1·30 ($1+40−10 premium). Allowance must therefore be made for this compulsory loss when calculating the break-even price above which shares can be sold to make a profit. In the example it is almost 7 per cent; in late 1974 it was up to 10 per cent and over!

CHAPTER 16

New Issues

BUSINESS on the Stock Exchange is not confined to buying and selling existing securities. There is a constant stream of newcomers, which adds to the overall volume of the market's 'stocks' and which in recent years has averaged upwards of £4,000 million in nominal value per annum. For the year ended March 1973 the total was an all-time record of just over £8,200 million, of which some £3,700 million was for company securities and £4,500 million for gilt-edged and foreign stocks. Various types of capital operation make up these huge annual additions:

Public issues, offers for sale, or placings on behalf of the gilt-edged type of borrower, companies already quoted, or newcomers to the Stock Exchange – all generically termed new issues.

Rights issues made to shareholders of existing companies, usually on favourable terms.

Conversion operations, under which existing securities, invariably fixed-interest, are replaced by new stocks.

Scrip issues, which represent the capitalization of a company's reserves and add nothing to its assets.

Securities issued by one company on the take-over of or merger with another or in payment of new assets acquired.

Exercise of options granted to shareholders, or to directors or employees, and of warrants to take up shares.

NEW ISSUES

Offers of new or existing capital of newcomers to the Stock Exchange, or of companies which already have quotations, can take four different forms:

A **public issue** invites investors at large to apply for stated amounts of shares or loan capital at fixed prices.

An **offer for sale** differs from a public issue mainly in that the block of capital offered at a fixed price per unit has previously been bought or subscribed by an issuing house at a lower price or for a round sum. It also includes what is called a *secondary offering*, which is a block of shares already with a quotation which are offered for sale at a fixed price by a big holder (or holders) wishing to reduce his interest, for estate duty purposes or some other reason.

A **placing**, as its name implies, means that blocks of existing or new securities are placed at a fixed price amongst insurance companies, pension funds, financial and investment trusts, other financial institutions, jobbers, brokers, and private investors. If a quotation is to be applied for, the Council of the Stock Exchange insists amongst other things that a reasonable proportion of the issued equity or of the fixed-interest capital should be placed, and that of this fair proportions should be made available in the market for clients of other brokers when dealings start. The Council also tries to eliminate possible abuses of this economical means by insisting that where there might be a rush for shares the method used should be an offer for sale.

An **introduction** is a means of establishing a market in securities which are sufficiently widely spread to justify such a step. There is no marketing in the normal way, though certain holders may undertake to make stock available at stated prices. This method is rarely used for equity shares, the main exceptions being where a market is already established on another recognized stock exchange, or when a quoted company segregates some of its assets by distributing to its shareholders shares in a subsidiary or associated company.

Before an application will be considered a company must have an expected market value of at least £500,000, and any one security for which a quotation is sought must have an anticipated value of not less than £200,000. To maintain an orderly market the Bank of England controls the timing of new issues which call for the raising of £3,000,000 or more money.

An essential part of any of these operations is that the investing public should be given adequate information on which to assess the merits of the offer. Such facts are given in a *prospectus*, or in the case of a placing or introduction in an advertised statement which is equivalent to a prospectus. The Companies Act lays down the minimum information which must be supplied. The Stock Exchange, which codified its rules in mid-1966, goes further by insisting on its own requirements. Before looking at these requirements, it is as well to consider first the various steps necessary to success before an offer reaches this 'end-product' stage.

An important part of our financial machinery is the *Capital Market*. Unlike other markets, it has no central place of trading. It is made up of finance houses whose sole or main activity is the sponsoring of capital issues; merchant banks which include these services amongst others such as the financing of trade, acceptance business, and foreign exchange dealing; stockbroking firms who have their own new issue departments, or who participate in other ways; and the much more widely spread but important participants such as the insurance companies, investment trusts, pension funds, financial institutions, brokers, and jobbers who shoulder vital responsibilities like underwriting. Although the bulk of the new-issue business is done in the City of London by merchant banks, similar facilities are available in some of the large provincial centres.

The starting point in an offer made under one of the methods already described is for the company seeking capital to consult an *issuing house*, which will advise on the terms and the best way of handling the operation. The preliminary steps will depend on the nature of the proposition. An issue of stock by a local authority, for example, will be a relatively mechanical task, the main problem being that of hitting the rate of interest which will just ensure success. But in the case of a company, much depends on its nature and whether it is a newcomer to the stock market or an established proposition known to the investing public and the issuing house. If the latter, most of the essential data is already available. The work to be done by the issuing house may therefore be limited to bringing up to date the facts to be given in the prospectus, and to settling the terms on which the offer should be made.

A newcomer, which may be a one-man business or a private company owned by a small number of shareholders, is a different proposition. Although its products may be household words, little may be known about its finances, profit record, management, and future prospects. The issuing house may therefore have to start from scratch. It will want preliminary details of the history of the business; its present size and scope; the extent of any export business; who is responsible for its running; the turnover and profits for at least ten years (if it has been in existence for that long); whether sales are going up or down; the nature, extent, and value of the assets; the total and nature of the liabilities; the size and nature of any commitments to build factories or for other capital development; whether the business can be expanded; and the reason for raising new capital, offering some of the existing capital, or otherwise 'going public'.

The issuing house will expect the potential client to supply most of this information in the form of audited balance sheets and accountants' and other reports. Should these preliminary data indicate that the proposition is worth pursuing, the next step will be to have a closer look at the business, the methods of operation, and the management. A principal, alone or with experts, will make on-the-spot inquiries and get the feel of the firm. His findings will decide the next step, which is to nominate independent accountants to report on the financial side, including the bases for arriving at the profits and for valuing the assets and liabilities, the adequacy of the book-keeping and costing systems, and the degree of control over stocks and expenditure. This second report, which will play a key part in drawing up the prospectus, will reduce the figures to uniform bases so that like can be compared with like after eliminating or including relevant adjustments. While this important work is in hand the issuing house will be making inquiries amongst its many and varied contacts about the standing, competitive nature, and future prospects of the business and the rating of its management.

When all this information is assembled, and not before, the first steps in the final stages can be taken. The best method of making the offer can be worked out. This is when the skill, experience, and knowledge of the issuing house and the stockbrokers with whom it is working will become important. Stock markets are live, volatile, ever-changing reflectors of financial and economic conditions. What may be suitable and successful today may be a flop tomorrow. What may suit one type of capital operation may be no use for another. And in the background, when a private business is going to the public, there may often be a tussle of personalities. An individual who has built up a successful enterprise, probably from little or nothing, may be reluctant to part with even a small fraction of the equity: he does not see why anyone else should get a slice of his cake. But if new capital must be raised or (a common reason) provision be made for death duties now or in the future, it will be pointless for him to try to get away with a fixed-interest offer when investors are only interested in equities. Delicate negotiations may thus be needed to reconcile personal with practical market considerations. Another factor which has to be watched is that some sudden unexpected development like a political crisis, a threat of war, or a slump in markets may call for a last-minute revision of the issue terms, or even for a postponement. It may therefore be close to the actual date of the operation before the final terms, nature, and method of the offer are settled.

During the later stages of all this work, another and vital part of the operation is under way. As already noted, the Stock Exchange insists on a great deal of information, some of which goes beyond the minimum laid down by law. As soon as the prospectus gets to the draft stage, therefore, the brokers to the issue will begin to submit documents to the Quotations Department, the section responsible for the 'vetting'. The objective of this is to ensure that there is effective machinery to enable shareholders to exercise their rights and that all the information needed for an investor to make a fair assessment of the offer is available. Over and above the routine matters already mentioned, where appropriate the Quotations experts will call for information on the arrangements made for continuity of management; the number of employees; the property owned or to be bought; large or controlling shareholdings; any options granted for the subscription of new capital; the basis of current and future profit estimates; any special arrangements with subsidiary or associated companies; clearance certificates for surtax and estate duties, and indemnities against such possible liabilities; whether uniform bases have been used for calculating depreciation and for valuing stocks and work in progress; and the treatment of extraordinary revenue or expenditure. The Department also inquires into the bona fides, standing, and reputations of the management and everyone connected with the offer. The Stock Exchange also insists that the directors of the company must agree to the General Undertaking which, as outlined later, insists on a great deal of information being given to shareholders in annual and other reports.

By the time the requirements of the issuing house and Stock Exchange have been met, every offer will have been subject to a searching probe. However, a gap of at least forty-eight hours between publication of the prospectus and the granting of the essential market requirement – the official quotation – gives time for anyone with vital knowledge about the offer to give it to the Council. But in spite of the care taken to ensure publication of all essential information, there can of course be no guarantee of the soundness of an offer. The individual investor or his advisers must judge it on the facts.

A key part of an offer is an assurance that it will be fully subscribed whatever the conditions at the time of launching. This is usually achieved by *underwriting*. The brokers or issuing house arrange with responsible institutions and individuals to guarantee to take up specific proportions of the offer not subscribed by the public. Payment for this service is an underwriting commission which varies with the type of security offered, but which may be, say, $1\frac{1}{4}$ per cent on the offer price of shares, and as little as $\frac{1}{2}$ or $\frac{3}{4}$ per cent on a first class fixed-interest stock. Sometimes the offer is fully subscribed or heavily oversubscribed, and the underwriters are relieved of all responsibility. Sometimes, however, the offer is a flop, in which case they have to find the money to take up their quotas of the portion undersubscribed. Underwriters may then have to sell at a loss or nurse their holdings until they can be realized at a fair price. Times for opening and closing the applications for public issues and offers for sale are given at the top of the prospectus. If there is a heavy response, the lists will be closed within a minute or so of the official opening time. But if the response is poor, they may remain open for the full time.

When an offer is oversubscribed, the issuing house is faced with the problem of the best way of allotting shares. Applications for a total of one million 25p shares at 75p each, for instance, may be four million. Scaling down by three-quarters might mean that applicants for small numbers would get unduly small allotments. At the other extreme, all applications up to say 500 shares could be eliminated and allotments confined to the larger applications, which would be unfair to the small investor, who can be a valuable prop to a company. Fair compromises are to allot in full all applications up to 100 shares, and to scale down bigger applications; or to ballot for allotments, with or without upper or lower limits to the number issued to successful applicants. Such decisions have to be made speedily by the issuing house, brokers, and clients.

A successful applicant receives an *allotment letter* setting out the number of shares or amount of stock allotted. This has later to be exchanged for a share certificate. Until then the securities can be bought and sold on the basis of the allotment letter, which provides for the renunciation by a buyer of part or all of the entitlement. When an allotment is sold to more than one buyer, or part only is realized, the letter is *split*, which means that the original has to be submitted to the registrars and new letters have to be made out. On the specified day, allotment letters have to be sent for exchange into share certificates which, on their receipt in due course, are the evidence of ownership.

Payment for securities marketed by a public issue or offer for sale may have to be made in full on application, which means that, if the price is 75p and 500 shares are applied for, a cheque for £375 must be sent. Alternatively, payment may have to be made by instalments, such as 25p on application, a further 25p on allotment, and the balance say one month later. Failure to make such payments in time may mean forfeiture of the shares.

The *stag* is another of the Stock Exchange 'animals', and he may make his appearance when a new issue is made. His aim is to sell an allotment at a profit immediately dealings commence and before any further money is payable. Stags can perform a useful service, or they can be a menace. The practice has unfortunately developed of very heavy stagging on offers which look fairly sure of success or which have obviously caught the public fancy. The problem of the stag is then to decide how to spread his applications, in order to have the best chances of obtaining an allotment. He can put in a single application for a big block. Alternatively, he can make a number of applications for different quantities; but this means considerable work and ingenuity in trying to guess the basis of allotment, if the offer is heavily oversubscribed. Reputable issuing houses do all they can to eliminate the stags, some of whom send cheques for amounts far in excess of what they could pay. One method of elimination is therefore to announce that all cheques will be cleared before allotments are made. While stagging can be a profitable or amusing venture, it can be a time-waster, because it ties up large sums of money. It is not a suitable method of speculation for the average investor. Figures given in 'Going Public '73', the *Accountancy Age* guide to company flotations, showed that two-thirds of all the 1971 and 1972 issues stood below offer price by the end of 1973 and of these 14 per cent had dropped by at least one-half. The sad story continued to unfold with the 1973 issues, of which less than one in four stood above their offer price by the year-end.

A form of stagging can be practised with placings. Certain proportions of a placing, as already mentioned, have to be made available to investors at large through the market at the placing price. The method of 'applying' for such securities is to get one's broker to 'put down the name' with one of the jobbers who will be dealing in them. Such applications are totalled up, and shares are parcelled out *pro rata*. Should there be little interest, an applicant is likely to get all or most of the quantity asked for. But if there is a rush, the 'allotment' may be heavily cut down or it may have to be ignored. In such cases a broker who has several clients on his list will probably apportion out what he gets as fairly as possible. Fingers can be badly burned on such speculations. Not all placings open at a premium over the original price. Equally, investors who buy 'at best' on the start of dealings can find that they have paid premiums which may be up to 100 per cent or more above the placing price and which will call for a lot of justification in terms of future trading results and dividends. Fortunately, the Stock Exchange does much to help by restricting placings to fixed-interest stocks and to relatively small equity placings. As already mentioned, the emphasis is on public offers for sale.

Assessing the merits of any kind of public offering calls for knowledge and skill. The prospectus or statement should be studied thoroughly, with particular attention to the items in small type. The key points which should be considered can be summarized:

Nature and history of the business: Is it old-established, with a solid foundation and (if a manufacturing concern) ample factory accommodation? Does it rely on any patents or special processes which might be superseded by new and cheaper methods of production? What is its standing in its particular industry?

Management: Are the directors and key personnel responsible for past successes continuing to serve the company, and if so have they long-term service agreements? What arrangements have been made to train new management to succeed directors who are getting on in years? *Management is the main key to the continuing prosperity of any business and its quality can be a decisive factor in assessing the merits of a company's shares.*

Sponsors of the offer: If the issuing house and brokers have a good record of successes, it can be taken that the offer has been well 'vetted' and has a good chance. If the sponsors are comparatively unknown, however, it may be as well to find out something about their standing in the City.

Capital structure is important. What relation does any loan or preference capital bear to the equity capital? What are the borrowing powers?

Terms of the offer: What is the price at which shares are being offered or placed? Does it seem reasonable in relation to the net assets and the expected dividend? Why is the offer being made?

Profit record: If profits for at least ten years are not given, the reason should be stated in the prospectus. See whether profits have been rising steadily, have fluctuated, or are falling, and whether any reason is given to account for changes.

Turnover: Details for up to ten years should be provided. It is vital that the trend should be upwards and that the reasons for any sharp fluctuations should be stated. With inflation at recent high rates it is even more important to know whether turnover in *real* terms, which usually means volume, has been rising or falling. A 10 per cent rise in monetary turnover is a fall in volume if prices have risen by an average of 15 per cent!

Future prospects should be stated, together perhaps with a forecast of the minimum profit expected for the current year. An indication whether turnover is going up, going down, or standing still is essential.

Dividend forecast and cover: What rate of dividend is forecast on the equity shares, and how many times is it covered by (a) current profits and (b) average profits of recent years?

Assets: How are these made up, and has there been any recent valuation of the fixed items such as property and plant? Is there plenty of cash in hand or in readily realizable investments?

Stock-in-trade and work-in-progress, as some débâcles have unhappily demonstrated, are vital items in financial assessments. They are the simplest assets to over-value, or to under-state, and their totals directly affect not only annual profits but longer term trends. The Institute of Chartered Accountants has formulated guidance rules for valuation, of which the key factors are consistency in valuation bases year by year and insistence on the use of realistic prices such as cost or market value, whichever is the lower. So, any qualification by the reporting accountants should be looked for.

Liabilities: Are these high in relation to the current assets comprising stocks, debtors, cash and other liquid items? Careful attention should be given to any short- and medium-term bank and other borrowing, particularly whether it is secured on assets of the company or is guaranteed by individuals or another company; and the repayment terms. Large loans and short repayment conditions can be a serious handicap if credit becomes 'tight'.

Purpose of the issue: If new capital is being issued, what is the purpose of the operation – to finance expansion, pay for the take-over of any other concern, or repay bank overdrafts or other borrowed money? The prospectus should show the net amount which any new issue will provide and how it will be allocated.

Net assets: What is the value of the net assets, after allowing for all liabilities and including any new capital raised by the issue?

Goodwill: Is anything included in the assets for goodwill, patent rights, or other items which have no tangible value and might be worthless if the company ran into difficulties? (A concealed good-will item can arise when ordinary shares are issued at a premium. For instance, if the total issued equity is £1,000,000 in 25p shares, of which some are offered at 75p each, and the net assets applicable to the ordinary are £2,000,000, the concealed goodwill is £1,000,000 – 4,000,000 shares valued at 75p, or £3,000,000, compared with net tangible assets of £2,000,000. This calculation can be most important – it can show that the market valuation of the equity is high in relation to real assets and future prospects. It should be based on the total equity – the shares retained by the founders and those offered or placed.)

Vendors' interests: What proportion of the equity is being retained by the people who are selling an interest in their business? If it is unduly low, there should be some good reason to account for the sale of say more than one half of the equity.

Contracts: Details must be given in the prospectus of special contracts entered into for the purchase of property, building of new factories, and other capital commitments, also of service agreements with the directors. The latter should be on terms which seem fair and reasonable in relation to the profit potentialities.

Professional certificates: The prospectus should state that auditors, reporting accountants, valuers, and other experts giving certificates have not withdrawn them prior to publication. The standing of such experts is also important.

Underlining its insistence on the publication of all relevant information on the progress of a company the Stock Exchange binds it to observe certain rules after its securities are listed. This Listing Agreement broadly requires immediate notification to the Exchange of dividends, profits (and losses), issues of new securities and other changes and information necessary to enable shareholders to assess the position of the company. Equally, directors should not divulge price-sensitive information so as to put anyone in a privileged position – all shareholders should be informed of developments. As well as annual reports, companies must also issue half-yearly statements.

More specifically, the Agreement asks for, or insists on, notification at least ten days in advance of board meetings to decide dividends and announce profits; release of such information during market hours; translation of profits available for equity shares into pence per share; disclosure of the interests of directors and their families in the company's capital; immediate announcement of the acquisition of 10 per cent or more of the voting capital by a particular party; publication of audited accounts, normally within six months of the end of a financial period; and inclusion therein of sectional and geographical analysis of turnover and profits.

CHAPTER 17

Rights and Other Issues

A FEATURE of post-war company finance has been the large amounts of new capital which publicly-quoted concerns have raised by direct offers to their share and stock holders. Such operations, which have a great deal to be said in their favour, may be an issue of debentures, loan stock, or convertible loan stock for which applications are unrestricted; or they may be the offer of ordinary shares or convertible loan stock in strict proportion to the number of existing ordinary shares held. The latter are known as *Rights Issues*; they give the shareholder the right to subscribe more capital on what are usually bonus terms.

An example will show the method and value of a rights issue. Suppose that a company whose 25p ordinary shares are quoted at 100p decides to offer shareholders one new 25p ordinary share for every two old ones held at a price of 55p each. This means that shareholders can increase their stake in the company on terms which, in effect, represent a bonus. In fact on taking up their allotment they will have two old shares valued at 200p and one new one costing 55p, or a total of 255p for three shares. The average worth of each share is then theoretically 255p divided by three, i.e. 85p each. The value of the rights per old share is thus 15p, and the ex rights price should open at around 85p. This would make the *new* shares worth 30p premium on the issue price of 55p.

Shareholders do not have to take up their quota of a rights issue. They can probably sell their rights at a profit. Generally, however, it is advisable to take up such an offer – for three reasons. First, it is a good rule to follow up a sound investment, and sales of rights reduce the proportionate stake in a company. Secondly, most companies put such new capital to profitable use. Thirdly, it can happen that the market price of old and new shares improves after a rights issue has been assimilated and the new money is being put to work. However, there are shareholders who for one reason or another do not or cannot take up their allotment. Providing there is a premium based on the price of the new shares, they can sell their rights. Sticking to our previous example, a holder of shares could get something like 30p each for handing over his rights to another investor, always providing he acted before the date the offer expired.

The important fact for shareholders is that action of some kind should be taken before the final date for applying for shares. The shares should be taken up or the rights sold. *Failure to act within the time limit can be costly*. Not all companies make arrangements to sell the rights of non-assenting holders and distribute the proceeds *pro rata* amongst them. If in any doubt on what it is best or feasible to do, consult a stockbroker or bank manager as soon as possible after receiving the documents.

A rights issue sometimes gives new investors an opportunity to buy shares at a slightly better price. A purchase of rights is not liable to stamp duty. Although the market allows for this in its quotation for the new shares, there can be a slight gain. It can also happen that the prices of both old and new shares are depressed until the issue is out of the way, largely as a result of sales of the rights. It can pay, therefore, to watch for rights issues by companies with good prospects.

Conversion operations are generally used to replace gilt-edged, debentures, and other fixed-interest securities due for repayment in accordance with the terms of issue; or (an arrangement which is growing) to enable a parent company to streamline its finances by making offers for the outstanding fixed-interest capital of its subsidiary companies. A typical instance of the first type would be where say a $7\frac{1}{2}$ per cent stock issued in cheap-money days falls due for redemption and the borrower has not the funds to repay the outstanding amount in cash, or for one or more reasons wishes to continue having the use of such capital. The new issue of stock will have to carry a current rate of interest if it is to appeal to new or old investors. Depending on the nature of the offer and the redemption terms, this may have to be, let us assume, 12 to 14 per cent; in other words not far short of double the rate on the old stock.

The methods open are to restrict the issue to a conversion offer to holders of the 7½ per cent stock, and to find other means of financing repayment of stock not converted; to make an issue of an equal amount of the new stock, giving holders of the old an option to convert and issuing the balance not so taken up to investors at large; or to make an issue of a larger or smaller amount of new stock, again with the option of conversion of the old in part or in whole. Acceptance of a conversion offer must depend on the attractiveness of the terms and on whether it is advisable to continue to leave the money in a fixed-interest stock.

The development of take-over bids has sometimes (for example in the brewing industry) led to the building-up of complex or diverse structures of fixed-interest capital. The existence of debenture stocks and preference share issues of subsidiary companies may make it difficult for the parent concern to reorganize, regroup, or otherwise deal with assets in the most economical and progressive way. Parent companies can cope with the situation by liquidating the subsidiaries and thereby repaying the fixed-interest capital, or – the usual way – by offering their own prior-charge capital in exchange for the issues of the subsidiaries.

Offers of the latter type can be a stock-for-stock offer carrying the same rate of interest, or the same thing with an appetizer in the form of a cash addition of say 5p per £1 share or £5 per £100 of stock; or if the offering company wishes to keep its own capital structure as simple as possible, conversion into one or two stocks on bases which give at least the same nominal value of securities and the same or a higher annual income. Offers for preference capital are sometimes in the form of loan stock, which means that the prior-charge capital will eventually be reduced by repayments of the new security. While, as we have seen, offers of this kind are generally pitched to give some benefit to holders of subsidiary companies' capital, it is advisable before accepting to make sure (a) that if there is any change in the interest rate it will produce the same or more annual income, (b) that the security is as good as or better than the present security, and (c) when the offer for irredeemable capital is into redeemable stock, that the latter gives a realistic bonus in return for losing a definite income virtually for good.

Scrip issues have been mentioned in Chapter 8 (see p. 136).

Because they come from accumulated reserves, they add nothing to the intrinsic value of the assets. They are paper transactions which simply bring the issued capital more into line with the net assets employed and theoretically do not of themselves add any-thing to the income received by way of dividends. Mostly, such 'free' issues are made in ordinary shares, or (where it is wished to restrict voting power) in 'A' ordinary or some other class of equity which has no voting power or has restricted voting rights. Because of increasing opposition from insurance offices and other insti-tutional investors issues of voteless equities are now very rare.

An example will show the effect. A company has an issued ordinary capital of £1,000,000 in 25p shares, and by ploughing back surplus profits, and by other means, it has built up reserves of £1,000,000. The net equity value of the company is £2,000,000, or 50p per share. The directors decide to distribute part of the reserves by a one-for-two (or 50 per cent) scrip issue. The effect is that the issued equity is increased to £1,500,000; shareholders have three shares in place of two; the reserves fall to £500,000; and though the overall net value is unchanged at £2,000,000, the net asset value of the enlarged equity becomes 33⅓p per share. Instead of having two shares with a total net asset value of 100p, share-holders now have three shares with the same total book value. Let us further assume that the dividend on the old capital has been 12½ per cent, and that it has been covered twice by available profits. If future distributions are to be kept at the same level, the *rate per share* will have to be reduced to 8⅓ per cent. What may happen in practice, if profits are maintained, is that the new dividend will be rounded up to perhaps 9 per cent, or to 10 per cent if the long-term prospects are good. Hence – although it must never be taken for granted – a scrip issue by a prosperous company may be the fore-runner to a stepping-up of the *effective* dividend rate.

As far as the market is concerned, therefore, the theoretical effect of a scrip issue is to reduce the price of the old shares proportionately. If the old shares mentioned above were standing at 75p immediately before the scrip issue, the price afterwards for old and new would be 50p – two old shares worth 150p becoming three worth the same total amount, 50p each. The 'ex' position should be carefully noted. There can be no quotation 'ex' the scrip issue until approval to the issue has been given by shareholders or they have authorized the necessary increase in nominal capital. Unlike dividends, which generally lead to an 'ex div.' price shortly after they are announced, shares may not go 'ex cap.' until some time after the proposal is made.

Although not issues in the senses already covered, two other types of capital operation, or reorganization, can take place. First is a *share-split* by a company whose ordinary shares have, because of profitable progress or a relatively small issued total, risen to an unwieldy level in the market. If, for instance, a £1 share is priced at £30, this may hamper purchases by small investors. If each £1 share is split into ten 10p shares there is no change in the issued amount of the ordinary capital; but, on a straight arithmetical basis, the 'split' 10p shares are priced at £3 and holders have ten new shares still worth the £30 equivalent of the old £1 share. In practical terms a split can mean a relative increase in value because of easier marketability and the price of the new shares might go to £3¼ or even £3½ each. Second is a *consolidation*, which is a reverse process of reducing the number of shares by, in effect, raising their par value. For example, if a 10p ordinary share is priced in the market at 3p, the consolidation of five shares into one 50p share would theoretically increase the price to 15p which, psychologically, could produce a better 'image' for the company.

Our final class of capital issue is mostly made in connection with a *take-over bid*, or an amalgamation of two or more companies. A take-over offer can be in various forms. First is a cash bid. Second is an offer of shares. Third is an offer of shares plus some cash. Fourth is the alternative of shares or cash. Fifth is an offer of a fixed-interest stock for an equity. Sixth is a mixture of shares and loan stock. Whatever the form of the offer, it can be successful only if it is attractive enough to appeal to holders of the capital which is the subject of the bid.

The directors of a company making a bid for the capital of another are expected to base their offer on the worth of the business they wish to acquire. They will take into account the value of its assets, its profit record, the future prospects, and – often the key factor – what it is worth to them for any particular or general purpose in mind. For instance, it may be profitable to pay a high price for the shares of a concern which has productive facilities, a technical skill, patent rights, or some other tangible or intangible asset which the bidder requires. There have been a number of instances where the primary objective has been to get hold of production facilities ready-made, in preference to waiting many months or years before the bidder could build his own plant – the time saved has been worth a lot of money.

On the other hand – and such cases need careful watching – the bid may be made solely in order to increase the size and importance of the take-over company. One man or a group of men may suffer from a megalomania which can lead to the payment of fancy prices, a growth which is uncommercial, and nasty losses when the chickens come home to roost. Most cases of such megalomania are companies which build up a hodge-podge of widely diversified companies into an industrial holding empire. Not all these holding companies (or *conglomerates*, as they are now called) are sufficiently well balanced, properly capitalized, or ably enough managed to survive as prosperous concerns. The collapse, or virtual bankruptcy, of many of these 'empires' has cost investors many hundreds of millions of pounds in recent months; and is a warning to step very very carefully when such shares are being recommended strongly or are showing spectacular rises.

A substantial number of bids, on the other hand, come from quarters which realize that the assets of a company are not being put to their most profitable use or that profits are being too conservatively distributed. An early example of this type of operation was Sir Charles Clore's bid for part of the ordinary capital of the Sears shoe business. Now, after reorganization and the sale of many of the shop properties under lease-back arrangements, Sears (Holdings) has become the largest footwear organization in the country and has used its surplus resources to spread into other activities – all with considerable profit to its shareholders. The only way in which bids can be fought successfully in such cases is for the directors to 'open the books' to show just what the company owns, to open the purse strings by stepping up the dividend, and perhaps to distribute some of the non-trading assets.

Deciding whether a take-over bid is fair may be no easy task. Clearly, if shares suddenly become worth more than their market price to one party, they may be worth still more to a second party or to retain. Fortunately, there is often a good measuring-rod these days. If the bid is inadequate, there is a good chance that a rival bidder will weigh in with a better offer, or the directors of the target company will produce facts to demonstrate the real worth of the shares. There have been a number of take-over battles in which the price has risen substantially before one of the rivals capitulated.

But should there be no rival bid, or if the directors of both companies are in agreement on the terms, the offer has to be judged on its merits. In such cases, doubts should be resolved by consulting an expert. But there is always one very sound rule with a take-over bid: *If in the slightest doubt, do not accept until the last twenty-four or forty-eight hours.* This gives time for the emergence of a rival bid, or if there has been sufficient vocal opposition, for the bidder to improve his offer.

During 1967 and early 1968 take-over tactics began getting out of hand, particularly through buying in the market and outside it. While the Stock Exchange could exercise some control through withdrawal of quotations and by reprimanding members involved in unethical tactics, its powers were limited by its very constitution. Some more widely based control was wanted. Government legislation would have taken considerable time to enact and, even if it had been a feasible step, there would have been great difficulties in the way of covering every loophole. Moreover, no practical person wanted hampering and time-wasting regulations of the type imposed in the U.S.A. through the Securities and Exchange Commission. The City met the situation in its traditional way of putting its own house in order. The Governor of the Bank of England reconvened a City Working Party, originally set up in 1959, and gave it the job of hammering out a code of voluntary self-discipline. All bodies involved – stock exchanges, issuing houses, investment trusts, insurance offices, banks, pension funds, acceptance houses and industry – took their part. The first *City Code* appeared in March 1968. After teething troubles had been sorted out there came amendments which, as fresh problems and loopholes emerged, have been changed and expanded. The *Panel*, as it is popularly called, has shown, and continues to show, considerable awareness of new tactics which might be against the interests of shareholders at large and, equally, speed in formulating new rules to stop or minimize abuses.

The present *City Code* is administered by the Panel on Take-overs and Mergers whose Director-General or his deputy is always ready to give rulings on points of interpretation as promptly as possible for the free working of take-over and merger business; and with the right of appeal to the Panel. The Stock Exchange, the Issuing Houses Association, other bodies directly concerned, together with the Department of Trade and Industry have amended their rules or undertaken to take steps to put strong teeth into action against those who disregard the Code or the advice given by the Panel. Particularly strong deterrents to infringements of the Code are the Panel's power to ask the Stock Exchange to suspend quotations during a take-over struggle and to refuse quotations for new securities to be issued under a bid. Two important basic principles are that (a) all shareholders of a company being bid for must be treated similarly and (b) every endeavour must be made by both sides to prevent a false market in their shares. A good example of the benefits of having such a Panel was seen in 1969 during the protracted and bitter struggle over the partial take-over of Pergamon Press by the American conglomerate, the Leasco company. The Panel did good work striving to get order out of chaos and to reconcile wide differences between the principals of the two companies. More recently, action and advice to one or both sides (and their merchant banker advisers) have been effective in big take-over struggles such as the Allied Breweries bid for Trust Houses Forte and Maxwell Joseph's battles to bring Trumans and Watney Mann, the two brewery groups, into his Grand Metropolitan Hotels empire.

Various rules have been made by the Panel. Apart from technical directions for the companies concerned and their advisers, their main tenor is that shareholders must be given the earliest possible warning, by Press notice and circular, of serious approaches, agreed mergers and moves through the share market; and that this should be followed up as quickly as practicable by a letter setting out the views of the offeree company's board. Formal offers must set out all facts essential to making decisions on the merits and demerits; profit forecasts must be compiled with the greatest care, be the sole responsibility of the directors and be examined and reported on by qualified accountants; asset revaluations must be supported by independent professional experts and the valuation basis clearly stated; and there must be competent independent confirmation that resources are actually available to meet a partial or full cash offer. Offers must initially be left open for at least twenty-one days after posting and any revisions for a minimum of fourteen days. Taking the realistic view that it would be unwise to fetter the share market, there are no restrictions on all parties to a take-over or merger, and their associates, from dealing (at arm's length) in the securities concerned. But all such deals must be disclosed to the Panel, the Press and the Stock Exchange, with totals of shares bought and the average prices paid or realized. If the bidding company directly or indirectly buys shares of the biddee company during the offer period at above the offer price it must offer to all accepting shareholders an increased price which must be not less than the highest price (not including stamp duty and commission) of shares so acquired. Similarly, if more than 15 per cent of the biddee company's shares are bought, directly or indirectly, within 12 months of the offer, the Panel may rule that an alternative cash offer (at not less than the highest price paid) should be extended to other holders.

A legal point which can cause concern is the treatment of holders who do not accept an offer. When holders of at least nine-tenths of the class of capital involved in an offer have accepted, the bidder can, within four months of making the offer, give notice that within two months he will acquire the shares of dissenters on the same terms. The effect of this is that if a bidder wants complete control the offer must be at least 90 per cent successful. Most offers stipulate that completion is subject to acceptances by holders of a minimum of perhaps 75 per cent or some other proportion of the shares. They are conditional on such minimum acceptance. When the acceptances pass this minimum figure, the offer may be declared unconditional, which means that the bidder accepts all the shares offered and will go on taking more on the same terms.

What happens to the minority holdings if a bidder who does not get a 90 per cent acceptance decides to accept all shares offered? The position depends on the proportion which is accepted. If it is substantial – say up to 75, or just short of 90 per cent – the market in the balance may become very restricted and 'one-way', particularly if the issued capital is relatively small. Dissenting shareholders may therefore find themselves left with an investment which is difficult to sell at a fair price. And if the company strikes a bad patch which means a reduction in the dividend or its passing altogether, there may be a very sharp fall in prices. In other words, the minority interests may be pretty well at the mercy of the majority. Against this must be set the fact that if the company prospers under its new control the value of the dissenting shares may become worth more than the take-over price, and they can be sold in the market at a good figure – or the take-over company may put in a higher bid for them. There have been cases of both things happening.

On the whole, however, it is usually good policy to accept a bid if the offer is extended after the bidder has not quite got his 90 per cent minimum. In the famous Courtaulds and Imperial Chemical Industries struggle, the latter was left with less than 40 per cent of the Courtaulds equity: such cases are of course a different matter – there is then little chance of the market drying up or becoming artificial.

CHAPTER 18

Shareholders and Their Rights

IT is an unfortunate fact that most shareholders do not take an active interest in the affairs of their companies until something goes wrong. So long as the dividends roll in, and the prices of their shares do not fall too heavily, they are content to sit back and let happen what may. They overlook the important fact that however small their holding, and however large the company, they are part proprietors – a portion of it belongs to them – and they have rights which are laid down by the Companies Acts of 1948 and 1967 and the articles of association that govern the legal running of the company.

The highlights of the share investor's calendar are usually the announcement of the annual profit figures and dividend, followed by publication of the annual report and accounts, and the holding of the annual general meeting. Other events that are also important are the declaration of any interim dividend, the issue of half-yearly or possibly quarterly progress reports, and the holding of extra-ordinary general meetings which may be necessary to approve an increase in the authorized share or loan capital or to transact any other business requiring the consent of those shareholders entitled to vote.

The *listing agreement* which companies have to enter into when their securities are given a quotation on the Stock Exchange lays down important specific rules and procedures designed to give prompt publicity to any developments likely to affect prices and to avoid artificial markets. Directors, for instance, are expected to announce profits, dividends, new issues and other key information as soon as possible after the board meetings at which figures are finalized or decisions taken. All information must be sent direct to the Quotations Department in London, or appropriate department of a provincial exchange, in a clear, unambiguous form and with any necessary comparative figures. Immediately

Exchange officials have cleared the announcements they are posted in the House and put on the Market Price Display Service which operates on a closed television link up to 5 p.m.; and copies are handed to the Exchange Telegraph Company News Service. Simultaneously, it is usual for companies to have copies of all announcements and documents circulated to the City Editors of the daily and evening newspapers, to other financial publications, and to the Exchange Telegraph and Reuter's ticker-tape services. In the case of dividends and profit figures the Stock Exchange expects notification of the dates of relevant board meetings at least ten days in advance.

Some days or weeks after publication of these preliminary details, the directors follow them up with the annual report and accounts, a copy of which is mailed to every share or loan-capital holder entitled to it. Annual reports vary considerably in size, style, comprehensiveness, the amount of information given, and simplicity or complexity. Some squeeze the bare minimum requirements of the Companies Acts into three or four small pages, and forgo any attempt at elaboration or trimmings. Others run to dozens of large expensively-printed pages giving pictures, charts, diagrams, masses of relevant and sometimes time-wasting information, and statistics. In between are excellent bread and butter efforts which strike the happy medium of presenting essential and useful information in a clear and understandable manner. It is an unhappy fact that in the effort to inform shareholders the directors of some companies have let their public relations experts, designers, and layout men run riot in trying to produce the lushest reports, sometimes almost unreadable because they use the wrong combinations of coloured ink and paper. There is a great deal in favour of the simple straightforward document which sticks to essentials. Shareholders who get an elaborate report from a company are entitled to ask what it costs to produce and mail, particularly if things are not going too well with the company.

The first item in the report is the *notice of the annual meeting* – the place, the time, and the items to be discussed. At least twenty-one days' notice must be given of the calling of this important event. Items to be discussed are usually as follows:

Receipt and consideration of the directors' report and the accounts gives those shareholders who trouble to attend the meeting the opportunity to ask questions about management; finances; past, current and future trading; and other relevant matters. They can also criticize items in the accounts which call for comment or are not clear.

Declaration of a final dividend: once declared by the directors, it is not easy to alter a distribution. All shareholders can in fact do is criticize the payment as being too parsimonious or over-generous, and reduce it if they get sufficient voting support.

The election of directors: the articles of a company provide that a certain number or proportion of the board must retire each year; retiring directors usually stand for re-election. Shareholders can, however, oppose the re-election and put forward other candidates. This is another opportunity to criticize or probe into management policy and to call for details of or to criticize the fees and other payments to directors. When a director reaches seventy years of age, notice of the fact should be given.

The remuneration of the auditors is fixed at the meeting. Although this is mostly a routine matter, it does give an opportunity to put further questions regarding the accounts. The auditors, as representatives of the shareholders, have the duty of seeing that the annual accounts give a true and fair view of the company's affairs and profits, and of drawing attention to any items or transactions which they do not approve.

Other business which may be transacted includes any motions put by shareholders and any ordinary resolutions that can be dealt with at an A.G.M. such as the conversion of shares into stock.

Not all shareholders may be entitled to attend the annual meetings. Preference shareholders (as noted in an earlier chapter) may be debarred unless some motion affecting their rights is up for discussion. Some classes of equity holders, such as those with non-voting 'A' ordinary shares, may be entitled to attend meetings but not to vote, or to have only a limited vote of say one per ten or fifty shares. On the other hand, some classes of equity, such as deferred shares, may have more than one vote per share.

Shareholders entitled to vote usually receive a *proxy card* which enables them to appoint someone else to vote for them, either specifically for or against a motion or generally without any direction. When such cards are sent out by the company, they almost always provide for the appointment of one or more directors as proxies. While it is safe to complete such cards when a company is doing so well that there is no cause for criticism, it is a different matter if things are not going well or there is a dispute between members of the board or between shareholders and the directors. The pros and cons must then be carefully considered before giving a free hand to the board, or of giving support to an opposition if there is one also asking for proxies. Company affairs are enlivened every now and again by a big proxy battle, with both sides striving to whip up support. This is another instance when expert advice should be sought in all cases of doubt. It is not enough to throw away a proxy card. All shareholders should take an active interest in the affairs of a company which is the centre of a dispute or is doing badly. To be effective, proxies must be lodged with the company a clear forty-eight hours before the holding of the meeting.

Resolutions are normally decided by a show of hands of the shareholders present, which means in practice that a tiny minority of the owners of the average company settles its annual business. However, shareholders or the directors can call for a poll, which then decides the matter on the number of votes cast for and against a motion. This is where 'absentee' control becomes effective through proxy voting. Each proxy represents the number of votes given by each shareholding. Extraordinary general meetings are called whenever it is necessary to get the approval of shareholders or loan-capital holders to changes such as increases of capital, variation of rights, or sale or purchase of assets. Proxies may then be particularly important.

When shareholders do act at an annual or other meeting, they often spoil their case by not presenting it properly. Opponents of a board should make sure of their facts, provide a workable alternative, put their case clearly and logically, and once on their feet should avoid being carried away by their own enthusiasm or being browbeaten by a forceful chairman. Too many chairmen and directors of companies forget that they do not own them – like their fellow-shareholders, they are only part proprietors.

After the list of the directors and other officials of the company, the next item in the annual report is the *report of the directors*. Both the Companies Act 1967 and the London Stock Exchange have had a material effect on the information which must be given to shareholders; and a good part now appears in this report. While, in practice, some of the information may be given elsewhere in the annual document, companies should now give details of: their principal group activites, main trade divisions, geographical spheres of operation, and the names of their major operating subsidiaries; significant changes in group activities and assets during the year; details of share and loan capital issued; details of contracts with directors, directors' share options and directors' shareholdings; contracts in which directors have, or have had, material interests; distribution of the year's profit by way of dividends and transfers to reserves; breakdown of turnover and profits by principal activities and geographically; particulars of exports; average number of employees and their total remuneration; a breakdown of directors', top employees', and the chairman's remuneration; details of charitable and political contributions exceeding £50; statement of the market value of buildings and land; and any other information necessary to appreciate the current state of affairs.

The directors' report may be confined to essential and statutory facts, including the names of directors up for election. Or it may be amplified by additional information on the year's trading, major developments, and future prospects and plans. Usually, however, such latter information is given in the *chairman's review*.

Thereafter the report turns to facts and figures – the accounts for the year or other trading period. The first account will probably be the *profit-and-loss account*. If the company has subsidiaries, as is the rule rather than the exception, the first item is the consolidated trading profit – the group's surplus of trading income over expenditure. This may show in detail the depreciation, directors' emoluments, and other items charged before arriving at the trading figure, or it may give the net amount only and refer to notes for the details. To it are added interest received, dividends from trade and general investments, and other non-trading income; and from it are deducted any interest paid on loan capital and non-trading expenditure. A recent development of considerable importance is that companies with interests in associated concerns should include their proportion of the profits in their own profit-and-loss accounts and in the allocation section show the amount of profit retained by the associated companies. The balance is the *profit before taxation*. Tax is next deducted, to give the net profit of the group, to which may be added or deducted items relating to previous years such as taxation overpaid or underpaid. The balance is the overall amount available for distribution. From it may be deducted (a) dividends paid to minority shareholders in subsidiary companies, and any portion of surplus profit due to them; and (b) profits belonging to the parent company put to the reserves or kept in the profit-and-loss accounts of subsidiaries plus, as already mentioned, the proportion of 'associated' profits not received by way of dividends and/or interest. The final balance is the amount available for distribution to the shareholders of the parent company. Out of it will be taken first any preference dividends, secondly the dividends on the equity capital, and thirdly any amounts put to reserve or added to undivided profits. A note should translate the amount available for the ordinary shareholders into the equivalent of pence per share – the *earnings*. Comparative figures will show the corresponding items for the previous year.

The vital points to look for in the profit-and-loss account are whether the various items, particularly the trading and net profits, are up or down, and the number of times the surplus covers the preference and ordinary dividends. Some accounts are clear and easy to follow. Others are confusing, because they have not been drawn up with care or because the directors for some reason do not want to make things easy to follow. There is no justifiable reason why profit-and-loss accounts should not show the total available for dividends, including the share of the parent's profits retained by subsidiaries, and how much is absorbed by dividends and how much left in the group.

A company with subsidiaries must give two *balance sheets* – its own, which amongst other items shows the interests in subsidiaries, and a consolidated statement which sets out the figures for the whole group. They may be two separate documents, or a composite one giving the figures of the parent in one column and those of the group in a second one. They may also be in the old-fashioned, and still the clearest and simplest, form of assets on one side and liabilities on the other; or the newer and sometimes confusing form of columnar statements squeezed on to one page to give the assets at the top and how they are represented by capital, reserves, and other items at the bottom. Additional columns show the comparative figures at the end of the previous year.

Although the parent company balance sheet should be examined to see what changes have been taking place, the consolidated statement is the more important. It provides a financial bird's-eye view of the financial position of the group at the year's end. On the assets side it will probably start with *fixed assets* – land, factories, office buildings, plant, machinery, and other items used for production, selling, or other purposes – shown at their cost price or valuation, less depreciation provided out of trading profits to cover their using up, wastage, and obsolescence. Included, or shown separately, will be any *trade investments* in other concerns which are not more than 50 per cent owned and therefore do not qualify as subsidiaries – as such assets can sometimes be very valuable by producing large dividend income in relation to their book cost, it can be important to know their nature, which may or may not be readily available information. Following modern practice, investments in *associated companies* should be shown at the net asset value equivalent to the company's interest therein. *Investments in subsidiaries* which it has not been practicable or possible to consolidate should be set out separately and an explanation given for their non-consolidation. *Current assets* are made up of trading items such as stocks of raw materials and finished goods, work in progress, and debts owing to the group for goods sold, together with cash at bank and in hand, deposits, tax reserve certificates, quoted investments, and other liquid items which can be turned readily into cash. Strong liquid resources are a sign of strength and ability to expand or meet emergencies without having to raise bank or other loans or call on shareholders for additional capital; weak ones an indication that more capital will be needed or that the group is getting into financial difficulties. Last amongst the assets may be *intangible items* such as the value put on patents and good-will, the excess of the cost of investments in subsidiaries over their net tangible value, and other items which have no physical existence – a prudent board of directors writes off as quickly as possible all intangibles, however valuable they may be as profit-earning assets or as items with a realizable value.

The other or liabilities side of the balance sheet will set out the authorized and issued *capital* and how it is divided into different categories of shares. Next may be the capital, revenue, and other *reserves* which belong to shareholders, nearly always the equity holders. Capital reserves may represent premiums received on capital issued at more than its par value, profits on sales of assets, and other items of a special or non-revenue nature. Revenue reserves are mostly built up from profits not paid out in dividends and thus retained in the business, to provide a buffer against bad times and (a feature of post-war company finance) to help to pay for new factories, plant, or other expansion of business. The average company generates well over half of every £1 of its capital requirements from profits ploughed back and from similar internal sources. As shown in earlier chapters, accumulated reserves have to be added to the issued equity capital when calculating the im-portant figure of share net asset values. Large reserves represent strength and prudent or sometimes over-cautious finance; small ones may be a signal that all is not well. *Future taxation* is a particu-lar form of reserve, representing the amount set aside for taxation on the current profits which is not due immediately and which often includes deferred liability resulting from capital allowances; prudent finance dictates that such provisions be made, although on a liquidation the liability might be smaller. *Minority interests*, which represent the interests of outside shareholders in the con-solidated net assets, may be made up solely of preference capital, or of such capital plus some equity and the relative proportion of accumulated reserves. *Debentures* and other loan capital represent the long-term indebtedness of the group; in other words, liabilities which are a charge on the assets before the shareholders are entitled to any payment. Finally will come the *current liabilities and provisions*, representing the sums owing to creditors for goods and services supplied, provision for taxation currently due, interest accrued on loan capital, provisions against some known or estimated liabilities, dividends due to shareholders, and bank loans or overdrafts. Such items should bear a reasonable relation to current assets, from which they are sometimes deducted in order to show the *net current assets*. If bank finance is high, it may be a signal that further permanent capital may have to be raised or that the company is getting out of its trading depth. In fact, very particular attention should be paid to all borrowings of a short-term nature; which can be those repayable at early notice or in up to, say, five years, and whether they are secured on any part of the assets. The apocryphal definition of a banker as 'someone who lends you an umbrella when the sun is shining and wants it back when it rains' can be only too realistic in times of monetary stringency such as that experienced in 1974.

Important items which appear as notes to a balance sheet are capital commitments in respect of fixed assets under construction or ordered, other possible liabilities and contingent liabilities such as on bills of exchange discounted, and guarantees of subsidiary or other company dividends which may never arise but which would involve payment if they ever did mature. The extent of capital commitments can be another indicator of the need to raise further capital.

So that the profit-and-loss account and balance sheet are not cluttered up with too much detail, additional information is given in *notes*, which should be looked through carefully. Data so provided can include changes in the reserves, details of depreciation and directors' remuneration, a summary of the fixed assets and minority interests, and the bases of valuing certain assets.

The report of the *auditors* is attached to the balance sheet or follows it. It should always be read, to find out whether the auditors direct attention to any feature of the accounts or point out that they have not received sufficient information to give a clean certificate, or whether they disagree with the way the directors have dealt with any particular item in the accounts. The strictures of the auditors can be the first warning that all is not well with a company.

Policy varies on the publication of the *Chairman's review*. Many companies make this a part of the report. Others leave it to the annual meeting. Whatever the policy, a Chairman with the best interests of shareholders at heart will deal in reasonable detail with trading and financial changes during the period under review, report on particular developments, comment on the present position, and where possible forecast the immediate prospects for both trade and profits.

A growing number of companies, as we have already seen, give a certain amount of extra information on general and specific matters thought to be of interest. There may be reviews of particular aspects of the business, or illustrated reports on new factories. One useful extra is a tabulation of profits and balance sheets for a period of up to ten years – simply done, this gives a good overall view of the progress or otherwise of the group. Another, which relatively few companies give so far, is a summary of share-ownership showing the type of shareholder and a break-down of the quantities held. A valuable feature which more and more companies are incorporating in their accounts is a *cash flow* statement. This is the amount of profit and depreciation retained. Its value lies in the fact that it shows to what extent a company is generating its own capital resources, particularly if details are added of the way in which expansion has been financed. Another addition that should be a 'must' in annual reports, is a *source and use of funds* table which, in effect, is a cash statement showing (a) the capital generated by retention of profits, depreciation allowances, issues of share or loan capital, bank borrowings, sales of assets and the like; and (b) how the money has been invested in new assets such as factories, machinery, subsidiaries, stocks and increases (or decreases) in liquid resources. It is a simple way in which to show how a company is financing its expansion.

The Council of the Stock Exchange, as already mentioned, has been most active in post-war years in pressing company directors to give shareholders ample information. In fact, the Companies Act 1967, an interim measure to fill in legislative gaps pending a complete overhaul of the law, is largely based on Stock Excha requirements under the *General Undertaking* which is a requisr of any new quotation being granted. Amongst the non-statutory requirements are two-way proxy voting forms, details of large shareholdings, ten-year or other long-term financial statistics, and the issue of half-yearly or quarterly interim reports on profits and trading. If half-yearly reports are not mailed to all investors the company must advertise them in two leading daily newspapers.

Equally, the Institutes of Chartered Accountants in England and Wales, and Scotland have been active in formulating practice notes on accounting procedure and principles, the value of which is being underlined by the problems which are multiplying as inflation upsets traditional rules. Valuation of stock-in-trade and work-in-progress ... treatment of deferred tax reserves ... disclosure of accounting policies ... treatment of associated company results ... putting extraordinary items and prior year adjustments through the profit-and-loss account instead of 'hiding' them in reserves ... and clear-cut rules for calculating earnings per share are all vitally important accounting procedures which have been laid down as definitely required or strongly advised.

A new Companies Act is on the way. Depending partly on the political complexion of its sponsors, it should close the blatant loopholes in company promotion, detail the facts which should be disclosed to shareholders, strengthen the powers of auditors, increase the penalties for abuses and fraud, try to lay down rules for valuation of stock-in-trade, fixed assets and other accounting items now open to various methods of computation, and cover the desire (or need) of accounting for inflation.

The morals of this chapter can be summed up:

Shareholders, as part proprietors, should take a constant interest in the affairs of the companies in which they invest.

They should attend annual general meetings whenever possible.

They should not sign proxies indiscriminately.

They should study annual reports, not throw them aside as tedious documents of no use or interest.

They should ensure that the auditors have not qualified their reports because correct accounting principles have not been applied.

CHAPTER 19

Keeping Track, Taking Advice, and Other Matters

ONE key to successful investment is to take an active interest in one's portfolio. Many things, as we have seen in previous pages, can happen to improve or mar the outlook for a particular security or group of securities and to affect market prices. Some developments may be temporary. Others may have long-term or lasting effects which can be avoided, minimized, or put to use by prompt action or intelligent anticipation. The best starting-point is to search out the essential facts about a security. Fortunately, there is an extensive pool of information from which to draw the basic data.

The first source of information, and the one which helps the investor to keep in constant touch with developments, is the daily Press. The national and provincial daily newspapers have City columns or pages giving the main company and financial news, and most of them publish the closing prices for the leading securities – some of these price-lists cover many hundreds of securities. Many of the evening newspapers also run City pages or articles, together with price-tables. The City articles of the Sunday newspapers are widely read and acted on. Finally, and perhaps most valuable, is the *Financial Times*, which gives a complete coverage of Stock Exchange, commodity, financial and related subjects, together with extensive coverage of the main provincial and overseas securities markets. Amongst the useful features of this specialist daily paper are the record of the previous day's markings; the full back pages of closing prices, dividends, dividend coverage, yields, and high and low points of the year; the '*F.T.*' daily price indices; summary of the most active stocks; list of new 'highs' and 'lows' for the year; unit trust prices and yields; full reports of all company, take-over, and financial news; and commentaries on daily developments and news.

Finally, there are also a number of weekly publications w. detailed reports and commentaries on company news; article. dealing with individual companies, groups of companies, and investment trends; recommendations of specific securities; and other features which enable the large or small investor to keep in touch with the investment world. The leading weekly concentrating on Stock Exchange affairs is the *Investors' Chronicle and Stock Exchange Gazette*. Another useful publication is the *Investors' Review*. Extensive coverage, together with economic and trade surveys, is given by the *Economist*. 'Mid-week' investment newsletters are issued by certain of the publications mentioned. Most of the daily newspapers and weekly publications also offer advisory services, which may be free to readers or for which small fees may be payable.

For individual advice, the best expert is a stockbroker. He is ready to give opinions on selections made by clients, or to make his own recommendations. It is perhaps not appreciated that a good deal of the advice given by stockbrokers comes indirectly. A recent survey of the technique of investors indicated that bank managers were the most frequently named source of advice. But who advises the bank managers? The stockbroker, of course. In most banks he is consulted when customers want investment advice. Stockbrokers are always ready to supply clients or prospective clients with recommendations, reviews of individual securities or groups of securities, and suggestions for portfolio layouts. In addition, a number of stockbroking firms issue detailed surveys, regular market reviews, and reports on individual companies, groups of companies, or industries to their clients.

Merchant banks have highly specialized investment departments but, because of the demand for their services, most of them have to insist on a minimum account of say £50,000/£100,000, or even £500,000. The commercial banks have trustee departments which will look after all kinds of investment work and which will take on much smaller accounts. There are also a number of portfolio management companies, some of which will handle accounts of as little as £10,000.

A good, and widely used, investment adviser is the City Editor one of the daily, evening, or Sunday newspapers or one of the specialized weekly publications. Many people, although they may claim to be acting on their own initiative, get their investment ideas from the City articles or by writing for advice to their favourite City Editor.

A point worth watching when acting on newspaper and similar recommendations is the effect of these recommendations on the market price. Jobbers are commercial people. They read the City columns just as closely as the keenest investor. It is natural therefore that after a recommendation they should anticipate a rush of business by marking up their prices. This ensures that they will be able to attract sufficient sellers to meet what may be an abnormal demand. A fairly good general rule is therefore to expect the price of a recommended share to open above its previous closing price. This does not always happen, of course, because investors may be feeling cautious as a result of some general uncertainty or for some other reason. There may therefore be no rush, and jobbers may have to revert to their old prices. Although it should not be taken as a universal guide, it can pay to wait for a reaction after a rush for a strongly recommended share; this can be a case for giving a broker a definite limit.

Jobbers produce a great deal of valuable material in the form of daily lists of securities on offer, market slips giving essential data on companies, reviews of industries and the public companies mainly concerned in them, and publications designed to help the individual or institutional investor. All such material must be obtained through brokers; jobbers are not allowed to contact the public directly.

Particularly useful aids for investors who want detailed information on the financial history and latest position of individual companies are the daily statistical services provided by Extel Statistical Services and Moodie's Services. Each service covers all, or nearly all, U.K. quoted companies, and leading Australian, Canadian and South African companies. Extel also provides cards for some 300 European companies, 250 Japanese market leaders and the bigger U.S. firms. Moodie's includes Australian, Canadian and South African leaders and International bonds, and publishes manuals for all the main U.S. industrial, bank, financial, pub, utility and transport companies. The publications for each company, in the form of handy-size cards or loose-leaf sheets, give details of the business and ramifications, directorate, authorized and issued capital, loan debt, profit-and-loss accounts for up to ten years or more, balance sheets for two or three years, net asset values, range of prices for up to ten years, gross yields and price–earnings ratios at different prices, latest dividends, chairmen's statements, latest news of concern to shareholders, and other information. Fresh cards or sheets are issued on the announcement of any news. Subscribers can take the whole of these services, sections of them, or groups of individual companies. Both companies supplement them with a useful taxation service which gives the basic information for calculating adjusted prices of securities held on 6 April 1965 when capital gains tax, as we know it today, began. Moodie's also publishes investment handbooks, and weekly and monthly market reviews.

Another, though more restricted, source of information is the monthly investment booklets published by two City firms of printers. These give details of issued capital, last two dividend payments, latest prices, dates dividends are due, and the highest and lowest prices for the current and previous years.

An individual investor may or may not feel the need for advice before buying or selling. He or she may have sufficient knowledge or information to act alone – women who are interested in markets often have a flair for picking good shares, simply because they tend to stick to companies whose goods they buy or see selling well. When, however, it becomes a matter of dealing with trust funds, the law may insist that competent professional advice must be taken. Up to August 1961, trustees who had not been given powers under a will or other deed to go outside the specified field were limited to a narrow range of investments, which so far as the Stock Exchange was concerned was largely confined to the gilt-edged and similar sectors. Post-war inflation inevitably brought the problems of the declining purchasing powers of the income produced from a fund, and the erosion of market values, as yields on fixed-interest stocks rose. The only way to contract out of the narrow

..ige of trustee investments was to apply to the Courts for a
.ariation of the terms, which could be a costly business.

The Trustee Investments Act 1961 brought welcome relief to
those trustees whose hands had previously been tied by the terms
of the trust and who wanted to go outside the old range of investments. The Act gives such trustees power to divide the fund, as
shown by an up-to-date valuation, into two equal parts – the
narrow range and the wider range. Where powers exist, there may
also be a special-range part.

Narrow range investments are sub-divided into two parts. The
first covers British Savings and similar Bonds, Savings Certificates,
and ordinary department accounts in Trustee Savings Banks and
National Savings Bank deposits. Trustees do not have to take
professional advice on such media. They have to get advice, however, before investing in the other, and much wider, narrow range
part which broadly covers gilt-edged securities; local authority
loans; debentures or guaranteed and preference stocks of water
companies which have paid ordinary dividends of at least 5 per
cent for each of the past ten years; debentures, loan stock, or notes
of U.K. companies which have an issued share capital of at least £1
million and have paid dividends on the whole of their equity capital
for each of the last five years; special investment department
accounts in Trustee Savings Banks; deposits in Building Societies
which have qualified for trustee status; mortgages on freeholds or
long leaseholds; and perpetual rent charges on land.

Wider range investments include share accounts in designated
Building Societies, designated unit trusts, and the share capital of
U.K. companies with issued capitals of at least £1 million which
have paid dividends on all their issued capital for each of the
previous five years and whose shares are quoted on a recognized
Stock Exchange. Competent professional advice is required on
these forms of investment.

While trusts set up before the coming into force of the Act can
now take steps to try to counter inflationary effects by investing in
equities, it does not always follow that up to the maximum of 50
per cent of funds should be so invested. Trustees must consider the
intentions of the trust. It may, for instance, be necessary to produce

a minimum income which is only assured by sticking wholly or mainly to fixed interest stocks. Alternatively, the loss on sales of irredeemable or long-dated stocks might be such that re-investment of the proceeds would produce a lower income. Factors which must be taken into account before the new powers are used are the interests of the life tenants, how the funds have to be dealt with on their deaths, and what capital may be needed for advances or other requirements.

Investment clubs are a form of mutual investment which help groups of people to save and at the same time to learn at first hand the mechanics of the security market. They started in the U.S.A. after the last war, and the idea spread to Britain a few years ago. The basis of operation is for a group of men and women to agree to pay in fixed monthly or weekly sums, and when sufficient funds are available – £100 is about the absolute minimum – to decide mutually how to invest them. Decisions are taken at meetings where investment suggestions are put forward and discussed before approval by the majority of members.

With anything up to twenty or more people concerned in the investment of funds, it is important that their interests should be safeguarded by clearly drawn-up rules. These should define the right of each member to an equitable share of the club assets, and the ability to draw out his or her share after giving notice to terminate membership; the voting rights; the keeping of proper books of account; the treatment of dividends and taxation; and the method of registering the investments. Care and thought must therefore be given to these and other matters before launching, or joining in, a venture which, without the essential safeguards, would run into disputes and difficulties. A unit trust may be a simpler and better means of regular investment.

CHAPTER 20

The Taxation Factor

TAXATION, as we have seen in previous chapters, is a factor which enters into many investment calculations. A retired person, or any other individual whose income is insufficient to attract tax, is better off in Local Council or Savings Bonds, and similar securities, than in Savings Certificates or building societies with their special exemptions. At the other end of the scale, anyone paying income tax and/or surtax is probably better advised to have the maximum investment in Savings Certificates. It is as well therefore to know something of the basic rules of income tax as they affect investment income.

When, in April 1973, the unified system of taxation came into force a generations-old distinction in types of income largely disappeared. With one exception, the division of income into earned and unearned categories was abolished. There is no longer any special relief for salaries, wages and other earned income; all sources are liable to the base rate, which is 33 per cent for 1974/5. Bank and similar non-annual interest apart, tax has always been deducted at the current rate from dividends and most interest on investments. This still applies; but in a somewhat different way.

The 'deduction' method still applies to interest – if the gross sum is £100, tax of £33 is deducted and £67 is paid to the investor; and the three figures are shown on the interest voucher.

But dividends (preference and ordinary) paid by U.K. companies are not, in effect, subject to tax deduction; the amount received by the investor is treated as having with it a *tax credit* which, for 1974/5, equals 33/67ths of the payment. Translated into gross terms, this means that, if the dividend cheque is £67, the investor has been *credited* with £33 tax and his gross income is £100; which is the figure taken into account when calculating his overall tax liability. As mentioned earlier in the book, there is a variation with preference dividends. When imputation began, many companies reduced the 'coupon' on their preference shares by lowering the dividend rate to the net sum after deduction of the then base tax rate of 30 per cent – a 10 per cent *gross* share became a 7 per cent *net* share. Now, with the base rate up to 33 per cent, the preference shareholder still gets his 7 per cent but is credited with tax at the higher rate and his gross income is 10·45 per cent for tax purposes.

The main exception to income distinction comes when gross income from investments exceeds a certain level, the figure of which is another political shuttlecock. Up to 5 April 1974 the level was £2,000. Over this amount an 'unearned' surcharge of 15 per cent was levied. For 1974/5 the 'threshold' is reduced to £1,000, but with the band from £1,000 to £2,000 surcharged at only 10 per cent. But taxpayers over 65 have as their threshold the higher amount of £1,500 and a reduced rate band of £500.

Another factor affecting tax liability is the total income from all sources. Again under existing rules, all income over £4,500 attracts higher tax rates which begin at 38 per cent and rise to a peak of 83 per cent, plus, where applicable, the investment surcharge. A simple example shows the effect. A married man with only the personal allowance has no income other than dividends of £2,680 with tax credits of £1,320. His liability will be:

	£
Dividends received	2,680
Add Tax credits ⅓ of £2,680	1,320
Total income	£4,000
Less Personal allowance	865
Taxable income	£3,135
Tax payable:	
£3,135 @ 33 per cent	1,034·55
£1,000 @ 10 per cent	100
£2,000 @ 15 per cent	300
	£1,434.55
Less Tax credits	1,320
Balance payable	£114·55

There are exceptions to the tax deduction and tax credit rules. The main ones, the interest on which is paid gross, are:

British Savings Bonds

$3\frac{1}{2}\%$ War Loan

Government stocks on the National and Trustee Savings Bank registers

Small amounts – e.g. £100 – of local authority mortgage loans

Savings Bank and other bank accounts

Hire-purchase finance-company deposits, the interest on which is not on an annual basis.

Interest on building society investment falls into a special category. With the object of reducing repayment claims, most societies (as we have seen already) pay income tax at a special 'compounded' rate, which is based on annual samples of the tax liability of the average investor. Interest, as explained in Chapter 4, is therefore distributed on a 'tax-paid' basis. One condition of this arrangement is that investors who are not liable to income tax cannot reclaim anything, and this can be an important consideration.

Interest and dividends, whether received gross or after deduction of income tax, have to be entered in annual tax returns. One reason for this is that the details have to be taken into account, where appropriate, for assessments to higher rates of tax. Another is that interest from which tax has not been deducted has to be assessed, where the investor is liable to tax. Three exceptions to the rule of returning all investment income are interest on Savings Certificates and Save-As-You-Earn contracts, and Premium Bond prizes: these are exempt from tax.

A common misunderstanding is that of the husband who puts investments in the name of his wife in the hope of reducing his tax bills. Although husband and wife can claim separate assessments, no tax is saved by having investments in a wife's name. Such income is still treated as part of the husband's income: *his* allowances and the total combined income thus decide the tax liability.

The investment income of children has become another game of political ducks and drakes. Between 6 April 1972 and 5 April

1975 children are assessed separately and receive the appropriate allowances. Parents lose reliefs, however, when a child's income exceeds £115 a year by a reduction of £1 in the appropriate child allowance for £1 in excess of this figure. It is proposed, however, that from 6 April 1975 all investment income of a child will be treated as part of the parents' income and taxed accordingly.

Certain interest in addition to that on Savings Certificates enjoys income tax exemption. This is the first £40 per annum on accounts with the following:

National Savings Bank *ordinary department*
Trustee Savings Bank *ordinary department*
Seamen's Savings Banks
Birmingham Municipal Bank Savings Department No. 2

The interest from all such sources, if there is more than one, must be totalled up when calculating the exemption relief. If, for instance, £22 is earned on a National Savings Bank account and £27 on a Trustee Savings Bank one, the £40 is deducted from the total of £49, and £9 is liable to tax. When husband and wife have separate or joint accounts, however, both can claim exemption on their respective portions of interest, to give a maximum of £40 *each* tax free.

It is important to note that this exemption does not apply to National and Trustee Savings Bank *special investment department* accounts, Railway Savings Banks, other banks, hire-purchase finance companies, cooperative societies, and National Development and British Savings Bonds. *All* such interest is liable to tax.

Where tax is deducted, investors whose gross incomes are less than all their tax allowances can reclaim part or all of it. The normal time for making claims is after the end of the tax year – 5 April. It is, however, possible to make interim claims half-yearly in October or quarterly in July, October, and January, a fact which is helpful to people with small incomes. An example shows the effect:

A spinster, 55 years of age, has a total *gross* income of £1,200 for the year ended 5 April 1975, made up of £400 from part-time earnings and £800 from dividends. Under the imputation system the net receipts from the latter totalled £536 and her tax credits at 33 per cent were £264. The only allowance due is the single personal one of £625. Her tax liability, and repayment, are:

	£	£
Earnings		400
Dividends received	536	
Add Tax credits	264	
	——	
		800
Total income		£1,200
Less Personal allowance		625
		——
Taxable		£575
Tax payable at 33 per cent		189·75
Tax credits		264·00
Repayment due		£74·25

Single people and married men who attain, or have attained, the age of 65 during the tax year ending 5 April 1975 may claim total exemption from tax if their incomes do not exceed certain limits, which are:

Single	£810
Married	£1,170

For a married man it is his age *or his wife's* which counts. Marginal relief operates where the income to take into account exceeds these amounts and can be of benefit where the total does not exceed £1,087 single and £1,627 married. Tax between the appropriate amounts is then payable at 55 per cent on the excess over £810 and £1,170, respectively. Above the maximum levels it is, however, cheaper to pay tax at the normal rates.

This, it should be noted, is the position for the tax year 1974/75 For the year 1975/6, beginning 6 April, an *age allowance*, more generous in its scope, takes the place of the long-standing 'age exemption' for the 65s and over with incomes up to £3,000 a year, whether from previous earnings or investments, or a combination of all three. The new, special, age allowances are: £950 for a single taxpayer, compared with the under 65 allowance of £625; and £1,425 for a married man, compared with £865. Marginal relief will apply if the total income exceeds £3,000 – for every £3 excess income there will be a reduction of £2 in the allowance. Assuming no change for 1975/6 in the normal personal allowances this will mean that marginal relief will be beneficial on incomes up to £3,488 for single 'old' people and up to £3,840 for married men. If the income is over these limits the normal tax allowances and rules will apply. It should be kept in mind that the investment income surcharge, as already outlined, will come into the tax computation *where applicable*.

An example shows the effect of the new age allowance. A married man aged 67 has a total gross income of exactly £3,000 from pensions, some small earnings and investments. For 1975/6 his tax bill will be:

Pensions		£1,500
Earnings		500
Dividends, etc. – gross		1,000
Total gross income		£3,000
Less Age allowance		1,425
Taxable		£1,575
Tax payable @ 33 per cent		£519.75

Under the old method the personal allowance would have been only £865 and the amount due on the taxable net figure of £2,135 would have come to £704·55.

Assuming that the total income is however £3,300, and the marginal relief applies, the 1975/6 tax due would be:

Total gross income		£3,300
Less Age allowance	£1,425	
Less ⅔ of £300 'excess income'	200	
		1,225
Taxable		£2,075
Tax payable @ 33 per cent		£684.75

Applying the old personal allowance rate of £865 the taxable income would be the larger amount of £2,435 and the tax £803·55.

Investors eligible for age exemption should look very closely at the way in which their savings are invested. They cannot, for instance, claim back any tax on building society investments because of the special arrangements applicable to the interest. Providing they do not go over their marginal limit it can therefore be profitable to switch from building society share accounts at, say, 7½ per cent to local council loans or to British Savings Bonds. Equally, there can be no point in holding Savings Certificates, the interest on which attracts no tax repayment. Perhaps more important, they should not keep very much in National, or Trustee, Savings Bank Ordinary accounts at only 4 per cent, despite the tax exemption on the first £40 a year of interest.

CAPITAL GAINS TAX

From 6 April 1965 profits on the sale of most forms of property, whenever acquired, may be liable to capital gains tax. The exceptions concerned with here are:

National Savings Certificates

Premium Savings Bonds

National Development, and British Savings Bonds

Contractual savings under the Save-As-You-Earn scheme

British Government and Government-guaranteed stocks held for more than a year

Owner-occupied houses – but if more than one is owned only the main residence is excluded

Normal life assurance policies on maturity or surrender.

Surpluses on such assets are exempt from the tax. And, for those interested, so are pools, lottery and betting winnings.

Until 6 April 1971 there were two forms of tax on capital gains – the short-term, which was charged through income tax on profits taken within twelve months of purchase; and the long-term. Now there is just the gains tax.

The long-term, as it was originally called, is charged on capital gains to the extent that there is a post-6 April 1965 profit. For individuals it is a flat rate of 30 per cent, with the alternative of a charge to income tax and surtax where favourable.

Losses can be set off against profits and when not used up in one year can be carried forward to subsequent years.

Example: If a profit of £100 is made on the sale of one holding and a loss of £200 on another no tax is payable for the particular tax year; and, assuming no further transactions, the net loss of £100 is carried forward until used up against any future profits.

Since inauguration of the tax two concessions for 'small' gains made by *individuals* have been introduced. The first, which was available for each of the tax years 1967/8 to 1970/71, gave exemption if chargeable profits *less* allowable losses in any year were not more than £50, with husband and wife being treated jointly. Beginning with the tax year 1970/71 the qualification for exemption was changed from a profits basis to a *proceeds* basis. While there was a choice for 1970/71 of either basis, the only one current since 6 April 1971 gives exemption if the aggregate amount or value of *all* sales in a tax year is not more than £500, again with husband and wife being treated jointly. If the total exceeds £500 by a relatively small sum the gains tax is however limited to one-half of the excess – on a total of say £520, the tax payable would be limited to no more than £10. The important point about the present exemption is that *the figure which matters is the total net proceeds, not the profit.* For instance, if shares bought for £300 were sold for £900 – a profit of £600 – tax would be chargeable in the normal way on the gain of £600. But if the net proceeds were only £500, and it was the only transaction in the year, no tax would be payable on the gain of £200.

Calculation of buying and selling prices is a basic part of any operation. Rightly, the incidental costs are taken into the reckoning. For new purchases and holdings at the time of the tax coming into being there are three general bases:

First is the all-in price of a specific purchase. If 250 shares were bought at 150p (before V.A.T. began and stamp duty was doubled in the April 1974 Budget to 2 per cent), the cost was not £375 but this amount plus the normal expenses, as under:

250 shares @ 150p	£375·00
Brokerage @ 1¼%	4·69
Stamp duty	4·00
Contract stamp	0·10
Total cost	£383·79

The starting point for gains tax is thus £383·79 or approximately 153⅝p a share. (In practice the tax inspector works to the nearest £1, giving the taxpayer the benefit of any pence.)

Second is the valuation basis of securities already held at the start of the new tax on 6 April 1965. This is the *higher* of the cost price or the closing price as shown by the daily official list of the London or another recognized stock exchange for 6 April 1965. Further, the latter, in the case of London, is the *higher* of (a) the middle of the closing quotations or (b) the mean of the prices of recorded normal bargains for that day. Thus, if the quotation under (a) was 197½–202½p, the middle price would be 200p. Similarly, if there were four normal deals marked on that day at 198½p, 201p, 200p and 197½p, the mean of 199¼ would be less and, for this part of the exercise, the price to take would be the closing quotation of 200p. Sticking to the purchase example above, it would clearly be better to adopt the closing price of 200p – equal to a cost of £500 – in place of the actual cost of 153⅝p, or £383·79. On the other hand, if the 6 April price had come out at only 100p it would be better to stick to the actual cost of 153⅝p for the gains tax valuation. It should be particularly noted that if a loss is shown on a sale the base value of the corresponding purchase would be the *lower* of the cost price or the 6 April 1965 closing price.

Third is the basis for securities bought *after* 6 April 1965. This is the all-in cost. Using again our example above, the tax buying cost is firmly £383·79 and profits or losses are worked from this level.

When securities are sold the gains tax figure is the price received less the normal selling expenses. Assuming that our 250 shares are sold in 1975 at 250p the net proceeds would be:

	£	£
250 shares @ 250p		625·00
Less Brokerage @ 1¼%	7·81	
V.A.T.	0·63	
Contract stamp	0·30	
		8·74
Net proceeds		£616·26

The profit to take into account would depend on the date of purchase. If this was before 6 April 1965 it would, as already shown, clearly be the 6 April closing price of 200p and the amount liable to tax would be £616·26 less £500·00, or £116·26. But if the shares had been bought after 6 April 1965 the cost would be the actual total of £383·79; and the profit to take into the reckoning would be £616·26 less £383·79, or £232·47.

These are the simple straightforward rules covering one purchase and one sale of a single block of securities. Other rules come into play when a holding has been accumulated at varying prices over a period, or there are partial sales. The task is to identify a sale with a purchase.

With the exception of those held at 6 April 1965, all purchases of an identical class of stock or share are lumped together at their average cost into a single block – the *pool*, as it is called. On a sale of part of the block a proportionate part of the total cost is treated as the cost of the sale. For instance, if 600 shares are bought after 6 April 1965 in three separate lots of 200 each at 120p, 135p and 90p, the pool price is 115p.

It is important at this stage to note the methods of dealing with sales from a pool. Sale of the entire holding in one lot is simple – the proceeds are set against the pool cost. But on part sales the rule, as originally conceived, was to work out the allowable cost by the following fraction:

$$\frac{\text{Proceeds of part disposal}}{\text{Proceeds of part disposal} + \text{Market value of shares remaining}}$$

271

Assuming a holding of shares cost £600 and part was sold for £240 when the value of the balance was £720 the gain would be:

$$£240 - \left(£600 \times \frac{£240}{£240 + £720} = £150\right)$$

or £90. The balance of the notional cost, £450, would be carried forward to set off against any future sale.

This somewhat complicated formula need not however be used. A simpler alternative is to take a proportion of the pool value as the cost of the shares sold. For example, if the average cost of 600 shares is 100p, or £600 in all, and 200 are sold for £300, the gain is £300 less £200 (the average cost of one-third of the holding) or £100; and the balance of 400 shares is carried forward at £400.

Problems can arise when selling quoted securities owned on 6 April 1965. The initial consideration is the date of sale – before or after 19 March 1968, from which date a right of *election* is open. Election firmly, and irrevocably, fixes the cost at the 6 April 1965 market value for the *whole portfolio*; or, as two separate units, (a) *the whole portfolio of ordinary shares* and (b) *the whole portfolio of fixed-interest stocks and preference shares*. The objective is to give investors the opportunity to opt out of what may be a difficult, if not impossible, task; that of tracking down the original cost of individual investments which may have been bought many years back, have been inherited without any note of the probate value, or which have changed their original form because of take-overs, mergers, conversion offers, scrip issues, rights offers, capital reconstructions, or other happenings.

Fortunately, investors selling after the key date have time in which to decide. They have up to two years from the end of the year of assessment in which such securities are *first* disposed of after 19 March 1968 to elect or not to elect. In view of the irrevocability of election it is unwise to make a snap decision. Tax could be saved, together with possibly a lot of research, through election. On the other hand, such a blanket decision could equally mean paying more. If practicable, it is wise therefore to work out the position for each individual investment on the basis of original cost and its 6 April 1965 market value. While a broad general rule would make this side of investment life simpler, there is no escape from the vital fact that the decision must depend on the make-up of a portfolio and the dates of acquiring *each separate* holding.

Subject to stringent reservations, the only two possible guidelines for securities acquired some years before April 1965 are: Ordinary shares *taken as a whole* might have increased in value, to make election profitable. But, in view of the fall in market prices of fixed-interest securities during most of the 1950s and 1960s, their cost would probably be higher than 6 April 1965 values and so make non-election the better choice.

This brings us to the treatment where there is no election. Again, there are two broad divisions. First is acquisition of an entire holding on or before 6 April 1965. Second is a holding bought partly before and partly after that date. The basic rules are:

When all acquisitions were made before 6 April 1965, the 'cost' figure, as previously mentioned, is the actual cost or the market value, whichever is most beneficial to the investor. The calculation is simple if there was only one purchase of the particular security; it is cost or market value and the appropriate figure is set against the net proceeds of sale. But if the holding was accumulated in two or more lots, sales have to be matched with purchases on the first-in first-out, or FIFO, basis.

Example: Purchases of the same class of shares in a company were made as under:

                1961:   600 @ 60p costing £360
                1963: 1,000 @ 45p   ,,   £450
                1964:   800 @ 70p   ,,   £560

The 6 April 1965 value was 55p a share.

Sales are made as follows:

                1974:   800 @ 65p for £520
                1975: 1,200 @ 52½p for £630

Under FIFO rules the 800 shares sold in 1974 comprise the 600 bought in 1961 and 200 of the 1963 lot. The 600 realized ¾ of £520, or £390, compared with a 6 April 1965 value of £330 (600 at 55p) and a cost of £360, to give gains of £60 and £30, respectively. As the latter gain, calculated on the actual cost, is

273

the smaller it is the figure on which long-term tax is assessed. The balance of 200 realized $\frac{1}{4}$ of £520, or £130, compared with a value of £110 and a cost of £90 (200 at 45p), to give gains of £20 and £40, respectively. As the former gain, the market value one, is the smaller, the figure to take into account is limited to £20. The total chargeable gain on this sale is thus £50 (£30 plus £20).

The 1975 sale is made up of the balance of 800 shares bought at 45p in 1963 and 400 of the 1964 lot costing 70p. The proportion realized for the 800 was £420 compared with a cost of £360 ($\frac{4}{5}$ of £450) and 6 April 1965 value of £440. As the first method showed a gain of £60 but the second a loss of £20, the 'no gain no loss' rule applies, and this part of the second sale is left out of account. On the balance of 400 shares, which came out of the 1964 purchase at 70p each or cost of £280 and market value of £220, the net proceeds of £210 show a loss of £70 on cost and only £10 on market value which, as it is the smaller, is the loss for the gains tax calculation.

Where a holding of similar shares has been built up by purchases both before and after 6 April 1965 and sales begin *after* 19 March 1968, acquisitions before 6 April 1965 are not pooled but those added after this date are pooled.

Example: Purchases of similar class shares were made as under:

```
1962:   500 @ 100p costing £500
1963:   500 @  90p    ,,    £450
1964:   500 @  70p    ,,    £350
        6 April 1965 value was 50p
1966:   500 @  50p costing £250
1967: 1,000 @  40p    ,,    £400
```

Sales are made of 1,000 shares each in 1973, 1974 and 1975 at 80p, 125p and 150p per share respectively, to produce correspondingly £800, £1,250 and £1,500.

Under the pooling rule the 1966 and 1967 purchases are taken as 1,500 shares costing £650 but the previous ones are taken individually, to give the following results:

The 1973 sale of 1,000 shares comprises the two lots of 500 each bought in 1962 and 1963 and the calculations based on (a) April 1965 value and (b) actual cost are:

	(a)	(b)
Proceeds of 500 (80p) bought 1962	£400	£400
Value 6.4.1965 (50p)	£250	
Cost (100p)		£500
Gain/loss	+£150	−£100
Proceeds of 500 (80p) bought 1963	£400	£400
Value 6.4.1965 (50p)	£250	
Cost (90p)		£450
Gain/loss	+£150	−£50

There is thus neither a chargeable gain nor a loss on this sale of 1,000 shares.

The 1974 sale of 1,000 comes from the 500 shares bought in 1964 and the 1,500 acquired in 1966 and 1967. The calculations are therefore based on (a) and (b) as above for 500 and on 500 from the post-1965 pool:

	(a)	(b)
Proceeds (125p) of 500 bought 1964	£625	£625
Value 6.4.1965 (50p)	£250	
Cost (70p)		£350
Gain	+£375	+£275

Proceeds (125p) of 500 from pool	£625
Cost 500/1,500 × £650 .. .. say	£217
Gain	+£408

The chargeable gain is thus £275 (the lower profit) + £408 = £683.

Proceeds of the 1975 sale of the balance of 1,000 shares at 150p gives proceeds of	£1,500
and with the cost the balance of the pool – £650–£217	£433
the chargeable gain is	£1,067

The tax rate for individuals, as already indicated, is 30 per cent on the net profits. Where beneficial in any year of assessment, tax will be restricted, however, to an amount equal to the income tax payable if a part of the net gains was dealt with as income instead of the whole net gains being charged at 30 per cent. The portion on which the 'notional' income tax may be calculated is (a) one-half of the net gains where these are less than £5,000 or (b) if the net gains are over £5,000 the sum of £2,500 plus the amount by which the gains exceed £5,000. Although the fraction notionally treated as income is looked on as the top slice of the investor's income, with tax calculated accordingly, the alternative should benefit those who are normally small taxpayers.

Two points should, however, be remembered. First, there is no choice of having part of a year's net gains charged at the normal gains tax rate and the remainder on the alternative basis; it is all or nothing either way. Secondly, the alternative basis is of no benefit if the income tax rate is already 63 per cent or more.

One general point about the choice of the purchase basis should be noted. When one method (actual cost or 6 April 1965 market value) would result in a profit and the other method would produce a loss, it is assumed that on a sale there is neither profit nor loss – it is assumed that the investor sold the securities and immediately reacquired them at the same value. Comparably, losses on sales are treated in a corresponding way.

Example: If shares bought at a cost of £500 before 6 April 1965, were valued on that date at £350 and were sold thereafter for £400 there would be a loss of £100 on the cost but a profit of £50 on the 6 April market value. Neither loss nor profit would be taken into account for gains tax, it being assumed that the investor sold the shares and immediately reacquired them at the sale price.

Abolition of the short-term tax brought a change in the treatment of gains on British Government and certain Government-guaranteed stocks. On sales after 15 April 1969 there was no tax liability if the stocks had been held for *more than* 12 months; but short-term tax was payable on gains realized *within* 12 months of acquisition. From 6 April 1971, which marked the exit of the short-term tax, the normal tax of 30 per cent is payable only on gains taking place within 12 months of acquisition. Gains from such stocks held for more than 12 months are exempt from gains tax.

Further rules for company securities look after capital distributions, scrip issues, mergers, and the like. A capital distribution in cash is dealt with as a part disposal of the shares concerned, and, unless liable to income tax, it is chargeable to gains tax. When the distribution is small however in relation to the value of the shares the tax inspector may treat it as a reduction in their cost and not bring the gain into account until the shares are sold.

The position is different when a scrip issue of shares is made. These add no value to the existing holding and are therefore not liable to gains tax on their distribution. For instance, if a one-for-one scrip issue is made in respect of a 25p share bought at 100p the two shares resulting from the 'paper' issue are taken into account at 50p each, or exactly half the price of the original share. The original cost is also stuck to on a conversion to some new security or a change resulting from a merger or take-over.

Example: Say 200 ordinary shares in Company A were bought at 125p, or for £250, and that on a merger with Company B they became 500 shares, their cost would still be the same £250. The price would come down to 50p for each of the new shares.

But when a take-over is for cash any profit (or loss) on the original or the 6 April 1965 price has to be taken into account for gains tax. Likewise, if the consideration is part cash and part shares the cash portion is treated as part disposal of the original holding. Calculation of the profit or loss then calls for an apportionment of the total cost between (a) the part represented by the cash received and (b) the portion retained in shares, on the basis of the market values of the two respective portions.

Though rare in recent years, a company which runs into difficulties may write off its losses against a reduction in its equity share capital. This could be, say, a writing-down of the par value from 100p to 25p. An investor who had bought the original 100p shares at 125p would still value the reorganized 25p shares at the same price of 125p (or the 6 April 1965 value) when computing his profit or loss on a sale.

Double charges to gains tax could arise on holdings in unit trusts and investment trusts. The trusts would pay on profits from changes in their portfolios and the investor on any increase in his or her sale price over the original cost. Up to April 1972 investors could take credit for their portions of the trusts' gains tax by deducting them from the sale price. For instance, if shares in a unit trust or an investment trust were bought at 50p, sold at 75p and the portion of net capital gains of the trust was 4p, the sale price was treated as 71p. The gain was 21p and not 25p. From April 1972 however, the trusts pay gains tax at half rate only and investors no longer get credits for their portion of the tax. On the other hand, they get a credit to set against their own liability on any gain from selling their holding. The actual position for the 1974/5 year, with its base rate of 33 per cent, is that the gains tax payable by investors will be reduced by whichever is the lesser of (1) the sum of that tax; (2) 16·5 per cent of the gains chargeable on sale of the units or shares; or (3) 16·5 per cent of all chargeable gains for the year.

It should be noted that the market value of unit trust shares is normally the lower of the two prices quoted by the managers. When it pays however to take the 6 April 1965 price, the market value is half way between the published buying and selling prices – with a quotation of 52½p–55p the gains tax figure is 53¾p.

Gains and losses of husband and wife are calculated separately, with losses by either being set primarily against his or her gains. Gains, less losses, made by a wife are normally assessed on the husband. Equally, a husband's allowable losses not used up against his gains in a tax year can be set off against his wife's net gains, and *vice versa*, unless either of them decides otherwise and applies accordingly before 6 July of the following year. Husband and wife, as with income tax, can apply at a similar time to have separate assessments for gains tax. These arrangements do not mean, however, that if each has a holding of similar shares they can be treated as one when it comes to sales; the two holdings must be regarded as entirely separate and a market sale of one cannot be identified with a market purchase of the other.

Anyone who dies after 30 March 1971 is not treated as disposing of his or her assets on death, as could happen up to that date. Hence, from 1 April 1971 there is no charge on unrealized gains at death – and no gains tax liability – and, equally, no relief for unrealized losses.

Glossary of Stock Exchange Terms

ACCOUNT: The period, usually two weeks and sometimes three weeks, into which Stock Exchange dealings are divided.

ACTUAL: The price at which a jobber will deal as a buyer or seller.

AFTER-HOURS DEALINGS: Transactions done between members' offices after the official close of the Stock Exchange at 3.30 p.m.

APPLICATION MONEY: The amount per share or £100 of stock payable on application for a new issue or offer for sale. It may be the whole amount, or a part to be followed by further instalments payable on allotment and/or by calls.

ARBITRAGE: The business of taking advantage of price differences in different markets by buying in one and selling in the other (or *vice versa*).

AVERAGING: The process of buying more securities on a fall or selling more on a rise, in order to level out the price of bull or bear transactions.

BACKWARDATION: A payment per share or unit of stock made by a bear to a bull for the loan of securities, to enable the bear to deliver when due.

BARGAIN: A purchase or sale done between a broker and a jobber.

BEAR: An individual who sells securities he does not own in the hope that they can be repurchased at a lower price before delivery is due.

BID: When a price is quoted as so much 'bid' it generally means that there are more buyers than sellers.

BLUE CHIP: A company, usually a fairly large and well-established one, regarded as a relatively safe investment.

BROKEN AMOUNT: An odd amount, such as forty-three shares, which is not a normal market quantity. As the costs of transfer are proportionately higher than for round amounts, a seller may have to accept less than the market price. For small quantities he may also have to pay transfer stamp and registration fee.

BULL: An individual who buys securities in the hope that they will rise in price. A 'stale bull' is one whose optimism is waning and who is ready to cut a loss.

BUYERS ONLY: If a jobber qualifies his price in this way it means he can buy, but not sell, stock.

CALL OPTION: The right to buy shares following the purchase of a call option.

CALLS: The amounts which may still be payable after allotment in order to make securities fully paid. There may be one, two, or more calls spread over a few months. Failure to meet them may mean forfeiture of the stock.

CASH SETTLEMENT: Unlike transactions for settlement in the normal way for the Stock Exchange Account, payment is due on the following day. This is the normal way of paying for gilt-edged securities.

CHEAP MONEY: When interest rates are low, money can be described as 'cheap' for borrowers.

CHOICE: The position where a broker can buy from one jobber at the same price as he can sell to another. Jobber A, for example, may be quoting 77p–79p while Jobber B's price is 79p–81p.

CLOSE PRICE: A narrow margin between the bid and the offered price.

CLOSING PRICES: The prices ruling at the official close of the House at 3.30 p.m. Business done afterwards is at 'after-hours' prices.

COMMON STOCK/SHARES: The term used in the United States and Canada for ordinary, or equity, shares. They often have 'no par value'.

CONTANGO: A rate of interest paid for carrying over a transaction from one account to the next.

COUPON: The warrant which has to be presented in order to collect interest or dividends on bearer securities, which usually have sheets of coupons attached to them. New sheets of coupons are obtained by presenting the 'talon', which is generally the last item on the old sheet.

CUM: Means 'with'. When a price is so quoted, it includes any dividend recently declared, a scrip issue, rights, or other distribution.

DEAR MONEY: Money is 'dear' when it is scarce and interest rates are high.

DIFFERENCE: The balance due to or by a client on the purchase and sale of a particular security during a stock exchange account.

DISCOUNT: The amount by which a security is quoted below its par or paid-up value. For example, if a 50p share, paid-up to the extent of 25p, is quoted at 22½p, it stands at a discount of 2½p. Similarly, fully paid-up stock standing at 97½ is quoted at 2½ discount.

DOLLAR PREMIUM: The premium over the normal exchange rate paid for 'investment' dollars, which have to be bought to pay for American, Canadian, other hard currency and Overseas Sterling Area (O.S.A.) securities.

DOLLAR STOCKS: A general term for American and Canadian stocks and shares.

EQUITY: Another name for ordinary shares, which usually take all the risks and most of the profits. What is left after meeting the demands of any other classes of capital belongs to the equity-holders.

EX: Means without. A price so quoted excludes any recently declared dividend, scrip issue, rights, or any other distribution.

FREE: Free of stamp and fee, which means that the seller pays such expenses, generally on the sale of small lots of securities. It also applies to new securities which change hands in allotment letter form free of stamp until they have to be registered.

FUNDS: A description for British Government stocks, which has the same meaning as 'gilt-edged'.

GILT-EDGED: A description for British Government and similar fixed-interest securities.

HOUSE: The Stock Exchange floor where business is transacted.

INSTALMENT: Payment for new issues of securities is often made up of application and allotment monies, followed by one or more instalments, thus spreading payment over a period of time.

INTERIM DIVIDEND: Companies may spread dividend payments over the year by distribution of an interim, or interims, followed by the final payment after the year end.

JOBBER'S TURN: The difference between the prices at which a jobber is ready to buy and sell. If the price is 77p–79p, the turn is 2p. This should be allowed for when calculating the cost of buying and selling.

JUNGLE: The West African mining market.

KAFFIRS: A name given to South African mining and related shares.

LIMIT: A client can 'limit' his broker to buying at a stated maximum price or selling at a stated minimum one.

LIMITED MARKET: Individual securities or groups of them are so described when, because of shortage of stock, or for some other reason, it is difficult to buy or sell.

LISTS CLOSED: Public issues and offers for sale have their application lists open for a specified time. Lists are closed when the time expires or the offer is fully subscribed. If it is a popular offer the lists may open at 10 a.m. and close at 10.01 a.m. the same day.

LONDON PARITY: The sterling equivalent of an American or Canadian price.

LONG: Anyone who holds an amount of a particular stock.

LONGS: Government and similar stocks with repayment dates more than fifteen years ahead.

MAKING A PRICE: When a jobber quotes or 'makes' a price, he is usually ready to deal in a reasonable market quantity, buying at the lower price and selling at the higher one.

MARKETABLE AMOUNT: The number of shares or amount of stock in which a jobber quoting a price would reasonably be expected to deal. Naturally, as circumstances vary considerably between active and inactive securities, the amounts vary.

MARKING: Brokers and jobbers may record the price at which a bargain is transacted by entering the details on a marking slip, which is used for entering the details of business done in the *Official List*.

MEDIUMS: Government and similar stocks with repayment dates of 5 to 15 years.

MIDDLE PRICE: The half-way level between buying and selling prices, e.g. 78p if the quotation is 77p–79p.

MONEY STOCKS: Very short-dated gilt-edged or other securities which are due for repayment at a definite date a short time ahead.

'MORE ONE WAY': When mentioned by broker or jobber, indicates that bigger business could be done for buyers or sellers.

NAME TICKET: The form which gives registration details on the purchase of securities and which the buying broker must pass to the seller.

NEW TIME: Purchases or sales in one account for settlement in the next account. Such transactions can take place during the last two days of the old account.

NOMINAL: A price is nominal when a jobber quotes it but is not prepared to deal. It then becomes merely an indication of the price.

N.T.P.: When a transaction is dealt in 'not to press' it means that the buyer agrees with the jobber that he will not put in motion the Stock Exchange machinery for obtaining delivery, if this is delayed beyond the normal time.

OFFERED: When a price is so much 'offered' it generally means that there are more sellers than buyers, or the price at which a jobber will sell.

ONE WAY: When a jobber says he is 'one way only' it means that he cannot deal both ways but can only bid for or offer stock.

OPENING PRICES: The prices quoted at the official opening of the Stock Exchange each day.

PITCH: The place on the floor of the House where a jobber is usually to be found.

POSITION: A jobber has a position when he holds stock (is a bull) or is short of stock (is a bear).

PREMIUM: A security is standing at a premium when the price is more than its paid-up or par value, e.g. a 25p paid-up share at 27½p is at 2½p premium.

PUT AND CALL OPTION: The right either to buy or sell shares under an option.

PUT OPTION: The right to sell shares following the purchase of a put option.

PUT-THROUGH: The sale of securities to a jobber simultaneously with the repurchase of them by the same broker.

RENUNCIATION: When a company makes a rights or similar issue to its shareholders, they are usually given the opportunity of selling their rights if they do not want to take up the offer. They then 'renounce' their rights to a buyer.

SCRIP ISSUE: A capitalization of reserves and retained profits in the form of a 'free' issue of shares. Sometimes called a 'bonus' or 'capitalization' issue, it is a paper transaction adding nothing to a company's assets.

SELLERS ONLY: Added to his quotation means that a jobber can sell, but not buy, stock.

SETTLEMENT: Payment for securities can be for cash – which means the day after purchase or sale – or account, which normally means eleven days after the close of the fortnightly or three-weekly account.

SHORT: Anyone is short when stock which is not owned has been sold.

SHORTS: Gilt-edged stocks which are due for repayment within five years.

SHUNTER: A broker who deals between London and other U.K. stock exchanges in securities quoted in both markets.

SIZE OF MARKET: The amount in which a jobber is making his price.

SMALL: An indication by a jobber that the price made to a broker is for less than a normal market quantity of shares or stock.

STAG: An applicant for new issues who sells his allotment – at a profit or a loss – on the commencement of dealings.

TO OPEN: A declaration that the order is to buy or to sell; or to get another party to 'open'.

TOUCH: The closest price quoted between jobbers, or the best price bid by one and cheapest price offered by another.

UNDATED: Government and similar stocks which have no fixed dates for repayment. Alternatively described as 'irredeemables'.

UNQUOTED: Securities which are not officially dealt in and which do not therefore appear in the *Official List* or *Monthly Supplement*. Such transactions can be specially marked under Rule 163 (1) (e). They are mostly in securities quoted on another recognized stock exchange abroad.

WIDE PRICE: A more than normal difference between bid and offered prices, such as 50p–62½p.

YANKEES: A term used to describe American securities.

MORE ABOUT PENGUINS
AND PELICANS

Penguinews, which appears every month, contains details of all the new books issued by Penguins as they are published. From time to time it is supplemented by *Penguins in Print*, which is a complete list of all titles available. (There are some five thousand of these.)

A specimen copy of *Penguinews* will be sent to you free on request. For a year's issues (including the complete lists) please send 50p if you live in the British Isles, or 75p if you live elsewhere. Just write to Dept EP, Penguin Books Ltd, Harmondsworth, Middlesex, enclosing a cheque or postal order, and your name will be added to the mailing list.

In the U.S.A.: For a complete list of books available from Penguin in the United States write to Dept CS, Penguin Books Inc., 7110 Ambassador Road, Baltimore, Maryland 21207.

In Canada: For a complete list of books available from Penguin in Canada write to Penguin Books Canada Ltd, 41 Steelcase Road West, Markham, Ontario.